Reviews fo

I read your book for the second time now; WOW is all I can say! The story blew me away, but your story telling talent is truly remarkable! So many emotions come through in a raw and powerful way. I couldn't get enough of it, the first and second time. I read it on my commute to work and before going to bed. In other words, every chance I got. Great Job!

*****

I love this book! It's sad, it's funny, and most importantly, it's real and heartfelt. You're writing ability and life experiences are fascinating and kept my interest every moment. It's an amazing story that will touch the lives of everyone lucky enough to read it.

*****

This book is a rollercoaster ride. I never read a book of this size so fast. Once I started I couldn't put it down. What an accomplishment to put all your experiences into words and make it flow like you did.

*****

Wow! I laughed, I cried, I was blown away by the mix of love, humor, and excitement. Once I started reading, I just kept going. And as I approached the end, I only wanted more. What a phenomenal story, what an awesome life.

*****

Your story affected me so deeply. You were capable of touching people's hearts and souls by being honest about your life.

*Hey Harmony —
Great to see you —
Enjoy the ride — and call
me back someday!*
Tony

THE NEIGHBORHOOD

BY

ANTHONY CARDARELLI

Copyright © 2007 by Anthony Cardarelli

All rights reserved. No part of this book shall be reproduced or transmitted in any form or by any means, electronic, mechanical, magnetic, photographic including photocopying, recording or by any information storage and retrieval system, without prior written permission of the publisher. No patent liability is assumed with respect to the use of the information contained herein. Although every precaution has been taken in the preparation of this book, the publisher and author assume no responsibility for errors or omissions. Neither is any liability assumed for damages resulting from the use of the information contained herein.

ISBN 0-7414-3729-5

Published by:

INFINITY
PUBLISHING.COM

1094 New DeHaven Street, Suite 100
West Conshohocken, PA 19428-2713
Info@buybooksontheweb.com
www.buybooksontheweb.com
Toll-free (877) BUY BOOK
Local Phone (610) 941-9999
Fax (610) 941-9959

Printed in the United States of America

Printed on Recycled Paper

Published February 2007

Chapter 1

Carmela Genelli

It was a very natural flow of events for an Italian family emigrating from their homeland. A homeland that was all they had or knew their entire lives. However, just as natural a flow of events as it was, it was just as unnatural in many other respects.

The family name was Genelli... and some fifty years after the first members of the family set foot on the docks of the city's West Side, it would become for them and their children, a much more interesting than natural, flow of events.

The first of the family to arrive in New York was Alfonso Genelli. He came to America like many of his countrymen, to get work and save money to send back home to his wife and children.

In Italy, his wife Carmela and her two sons, Donato and Anthony lived in anticipation of the day when they could join their father in America. Alfonso was able to find work in his new country and sent money back to his family. He also enjoyed the free lifestyle of a man with the Atlantic Ocean between himself and his wife and children.

As planned, Alfonso sent for his family. They arrived and were set up in an apartment on the West Side. As time went by, Alfonso began to feel the strain of someone who had enjoyed relative freedom even though he was married. He had had other lovers while his family was in Italy, and his most recent woman not only lived in the same apartment building, but directly across the hall from his family's front door.

Alfonso's wife was not an unintelligent woman by any means, so it became obvious. It was only her relentless sacrifice for her children that kept her going so that she could provide for her children as best as she could.

Before a years time, Alfonso took a drastic step that would affect the family for the next two generations. One day, he suggested to his wife that he would take the children, Donato and Anthony, shopping for clothes. He said that they would all be back in time for supper. What Carmela did not know and could not have possibly suspected, was that her husband had taken the children down to the West Side piers and booked passage for them and himself on the next ship bound for Italy.

Carmela went about her daily business and waited for them to return. All night long she waited, spending hour after hour leaning out the window and wondering what was keeping them. They never came back that night nor did Carmela see her two sons for another seven years.

Donato and Anthony Genelli

Incredibly, this woman, who had been so cruelly abused by her husband and, who couldn't speak a word of English, somehow had the insight to start checking down at the piers for ships leaving for Italy. Perhaps knowing even more about her husband than even he would have suspected. She did indeed learn, by showing photos of her husband and children to a customs manager at the Al Italia pier that they had in fact, all departed for Italy. The unbelievable rush of fear, anger and outrage washed over her all at once, and she withstood it, just as she would eventually overcome it.

Alfonso's shocking move was not only one of pure spite, but far worse. He had thought that by bringing his children back to Italy, his wife was sure to follow, thereby allowing him to go back to America a free man again.

* * * * *

Two children traveling across the Atlantic Ocean. That's what they were now. Their father was with them, but that was only temporary. They would have only themselves to rely on. An eight-year old child and his four-year old brother. That was it. Within the next couple of weeks their father would abandon them, leaving them with relatives in Italy. He left his children to fend for themselves in a household that didn't genuinely want them.

The children's fate was set early in their lives. A fate that would be extremely difficult for an adult, let alone two children with no idea why they were even there. How they eventually went on with their lives under these conditions is hard to imagine. To be that age with nobody to look to for love and encouragement is something no child should ever have to experience. Imagine the confusion, loneliness and fear these two kids must have felt. In those days a trip to Europe by ship could take more than two weeks. The feeling of emptiness was compounded by the fact that they were taken from their mother. Their father obviously had no shame. He had already begun to fill their heads with lies, telling them that their mother no longer wanted them with her.

Every night for the rest of their lonely voyage, they both cried themselves to sleep. These two young boys huddled together in their tiny sleeping quarters while their father sought out what ever nightlife there was on this ship to nowhere.

They had each other, thank God, but that's all they had. They didn't know it then of course, but that's all they would have for the next eight years. They also didn't know that their father had set them up for even more misery. He would abandon the two boys again only a few days after bringing them to his parent's home in Italy. He told them he would be back in two weeks to take them back to America, but of course, that was total bullshit. Then he was gone again. And I mean gone. Without a word. Gone.

So now the boys were alone again. But now it was worse because their father was gone too. Even though he was a jerk, he was still their father. With him there, they could at least feel connected to someone. Once he was gone, they were without both parents. How much could these kids take? They couldn't help feeling unwanted. As far as they knew, they were abandoned by both of their parents. They were both born in Italy, so being there was not what was strange, but everything else was. They spent the first part of their lives there. When their father left for America, the plan was for the family to join him there once he got settled. Once they got there, it was only a few months later that their father took them back. Only to leave them alone again. They had their grandparents, but that could never make up for their loss.

* * * * *

Back in New York City, Carmela was furious. She learned that her husband had boarded a ship with the two boys that was bound for Italy. Once she was sure of this, she notified the police. Again, this was done with great difficulty since she barely spoke any English. Imagine what this woman was dealing with while enduring the heartbreak of having her children taken from her. Then there was the embarrassment that it was her husband that had done it. On top of that there was the hopeless feeling of being in a strange country without any money at all.

When she finally got customs and the New York City Police Department to take her seriously, it was too late. The ship carrying her sons was too far out at sea and beyond the jurisdiction of the United States. So despite the efforts of the New York City Police to force the ship back to New York, it was too late... How can one describe what she was feeling once she realized this? Not only was she torn from her children and alone, which of course was the worst of it, but she was going home to an apartment that she had no way of paying for. It's almost impossible to put this situation into words. She had no money, no job and she barely spoke a word of English. The only reason for her being in this country in the first place was gone. Didn't exist. What could she do now? To even attempt to understand what this woman was going through, you have to somehow try and imagine the emptiness of that first night, if that is even possible. And I'm not sure that it is. Now maybe you're there with her. Walking back from the docks of the West Side to her empty apartment. Walking with the pain in her heart that she felt for her two sons. Her children on a ship that was forcing an ocean between them. Now, you're walking with her.

It was the middle of January. The bitter cold walk from the docks on the West Side was brutal, but it was nothing compared to the chill she felt when she opened the door of her now empty apartment. She took off her coat and sat down in her chair by the window. She sat there starring out the window looking at nothing. It was the same window at which she spent hours waiting for her sons to come back earlier that day. Now nobody was coming back. She sat there for hours. And that's where she woke up the next morning. She opened her eyes and the first thing she saw was that window, which by now had become a symbol of her agony. She looked at it for a few moments as the first thoughts of the day took shape. She thought about her sons on the ship. She realized that feeling sorry for herself would not help her get them back. She had not yet moved from the chair she had woke up in. She wanted to think. Without realizing it, she knew she couldn't get up from that chair until she had a positive feeling. She decided to devote the rest of her life, from that moment on, to getting her boys back. How? She had no idea. But it was that thought that enabled her to get up from the chair and begin that first day. And that first day was brutal, but she expected it to be.

She had some good friends and a few relatives in the neighborhood that offered to help her. The easiest thing for her to do would have been to borrow the money she needed to go back to Italy. But she had gone through so much to get to this country with her children and she dreamed of the day when she could become a citizen. She had begun that process months earlier and was waiting for her citizenship to come through when her children were taken from her. If she had left then, she would have given all that up. Now that may sound selfish, and you might think that being with her children should be more important. You also have to realize that in those days, becoming a citizen wasn't as easy as it is now. It was a long process, and she was a stubborn woman. She had a bigger plan for her and her children. She refused to give in and do what her husband expected her to do. It was not an easy decision by any means. She decided to wait. She would take any job and save every penny. She felt strongly that she would be contacted soon about where her children were. She was sure she had already figured out what this bastard was trying to do. She was proud and she was very smart. And her belief in herself would eventually pay off for her and her children.

Time passed slowly, as it always does. For Carmela, time passed by cleaning the bathrooms of the cities many movie theaters. It was the only work someone in her situation could get. Her workday began after midnight and lasted as long as it took her to finish. She did this seven nights a week. Everything she earned, other than the rent and bare essentials, went into the bank.

As she had expected, a telegram arrived after about three weeks informing her of her children's whereabouts. It came from her husband. He said they were at his parents' house and if she ever wanted to see them again, she should go back to Italy right away. He, of course, would not be there. He left no other information about himself. The telegram went on to say that the boys were fine and that she could contact them there. The address was also included.

The telegram was cold and heartless, but that's exactly what she expected. The letter infuriated her but at the same time she took comfort in knowing that the boys were OK. She also enjoyed the satisfaction of being able to predict what he would do. It wasn't much, but she drew confidence from it. She put the telegram down and felt sure she had cleared the first hurdle. Now she was working. She was putting money in the bank and she knew her children were safe. Those were her priorities. She had also not given in to what he wanted her to do. It was a feeling of accomplishment. Her first, on her own. And in her mind, it justified her sacrifice. But there was another freight train heading straight for her.

Within the next couple of days, she found out she was pregnant. Under normal circumstances, this would be something to be happy about. But her life at this point was anything but normal. She was devastated. She was a very religious person and so she felt guilty about not being happy about the baby. But how could she be happy. The father of this baby had just kidnapped her two sons. With all that was going on, she hadn't noticed the first signs of pregnancy. Now she was torn between her feelings of motherhood and the fight she had begun to get her other two children back. She decided to apply herself equally to her sons and to the baby. She thought about her walk back home from the docks that night, when she thought there was no hope. And somehow, that helped.

Carmela knew that with the baby coming, she would only have a couple of months to continue the work she was doing. After that, she had no idea what she would do. It seemed every time she had made some progress in her life, there was another setback. But this was a baby and she refused to think of the child in a negative way. Although she had friends and some relatives in the neighborhood who were willing to help out, the situation still seemed impossible. The people she knew were not that well off and they had their own families to think about.

It was during this time, when people were trying to help, that word had begun to spread about what this woman was going through. One of the people who took an interest was a man named Pasquale Pia. He, like a lot of other people was outraged at what this woman had been through. He was a good man and he decided to try and help.

He was a hard working man. He was the superintendent of about eight or nine buildings in the neighborhood. He also had a lot of connections. He seemed to know everybody. He wasn't well off by any means. He busted his ass every day maintaining all of those buildings. The building Carmela lived in wasn't one of those he took care of, but he knew the landlord. So he went to see him to try and work something out for her. He explained to her landlord and worked out a deal with him. I'm not sure what he did or how he did it, but when the meeting was over, it was agreed that she would not have to pay the rent until after the baby was born and she was able to work again. Because he didn't know her himself, he had one of the neighborhood women explain the situation to her.

This was the kind of man Pasquale was. He didn't even want her to know who had done this for her. He was genuinely trying to help. He was not looking to take credit for anything. When Carmela was told of the good news, she couldn't believe it. When she asked who the man was that had done this for her, her friend said he didn't want her to know. He just wanted to help. She was so happy that such a burden had been lifted from her. But she was frustrated because she wanted to at least thank the man. Her friend told her that she had to respect his wishes and couldn't tell her who he was. But she would thank him personally.

Carmela's life was one, filled with challenges. Some of them were immediate and others were subtle in their effect. But all of them were life altering. She was a woman that had to be respected. Her lifestyle and her sacrifice demanded it. Because there is nothing more admirable than putting yourself aside for the sake of your children. This is a fact even under normal circumstances. But when you factor in everything else in her life and why she was even faced with this situation, you had to just stand back in awe.

Chapter 2

Carmela had her baby toward the end of the summer. It was a time of mixed emotions. Now she had a daughter, she named her Mary. In tribute to the Blessed Mother of God, who she prayed to every night for the safe return of her other two children.

I write about the plight of this special family for a lot of reasons, but mainly out of complete and undeniable respect because it is my family. And as I write about what they were faced with everyday, over a period of nearly eight years, it is with a feeling of utter disbelief that they were able to endure and eventually overcome this impossible situation. To know that the older boy on that ship, who was taken from his mother and then abandoned by his father, was my own father is unbelievable. And no matter how hard I try to put their situation into words I could never really capture what they went through. I only hope that I can somehow, respectfully do justice to their story.

* * * * *

Almost six months had passed since the birth of her daughter when Carmela finally got to meet Pasquale. True to his word, he had allowed her time to concentrate on the baby and get her life in order. He stopped by her apartment one day to see how she was doing. It was amazing that after all this time and everything he had done for her, he had still never met her. She had no idea he was going to be there and was stunned when she answered the door and he introduced himself. She had imagined what it would be like to finally meet the man, over and over, in her mind. And how she would try to thank him for everything he had done for her. But now that he was standing in her doorway she just stood there looking at him. She didn't know what to say. He apologized for showing up unannounced and said if it was a bad time he would come back another day. She got hold of herself and asked him to come in. He had come with bags of groceries and gifts for the baby. It was an awkward moment, which was understandable. She put on a pot of coffee and they talked for hours.

Carmela was relieved to finally meet him and be able to thank him for what he had done. He told her it was nothing and that he was happy to help. She felt comfortable talking with him. She was relieved and felt sure his generosity was genuine. He expected nothing in return. It was only natural for a woman in her situation to be skeptical. In the back of her mind, she had always wondered why this man was doing these things for her. She knew that meeting him was the only way she could be sure of his intentions. She would only have to look in his eyes. She believed only in herself. She would know.

Now she could relax. She found out what she wanted to know. Before he left, Pasquale told her he had friends in Italy near the town of St. Donato. He said if it was all right with her, they would check on the well-being of her sons. The rush of emotions she felt when she heard what he had said backed her up. She felt for the kitchen table and sat down on one of the chairs. When Pasquale saw her reaction, he sat down next to her and apologized for speaking out of line. She said that the thought of being able to reach out to her boys was too much to absorb. He told her to take her time and think about it. He gave her an address where he could be reached. Before he left, he asked if it would be all right if he stopped by to see how she was doing. She said yes and they said their goodbyes.

After he left, she needed time to think. It was time to feed and change the baby and she went to her. Carmela tended to her daughter with her mind racing. When the baby was fed, she got her ready for bed. Before she put her in her crib for the night, she took her in her arms and sat in her chair. She held her daughter close to her and thought about what Pasquale had told her. As she watched her baby's eyes drift into sleep, her mind wandered across the ocean to the town of St. Donato. And she thought about her two boys. She felt close to them for the first time since they had been taken from her. And with that thought in her mind and her baby in her arms, she fell asleep.

* * * * *

Back in Italy, Donato and Anthony went about their lives. Such as it was, with no feeling of belonging anywhere. They had no idea what was going on. They had one thing in their favor. They were young and children have an ability to adapt to a situation without much thought. It's just part of being that age. It wasn't much of an advantage but it was the only one they had.

In the years that passed, Donato and Anthony lived in their grandparent's house in Italy. Their grandparent's were old and there was no form of family life at all. Also there were other relatives in the house, another whole family actually; an aunt and uncle and their two children. Donato and Anthony bore the brunt of being two children unusual in the fact that their parents weren't there and they weren't genuinely wanted.

When it was dinner time, they were allowed to eat only the scraps of food that were left by the other two children. In fact, even the packages Carmela had managed to send to them (by then she had learned of their whereabouts), were opened first by the relatives and enjoyed by their kids before the boys got to see them.

By now they had been placed in a local school. This at least, gave them some feeling of normalcy. It also gave them something to do. And with that, came their first sense of belonging. Not surprisingly, they did do well in school, even though their home life was a disaster. The town they lived in was small and everybody knew their situation. They went to school to escape their home life, and they went home to escape the ridicule they went through at school. There was no one to comfort them through this difficult time in their young lives. It's hard to imagine what they felt like. They were young and innocent. They were in this situation through no fault of their own. They were being robbed of their youth and they were denied the opportunity that every child deserves; to experience their youth and to grow and learn with the support of their parents. They had nothing but themselves. This hardened them.

* * * * *

Back in New York, Carmela, never a woman to waste any time, had begun working at any job she could find. She had found a woman in her building that she trusted to watch her daughter. As she had done before the baby was born, she began to save every dollar she didn't absolutely need. She had also begun paying her rent, refusing to take any more money from Pasquale. She was too proud. She just felt better paying it herself. It was the beginning of years of sacrifice and hard work. And she thought, the sooner she got used to the struggle, the better. She saw no point in putting off the inevitable, what good would it do her? She began cleaning at the movie theater's again. She did this in the evening after they closed. She also took a job washing dishes at a restaurant during the day. This restaurant was in the neighborhood and it allowed her to check on her daughter from time to time. The two jobs took up most of her time. The baby took up the rest. But she was driven. She felt the more she worked, the closer she would be to getting her boys back. She worried about them constantly. And she missed them so much it hurt. If she thought about them long enough, she would begin to cry. So she fought that too.

This unimaginable situation that had been going on for three years now, continued. Who knows how, it's almost impossible to understand how this woman dealt with her difficulties. Which was worse? Struggling to make ends meet in a foreign country with a newborn child, or was it the heartache she felt everyday for her two sons. Two young boys robbed of a mother's love and living in Italy with people who didn't want them. Either one was enough to break a person. A woman alone, faced with both couldn't possibly have a chance. But this woman was stubborn. She had a fire in her heart. It was put there by a man that had wrecked her life and stolen her dreams. She hated him for that.

But that was secondary to her. She could deal with her own pain and sorrow, but what he had done to her children was a different matter. To steal their childhood years and use them as leverage for his own selfish reasons was unforgivable. Somehow, some way, someday, she was going to make him answer for that. She was furious and decided to use that emotion for the sake of her children.

So she went on. Day by day, month-by-month and so on. As the months slowly turned into years she was driven by her determination. She drew strength from the passage of time. The longer she went on, the stronger she got. It became an obsession. But then she knew it would, it was the only way. How else could you put yourself aside and think only of your children. She developed a mindset and would live by it, no matter what. She was living life for one reason, to get her kids back. She would allow herself only one distraction, her daughter. She devoted herself evenly to both of these responsibilities. Raising her daughter and getting her sons back. To consider her own feelings would be a setback to one or the other. This approach would be very difficult. After everything she had been through, whatever she decided would have been understandable. Her decision to continue to deny her own needs for the sake of her children portrayed her perfectly. It was this aspect of her personality that would enable her to endure what she was faced with. Not that it would be easy, but she knew it was the right thing to do. Knowing it would take years of sacrifice worried her, but it didn't change anything, it couldn't. It had to be done. The bottom line was how could you not do this for your kids? So, without really knowing how, she went on.

What can you say about a woman like this? Any attempt at describing her struggle had to come up short. To try and put into words what she was going through is very difficult. Because writing about something or reading about something, no matter how hard you try, could never really capture what it was like for her. What she eventually accomplished, considering the situation was amazing in itself. On top of that, she did this for eight years! Eight years! Think about that. It's hard to do something you like to do for that long.

By the end of his fourth year in Italy, my father was almost thirteen years old. The same age I was when my mother died. I mention this because it was something I drew strength from years later. I was twenty six years old when I started writing about my family. I still couldn't accept my mother's death. Not that I can now. But once I started writing about everything, my father was always on my mind. What he had gone through at such an early age and everything else after that. Thinking about that and what my mother must have felt like knowing she was dying and would have to leave us, would never be lost on me. I never felt sorry for myself because of what happened to my mother. I wouldn't allow it. Believe me, I knew how fucked up it was, but knowing what my mother and father had been through, I just felt that they had suffered much more. For me to pity myself would be selfish and would somehow downplay what they went through. I wasn't going to do that, no matter what I was feeling. I loved them both so much. I could tell my father that because he is still here, and I do. But I would never see my mother again. And putting her feelings before my own was the only way I could think of to tell her the same thing. That's the way I felt and I would live by it. It was all about respect.

It was the end of January. Somehow three years had passed since Carmela had seen her sons. She felt the strain of working two jobs for so long, but she ignored it. Although she hated this time of year because it was the anniversary of when her boys were taken, it was also a relief because the holidays were over. Christmas and New Years were the hardest for her. She battled against her sorrow for the sake of her daughter, Mary. She wanted her daughter to enjoy the holidays, as every kid should. But what an impossible situation. To celebrate the holidays with your daughter while at the same time, feeling the agony of missing your sons. She was also working two jobs, six days a week, for the past two years. She was exhausted from her work schedule and the emotional strain of her everyday struggle. But there was no time for her to worry about herself. She wouldn't allow it. She had set her goals. She didn't know how long it would take her to get her boys back, but she wasn't going to stop until she did. So she went on, nobody knows how, she just did.

A lot of people deal with hardship in their lives. Some worse than what Carmela was facing, others with less drastic situations. But usually, there is some type of support from somewhere. A family member, or a close friend of the family, somebody. She had no one. Courage and belief in yourself, can only come from within. She had that. But even that can run a little dry over time. How she went on year after year with only herself to rely on is really hard to imagine.

It had been three years since the boys were taken from her. It would be another five before Carmela could afford to pay for their return. You might wonder how it could take eight years to save enough money to pay for two kids to get here from Italy. To put things into perspective, the year was 1933, to get here by ship, which was the only way at the time, cost two or three hundred dollars. Carmela was making about nine dollars a week and she had a daughter to care for. Also, for two kids it would be about five or six hundred dollars. Think about that. Her annual salary was about four hundred and thirty dollars. Take out living expenses for her and her daughter and then you could understand. Maybe.

Carmela Genelli and Pasquale Pia

Chapter 3

Carmela was modest, so she went on. Continuing her struggle. Not with any self-pity, but with an acceptance that this was what she was faced with. And what she would somehow have to overcome. It was during this point in time, as she dealt with her ongoing struggle that she received an anonymous letter. It was from a woman in the neighborhood. She explained that she was aware of her situation. And that she knew the whereabouts of her husband. She went on to say that she couldn't live with herself, unless she told what she knew.

Carmela, still standing where she opened the letter, read on. The woman went on to say that Alfonso Genelli was working as a tailor at Wannamaker's, then, a big time clothing manufacturer in Manhattan. As I said, the woman did not leave her name at the end of the letter. There was no other way to contact her. She closed by saying that she didn't want to get directly involved. Then she said that she hoped and prayed that this information would help Carmela in some way during this time of hardship. Carmela folded the letter and put it back into the envelope it came in. Then she sat down and began to think about what she would do next. Her mind was flooded with emotions. The idea that she knew where her husband was took a while for her to digest, but there were other feelings for her to confront. Wanting to find someone who had caused so much pain and cruelty on you and your children, was one thing. But knowing that now it was a reality, especially after all these years, was something else.

The next day, she walked to the local police station and told her story. It wasn't easy because of the language barrier. There was an Italian police officer on duty that day that took an interest in her story. She spoke to him in Italian and told him everything. Starting with the day her son's were taken from her and ending with the letter she had just received.

The officer's name was Frank Malzone. And when she was done with her story, he just sat there. It was an awkward moment. Then he stood up and asked her if she wanted a cup of coffee. She looked at him for a moment, and then she said, "Yes, that would be nice." Then he left the room. While he was gone

Carmela had time to think. She thought about the officer's reaction as she told her story. Especially the look on his face when she was done. And she understood that too. She was so used to dealing with her struggle on an everyday basis, after accepting the reality so long ago, that she had somehow forgotten how horrible it was. And how someone hearing it for the first time would react. She also realized something else. She was sitting in a Police Station. And that in itself, always had some kind of effect on a normal person. It was the first time she had ever begun any kind of legal process against her husband. And underneath it all, fueling everything, she knew where this bastard was! She had mixed emotions about almost everything that was going on. It was a lot to think about. But somewhere along the line she had gotten used to that. She had to because she had no choice. With all these thoughts slamming around inside her head and the anonymous letter in her hand, she sat there. She was lost in her thoughts. She thought about her boys again. Her mind was across the ocean when the door opened and broke her concentration. Officer Frank Malzone walked into the room and closed the door behind him. Then he sat down in front of her and looked into her eyes. He had a smile on his face, then he said, "Let's go get him!" She sat back in her chair and covered her face with her hands. Officer Malzone leaned forward and put his hand on her shoulder. Then he said, "Carmela, we don't have to do this today. We can do it another time. I just want you to know that you can. And whenever you feel up to it, I'll go with you." She had started to cry, but fought that too. Then she took her hands off her face and put them in her lap. She looked back at him. Her eyes, red and filled with tears. He knew she was upset; maybe even a little shaken but there was something else. He had been a Police Officer for many years and had a trained eye. Before another word was spoken, she had his respect. Because what he saw in her eyes was obvious to him. It was pure determination. A belief in oneself. A characteristic in her personality that enabled her to get to this point in her life. She looked at him and said, "I want to thank you for your support because I really do appreciate it. But don't ever feel sorry for me. I don't want or need your pity. And do not view my grief as a sign of weakness." He sat back in his chair. His respect for her, growing with every statement she made. She told him she would need a day or two, to gather her thoughts before she could confront her husband. Then, she would be ready. He wrote down his phone number on a piece of paper and handed it to her. She took the phone number from him and put it in her pocket. Then she stood up and said she would call him when she was ready. He got up from his chair and said, "I admire your strength and I'll be waiting for your call." She thanked him and walked toward the door. When she got to the door, she opened it, turned to look at him. Then she said, "I admire your compassion and I thank you for that." Then she walked out the door. When the door closed behind her, Frank Malzone sat back down in his chair. A few minutes later, the door opened again. His partner, Jack Ryan, walked in and sat down across from his desk. The two men sat in silence for a few seconds. Then Jack said, "Hey Frank, are you okay?" Frank said, "Yeah." Then he just sat there. Jack looked at him and said, "Who was that woman that just left?" Frank stood up and said, "Put aside whatever you're working on for a couple of days. She needs our help and we're gonna give it to her."

Carmela went back to her apartment. On the way, she stopped to buy some pastries for the woman across the hall, who was staying with her daughter. She had no way of knowing that the woman who had sent her the anonymous letter about her husband, had also sent word to her husband that she had done so. For whatever reason, that's what she did. This gave Alfonso time to think. Time, he clearly did not deserve. Knowing that Carmela knew where he was, Alfonso began to prepare himself. He knew she would come after him. He just didn't know when. He knew he was going to have to deal with her, sooner or later.

Of course, he had begun to prepare for this moment years ago. Because that was the kind of person he was, a real scumbag. He took advantage of Carmela's trust in many ways. The worst of it, of course, was the day he took her children. But to really understand what kind of scumbag he was, you have to factor this in. The same day he kidnapped her two sons, he did something else. Something almost worse than taking her kids, if that is even possible. Before he left with the boys, he asked her to sign some papers. He told her they were for the lease on their apartment. She couldn't read English, so she just signed them. He knew she couldn't read and he also knew she would believe him. The legal documents he gave to her to sign were divorce papers. But even worse than that, the way he had the documents drawn up, she was not only agreeing to the divorce, but also granting him full custody of their children. It was a despicable display of deceit. But like I said, he was a scumbag and had planned for this very day. So, from the day he learned that Carmela knew of his whereabouts and every day after that, he carried the documents with him everywhere he went.

Carmela went home and went about her daily routine as best she could. She worked everyday, so she had no idea when she could find the time to confront Alfonso. If she took any time off from work, she knew she could lose her job. She also knew this was something she had to do. It's important to try and imagine the stress and pressure of a situation like this. Especially for someone in her position. A woman who finally had the opportunity to bring her husband to justice. The man that had handed down so much cruelty and shame on her and her children. But to do it, she might have to lose her job. I mean, how fucked up is that? On top of that, it's not like she could just get another job. In those days, a woman with the limitations of her situation was lucky to even have a job.

So, there she was. Faced with another situation. One with the possibility of no up side for her. When she thought about how many times she was faced with this kind of thing, it made her crazy. But what it did not do, what she would not allow it to do, was make her give up. So, she did what she always did. She drew upon an inner strength. Her inner strength. A feeling inside her that was born on the day her children were kidnapped. And had been with her ever since. And it grew with every obstacle she was able to overcome. She had withstood so much and yet, here was another test. It's interesting to understand the human spirit at times like these. Because just like anything else, the more you have to deal with something, the more normal it becomes. It just gets easier. No matter how fucked up it is. This was no different. It was another avenue of thought she was traveling. It was then; she decided to call Frank Malzone.

Without realizing it, she decided to go after him. It was a gut reaction, based on a feeling deep inside her. For some reason she felt that this might be her only chance. The one opportunity she may ever have. She didn't know why but she had a strong feeling that if she waited for a more convenient time, it would be a mistake. A mistake that might give him one more chance to slip away. If she lost her job, so be it. She would find another one, somehow. Just as she had somehow found a way to do everything else.

The next morning, she made the call. A single phone call that would begin to bridge an eight year gap in her life. As she dialed the phone number to the Police Department, she realized her hand was trembling. She remembered thinking how weird it was that dialing a single phone number could cover so much time. She was lost in thought when he answered the phone. "Frank Malzone, Manhattan Central." She hesitated for a second, then said, "This is Carmela Genelli, do you remember me? I came to see you a few days ago about my husband. If you're busy, I'll call back another day."

Detective Malzone stood up and closed the door to his office. Then he said, "Carmela, how are you? Of course I remember you. How can I help you?" He was a very busy man. And had been involved with several new cases since the last time he had talked to her. But he was happy to hear from her. He had hoped that she would contact him again, for two reasons. The first was because so many women in her situation never follow up or even get back to him. And usually end up dropping the whole thing. Either because they're ashamed of themselves or don't think it's worth the trouble. Because they are afraid of the whole process. That they may have to face added humiliation without accomplishing anything. The second reason he was glad she called was because he had been genuinely moved, by what she had been through. He was a New York City cop and had worked the streets for more than fifteen years. But he had never come across a story, quite like hers. Like I said, he was a cop. But more than that, he was a good man with street smarts. He was motivated by the facts of the case but also by her courage. He saw something in her. He wasn't sure what it was but he really wanted to help her.

She said, "I've been under so much pressure between the baby and my job, and trying to decide what to do. But I'm tired of thinking now. So, if you can find the time to help me, I would like to figure out a way to confront my husband. I am afraid that this decision could cause me additional pain and hardship. But I've been afraid of so many things for so long that even if it does, I don't care anymore. I have to start to make him pay. At least try to, in some way, for what he's done to us. Not for me, but at least for the kids. To allow him to just go on with his life as if nothing had happened, as though we didn't matter, would insult my very soul. Everything I believe in and the lives of my children are being challenged. And I will not stand for that. I couldn't live with myself, if I did."

Frank Malzone sat there and listened to her as she expressed her thoughts and reasons for her decision. It seemed to him that every time he talked to her, he respected her even more. He told her that he understood everything she was talking about. He assured her that he would be available to her whenever she felt ready, no matter how busy he was. Then he said, "It's true, I am very busy. So all I ask is that you let me know when you want to do this. When are you thinking of going to where your husband is working?" She thanked him again, then she said, "Tomorrow morning." He started to laugh, for no other reason than pure surprise. He stopped when he heard her say, "If you think there is anything funny about this, Mr. Malzone, I would appreciate it if you could refer me to another police officer." He knew he had unintentionally insulted her. He didn't need another display of her determination. But he got it anyway. He said, "Carmela, I'm sorry. I shouldn't have laughed. I sincerely apologize for that. And it surely was not because anything was funny. It was a reaction of surprise and pure respect for your resolve." She waited a few seconds before answering. Then she said, "I'm not sure I understand what you said. My English isn't so good. But if you can still help me, I would like to move forward." He said, "Of course I can. Please continue." He remembered thinking, for a woman with such a burden on her; she sure knew how to put someone in their place. Then she said, "If you can pick me up in the morning, I'll take you to where he is working." He said, "What time would you like me to be there?" She said, "Nine o'clock but please don't be late. I'll have to make arrangements for someone to watch my daughter and I have to be back as soon as possible. I have to go to work after that. And hopefully I won't have to lose my job because of this decision." He said, "I'll be there." She thanked him again, and hung up the phone. He sat there for a moment, thinking about what she had said. Then he called his partner into his office. Jack Ryan came through the door and said, "What's up, Boss?" Frank looked at him and said, "Put everything on hold. We got something important to take care of." Jack said, "Are you sure, Frank? We're pretty busy tomorrow." He said, "Yeah I'm sure. There's a woman who needs our help and we're going to do, just that. I don't care how busy we are. She's more important. We're gonna help her bring that dirtbag to justice. We gotta pick her up tomorrow morning at nine o'clock. Then I'm gonna drive her over to where this guy works and take him in. And I want to put the handcuffs on him myself. I'm looking forward to it."

    The following morning Carmela got herself ready for the events of the day. First by seeing to it that her daughter would be cared for. Then, by trying to cope with what she would actually be doing that day. She had waited so long for this day to come. To be able to look into the eyes of the person responsible for the last eight years of her life. Of course, she could also lose her job for this opportunity but she managed to put that aside. But thinking about confronting someone like this for so many years, and actually doing it, were two different things. This was a person she had been married to for a number of years. A man she had three children with and had planned a life. What would she see in his eyes? How would she cope with what she saw? Of course, she wouldn't know until she did it. But these were her thoughts as she got her daughter ready. As she thought about maybe losing her job and as she waited for the police car that would take her to the next chapter of her life. As she dressed her daughter and kissed her, she knew she would find a way. What a remarkable woman. Whatever the outcome, this was a woman that had to be respected.

At 9:00 AM, a New York City police car pulled up in front of Carmela's apartment building. Of course, she was standing in the doorway, waiting for them. Frank Malzone got out of the car and said hello. She thanked him for coming and got into the car. Jack Ryan drove to the corner and turned right onto Broadway, then headed downtown. The mood inside the car was tense. Frank asked Carmela how she was doing and she snapped at him, "Don't worry about how I'm doing, just make sure your friend knows where he's going. Does he have the address I gave you?" Frank said, "Yes he does. Carmela I know you must be upset. It's only natural under these circumstances but try to relax and everything will be okay." She said, "I'll relax after I get my hands on that bastard. Just drive the car." Frank looked at Jack for a second, then told him to drive on. Frank was a little worried about Carmela's state of mind and what she might do when they got there.

But he decided to leave her alone for a while. He didn't want to get her any more worked up than she already was. A few minutes later they pulled up in front of the department store where he worked. Frank turned around and asked Carmela if she was okay. He could see that she was nervous but he expected that. They were minutes away from what would be a very emotional confrontation. She told him she was fine. Then she opened the door and got out of the car. Frank looked at Jack and said, "Put the cherry on top of the car and let's go do this." Jack reached under the front seat and pulled out the magnetic police beacon and attached it to the top of the car. Then he hit the switch and the circular red and amber lights lit up the entrance to the building.

They walked into the building and got on the elevator. Frank pushed the button for the sixth floor and stood next to Carmela. When the doors opened they walked up to the reception desk. The secretary said, "Can I help you with something?" Carmela said, "Look at her, acting like nothing is wrong." Frank put his arm around Carmela's shoulder and said, "We're here on official business. I'm Officer Frank Malzone and this is Officer Jack Ryan. We would like to speak to someone in authority from your company." The woman stood up and said, "I'll go get my supervisor, please wait here." A few minutes later a man walked into the room and said, "Gentlemen, I'm Mr. Myers.

Can I help you with something?" Frank Malzone said, "Yes, I believe you can. We're Police Officers from Manhattan Central. We're here to speak to an employee of yours. His name is Alfonso Genelli. We know he works here and we would like you to bring him down here. We need to speak to him and we need to do that right now." Mr. Myers said, "What is this about?" Frank looked at him and said, "Mr. Myers, what this is about is none of your fucking business. What you need to do is bring Mr. Genelli down here right now. If you do anything else but that, you will have problems of your own. Are we clear on that?" Mr. Myers said, "I'm sorry for asking, I'll go get him." He started to walk toward the door when Frank said, "And Mr. Myers, if you tell him anything, other than you need to see him in your office, I'll make your life a living hell!" Mr. Myers reacted like the chump that he was, and said, "I don't want any trouble, and I'll do exactly what you say." Then he walked out the door.

They sat in the office and waited for him to come back. Without saying a word they all knew they were about to experience an extremely emotional moment. They were there on Carmela's behalf, no doubt about that. But this moment was not lost on any of them. What aspect of that moment would be more intense? Would it be Carmela seeing the man who had wrecked the lives of her and her children, after all these years? Or would it be the look on her husband's face, that heartless bastard, who had no idea what he was walking into or who he would be seeing? As these thoughts danced through all of their minds, the office door opened. Jack Ryan stood in front of the doorway. Behind him, Frank Malzone put his arm around Carmela's shoulder and held her tight. Mr. Myers walked in, with Alfonso behind him.

The door closed behind them. Jack Ryan stood in front of Alfonso with his arms folded on his chest. Alfonso looked at him and said, "Who the hell are you? Mr. Myers, what's this all about?" Then Frank Malzone said, "Is this your husband?" That's when Alfonso saw her face. He looked into Carmela's eyes and stood motionless for a few seconds. Then he said, "Carmela, you look good. But what are you doing here? This is where I work. You come to my job and embarrass me like this?" Carmela's eyes widened as she felt the blood rush to her head. She pushed Frank Malzone's arm off her shoulder. Then she walked toward Alfonso and said, "Sommanabitch, what am I doing here?" She pulled her arm back and punched him right in the mouth. Alfonso fell backward as his front tooth flew out of his mouth and blood poured down his face. When he hit the floor, Carmela was all over him. She was kicking him and cursing his name when Mr. Myers said, "What are you doing, this is my office!" Jack Ryan smacked him in the back of the head and said, "Shut the fuck up!" Frank Malzone grabbed Carmela and pulled her off him. She was still kicking him, saying, "That's what I'm doing here, you bastard!"

Jack Ryan looked at Frank and said, "What do you want me to do, boss?" Frank said, "I'm gonna take Carmela downstairs for a cup of coffee. Handcuff that piece of shit and read him his rights. Then, bring him downstairs. I'll have a paddy wagon waiting for him when you get there." Jack said, "No problem, I'll bring him down." Frank left with Carmela and Jack walked back over to Alfonso. He was still sitting on the floor with his hands covering his mouth. He looked at Jack and said, "Did you see what she did to me? I want to press charges against her. Make her pay for what she did to me. You're a police officer, you have to help me!" Jack looked at him and said, "What are you talking about? When you tried to assault your wife, that's when I punched you in the mouth. That's what happened. Don't try to blame her for any of this." Alfonso said, "That's not what happened. Mr. Myers, you saw what she did, tell him." Mr. Myers looked at Jack Ryan, not knowing what to do. Then he said, "Officer, I have to tell the truth, that's not what I saw." Jack walked over to where he was standing. He bent down and looked into his eyes and said, "Is that right?" Then he reached out with one hand and grabbed him by the throat. Mr. Myers tried to say something, but couldn't. It was no use. Now he was gasping for air. Jack squeezed his throat a little tighter and said, "When I let go, you're going to tell me what you really saw. Do we understand each other?" Mr. Myers couldn't talk, so he just shook his head up and down. Jack let him go and he fell to the floor. He was coughing and trying to catch his breath. Jack looked down at him and said, "Time is up, Asshole! This is where you tell me what you saw." Mr. Myers stood up and said, "I was standing right here when Alfonso tried to attack that woman. You had no choice but to try and defend her. That's when you punched him in the face." Alfonso said, "That's not what happened. Who the hell does he think he is, lying like that?" Jack said, "I don't know who, he thinks he is, but I think he's an eye witness. And that's all that matters." Then he picked him up by his shirt collar, turned him around and handcuffed him. Then he said, "You have the right to remain silent." Alfonso said, "What does that mean?" Jack said, "It means, shut the fuck up!" Then he read him the rest of his rights. Jack walked Alfonso, his hands cuffed behind him, through the office and onto the elevator that would take them downstairs.

Carmela and Frank Malzone sat inside the coffee shop across the street from the building Alfonso worked in, sipping cappuccino as they talked. He had managed to calm her down, somewhat. But her temper was still raging. By now, he knew her well enough to sense that. He put his coffee down and said, "Carmela, they should be coming down any minute now. When they do, I want you to try to control yourself. It's very important, please." She said, "Control myself? That sommanabitch, he's lucky I only hit him once!" Frank said, "That's what I'm talking about. Forget about that. You can't hit him anymore. Jack and I will figure out a way to conceal the fact that you hit him in the first place, if he hasn't done that already. But you can't hit him again. It will hurt your case against him, trust me. If you do, you'll be helping him. And I know you don't want to do that! Besides, that was a pretty good shot you hit him with upstairs. You knocked his tooth out, for God sakes! Trust me; you can hurt him more by not hitting him." She looked at him and said, "OK, policeman. I try not to hit him. But I no promise nothing, OK?" He looked at her for a second and just smiled. He was amazed by her. He thought, so much strength and conviction from someone who hadn't caught a break in years. A rare display of courage from a woman in her situation. No self-pity, which would be understandable. A kind of courage that had been born out of despair. He was lost in thought when he heard her say, "Hey Policeman, you smile at me. You think it's a funny?" He started to apologize when he saw Jack Ryan bringing Alfonso out the front door of the building. He leaned over and grabbed both of Carmela's hands. He held them tight, looked into her eyes, and said, "There's something I've wanted to say to you but haven't had the time. Unfortunately, I don't have the time now either. In a minute you'll know why. But it has to be said right now! I have more respect for you than any woman I have ever met, in my sixteen years on the job. Please believe me, Senora. But right now, we got work to do. My partner just brought your husband out of the building." Carmela looked right back into his eyes and said, "Thank you for your kind words, I do appreciate them." Then she pulled her hands back and stood up. She looked across the street and saw her husband, standing on the sidewalk in handcuffs. She picked up her pocketbook and said, "Andiamo!"

    Carmela headed straight for the front door, as Frank hurriedly paid the check. He called out to her but she kept walking. He caught up to her on the sidewalk outside. He grabbed her by the arm and said, "Carmela, please, remember what I told you." She pulled her arm away and walked across the street. Frank followed her, expecting the worst but hoping for the best. When she got to the other side of the street and stepped up onto the curb, she was face to face with her husband for the second time that day. Frank caught up with her and stood between the two of them. As they stood there the police paddywagon pulled up to the curb, right behind them. When Alfonso saw this, he looked over Frank's shoulder at Carmela and said, "You're not gonna let them take me away in that thing, are you? Don't embarrass me like that. After all, I am your husband. Doesn't that mean anything to you?" Jack Ryan saw Carmela's eyes widen with rage again. He grabbed her husband by the arm and led him over toward the paddy wagon. When he got to the door of the police van, Carmela rushed toward him. She grabbed him by the neck and slammed his head against the van door. The bridge of his nose split open and blood poured down his face. He started screaming, "Get her away from me!" Frank ran over and put his arms around Carmela. Then he said, "Senora, please calm down!" She wanted to go after him again but couldn't break free. Then as they were putting him into the paddy wagon she said, "I hope I didn't embarrass you too much, you sommonabitch!" The scene was unbelievable but Frank was used to it by now. Not because it was easy, it wasn't. But he had no choice. He knew she was beyond his control. By now, that was obvious. He just admired her and hoped everything worked out okay.

Frank and Carmela stood in the street. He still had his arm around her. They watched as the paddy wagon drove off with Alfonso inside. Carmela looked at Frank and said, "We got him, right?" Frank looked back at her and said, "No Senora, we found him. We still gotta get him." When she looked back at him, he could see that look in her eyes. The same look he saw when he first met her.

It was a combination of determination and strength. But like that first day, he also saw in those eyes a trace of weariness and acceptance for whatever would come next. It came from what she was forced to become used to. She wouldn't, or couldn't, let herself trust any feeling of accomplishment. Because something always happened next. He wanted to tell her that he understood what he saw in her eyes. But he knew he couldn't. He knew she wouldn't admit to what he saw. She would never let him get that close. So he just smiled at her and said, "Jack will be here in a couple of minutes. Let's get in the car and wait for him there. Then we'll go down to the police station." She looked at him and said, "Maybe I'm a no have the chance to say this before. You a good man, Frank Malzone. 'Grazia Tante.' Thank you for all your help, OK?" He looked back at her and said, "Yeah Senora, OK."

When they got to the car, Jack Ryan walked over to where Mr. Myers was standing. He grabbed him by his shirt collar and pulled him until they were face to face. Frank opened the car door and helped Carmela inside. Then he told her to wait for him there. He closed the door and walked over to where Jack was standing. When he got there he heard Jack saying, "If I find out you did anything to help this guy hide from his wife, I'm gonna come back and break your neck. Do you hear what I'm telling you?" Frank put his arm around Jack's shoulder and said, "Let's go Jack, we got work to do. And Mr. Myers, you better pay attention to what this guy just told you. He is a crazy bastard and I can't watch him all the time." Then Jack let go of Mr. Myer's tie and he was petrified. As Frank and Jack walked toward the car Mr. Myers said, "I won't do anything, I swear. In fact as of right now, he's fired. He'll never work for this company again. I hope that proves my innocence in this matter!" When they got to the car, Frank got in the back seat next to Carmela. Jack opened the driver's side door. Before he got in he looked in at Mr. Myers and said, "You better hope I don't find a reason to come back here!" Then he got in the car and they drove off.

Inside the car, the attention shifted back to Carmela. She had been through a lot and it was beginning to take effect. You could see the strain on her face. As they drove toward the police station, she started to cry. Frank thought about saying something to comfort her but didn't. Carmela wiped the tears from her face. Then she looked at Frank and he said, "When we get to the station house, we'll file formal charges. Starting with kidnapping, child endangerment and nonsupport. Then we'll go from there. Don't worry Carmela, we got plenty on that bastard." She smiled, then looked straight ahead. Frank felt confident about what he had told her but there was something he couldn't put his finger on. An uneasy feeling he had but didn't know why. He couldn't explain it but he knew she felt it too. He also knew that she was already thinking about having to get back to her daughter. By now, he knew her that well. He looked at her and said, "Don't worry Senora, we won't take any more time than we have to. I know you have to get back home." He knew she heard him but she said nothing.

Jack Ryan turned left on Twenty-Third Street and pulled up in front of the station house. There was the usual activity in front of the building. It just added to the overall chaos of the situation. Frank asked Carmela if she was ready to go inside. She said, "We don't get anything done from inside the car." Then she opened the door and got out of the car. Jack looked at Frank through the rear view mirror and said, "I'm really starting to like that woman. She's really something, ain't she?" Frank said, "Yeah, she sure is. We better go catch up with her before she starts a fucking riot in there."

They got out of the car and walked into the building. They caught up with Carmela just as she got to the sergeant's desk. She had already begun to raise her voice as she told the officer she wanted to know where her husband was. Frank put his hand on her shoulder and said, "Carmela please, calm down and let me handle this." She pushed his hand away and said, "No, I talk for myself. And this is as calm as I'm gonna get. And nobody gonna tell me what to do anymore. You hear what I'm saying to you." Frank looked at her and saw that look in her eyes that always made him nervous. There was a rage in her that was always close to boiling over. Then the desk sergeant said, "Excuse me Ma'am, but you will listen to me!" Carmela turned around to face him. She looked right at him and said, "No I won't listen to you or anybody else, ever again. I don't care who you are or what you think I should do. I know what I have to do. I'm here to find the animal that took my children from me. And you are gonna tell me where he is. And if you don't I will find somebody who will. Because from this moment on, the person who tells me where he is, is the only person I will listen to. Do you understand me now, you SOMMANABITCH?" Frank stepped in front of her and begged her not to say another word. The desk sergeant looked at them for a moment. Then he called Frank over and asked him to fill him in on the details of the situation. Frank walked up to the desk and told him everything he knew about Carmela and what she had been through.

The desk sergeant's name was Philip Russo. And he was genuinely moved by what he had just heard. He came out from behind his desk and walked up to Carmela. He was an extremely large man. Which made the way she stood up to him even more remarkable. He stood in front of her and grabbed both of her hands. Carmela looked up at him and he said, "Senora, I'm very sorry for everything you have been through. I admire your strength and courage. And I will do what I can to help you." Carmela said, "That's very nice and thank you for your kind words. But when will you start doing what you can to help me? I have to get back to my daughter, Maria. Because she is just as important as all of this business." Sergeant Russo looked at her in disbelief. He was taken back by her straightforwardness and the ease at which she could put someone in their place. Frank Malzone broke the silence by saying, "Sergeant, I had the same reaction at first. But trust me, she's the real deal. And she deserves our help." Sergeant Russo looked at Carmela and smiled. Then Carmela said, "And now that everybody likes me, can we do something?" She was relentless in her approach. Sergeant Russo looked at Frank and said, "I see what you mean. Let's get started. You stay here with Carmela and I'll go across the hall and find out what I can about her husband."

Frank and Carmela walked across the room and sat down on one of the benches against the wall. She immediately started questioning why everything was taking so long. He tried to calm her down but by now she was really fired up. They weren't there five minutes when they saw Alfonso, still in handcuffs, being led into one of the interrogation rooms. Carmela went nuts and had to be restrained by Frank Malzone. She tried to go after him but couldn't break free from the hold Frank had on her. She was screaming at him, "You should die, you bastard!" They quickly got him into the interrogation room and Frank eventually got Carmela to sit down again. He started telling her that she should try to calm down when she said, "Don't bother me, Policeman. When I see you start to get something done, then you can tell me what I should do! Until then, I'll decide how I should act, OK?" He couldn't tell her, of course, but he loved her attitude.

They sat there for the next twenty minutes, basically saying nothing. The only time Frank said anything to her was when he had to answer her only question, over an over. "Why aren't you going in there to find out what's going on?" He kept telling her, "Because we have to wait here until they come out." "Why" Carmela would say. After this exact dialogue went on for about the fifth time, Sergeant Russo came out of the room. They both got up and walked over to him. He looked at them and said, "We all need to go inside and straighten this out." Frank and Carmela followed him into the room.

Once inside, Frank noticed that Alfonso had a lawyer with him. This was not unusual under the circumstances. But Frank's years of experience on the street and in the courtroom, forced him to notice it. It wasn't a big deal but in his mind, he saw it as a negative. It was almost like Alfonso was expecting this, somehow. And it bothered him. They all sat down at a table across from one another. It was a very intense situation and the atmosphere in the room was electric. You had Alfonso, who had to still be in shock that his wife had actually found him. Frank Malzone and Sergeant Russo had been through this kind of thing before, no doubt. But they both knew that this was a unique situation. One that neither of them, despite all their experience, had ever come across before. So they didn't know what to expect. Then there was Carmela, who obviously, had the most to win or lose. She had more at stake than anybody there. Her blood was boiling. It was extremely difficult for her to sit across from the man who had wrecked her life and the lives of her children. She could not control her emotions. In her mind, this was all bullshit. It was obvious what this man did. So, what the hell was there to talk about? As she felt her heartbeat pounding in her chest, she glared at Alfonso. He, of course, could not even look at her. As she tried to control her emotions, a thought crossed her mind. What if he, somehow got away with this. She had no idea why that thought crossed her mind. But it did and it infuriated her. She could barely sit still when she said, "What the hell is everybody getting ready to talk about? You all know what he did! I know what he did! And he knows what he did! That bastard took my children and left them in another country! Why are we going to talk now?" She was standing at the table looking right at Alfonso when Frank Malzone stood up and tried to comfort her. He said, "Carmela please, sit down or we'll never get anything done." She sat down and opened her pocketbook. Then she took her rosary beads out and held them tightly in her hands. She began to pray and felt as though she wasn't really there. Like she was somehow watching this whole scene from somewhere else.

    Alfonso's lawyer stood up and said, "Sergeant, I realize this is a difficult situation but my client was well within his rights when he left with his children." Right then, all hell broke loose. Frank Malzone stood up and went after Alfonso's lawyer. Sergeant Russo stood up and got between them just as Frank was about to grab him. It was a crazy scene. Frank was out of control. Sgt. Russo was a much bigger man and was able to hold him back. Frank was screaming at him, "You lowlife Son of a Bitch. How can you defend that piece of shit and what he did to this woman and her kids?" Sgt. Russo finally got Frank to calm down but everybody was on edge. Throughout this whole scene, Carmela never moved. She just sat there. She felt a chill, and a sense of dread came over her. She felt a pain in her heart and she knew. She held her rosary beads up to her heart and she cried. She didn't know how yet. But she knew that this lawyer would wreck her life again. She was sure of it. She knew there was no way he would have said what he said, if he didn't have something to back it up.

    Eventually, Sgt. Russo was able to get everybody seated again. But the room was far from orderly. There was hatred in the air. And everybody seemed to be waiting for the next outburst of emotions. It was hard to believe but Carmela was still the calmest person in the room. It was almost like, she and Frank Malzone had traded personalities. She just sat there, as

Frank seemed to be ready to explode at any moment. Sgt. Russo kept an eye on him as he motioned to Alfonso's lawyer to continue. The atmosphere in the room remained tense. Alfonso's lawyer was an overweight, sloppy looking man, which didn't help. His name was irrelevant and as he stood up to speak again, you could see the strain on his face. He was scared shit. And as the tension rose again, he began to speak. "Sergeant Russo, I have here a signed document granting sole custody of my client's children to him." The room went dead silent. Sgt. Russo asked, "A signed document? Signed by whom?" The lawyer looked at him for a few seconds then walked towards him, holding the document out in front of him for Sgt. Russo to see. Then he said, "They are signed by Carmela Genelli!" Frank Malzone jumped up and said, "What the hell are you talking about? She would never sign something like that!" Sgt. Russo leaned forward and grabbed the document. He looked at it for a few seconds and said, "This document is at least a couple of years old. You'd better have a very convincing explanation for this, Counselor." The lawyer said, "I do, Sergeant. This document was signed by my client's wife, the same day he left with the children! Obviously, my client is innocent of any wrongdoing. And he should be allowed to leave, immediately!" Sgt. Russo looked at Frank Malzone and said, "Frank do you know anything about this?" Frank could not believe anything he had just heard and said, "No, I don't know anything about it. But I'm sure it's all bullshit. But if it is legal and binding, I'm sure there's forgery involved. This woman loves her children. Everything she has done since they were taken from her proves that. Her husband took her children and abandoned them. Left them in another country and came back to America. Everything he has done proves he doesn't give a shit about them." From the moment Alfonso's lawyer produced his document, Carmela sat silently clutching her rosary beads. Her only reaction as it was revealed that it was her signature on the document, was a deadly glare at her husband. Sergeant Russo said, "Obviously we need to have this document and the signature verified. Until then, there is nothing else we can do here today. I want to see everybody back here tomorrow morning at nine o'clock." At that moment, time stood still for Carmela. She didn't need to wait for verification of the document. She knew she had signed something the day her husband left with her children. She just didn't know what it was. She didn't know what it was because she couldn't read English. But she knew now, for the first time, that her not being able to read was all part of his plan. He had taken advantage of her in an unspeakable, despicable way. As she sat there, she realized two things. Everything he had done to her was even worse now. Because of the way he had manipulated her and set her up. She also knew that her situation was hopeless again because she had signed that document that she couldn't read. All of these thoughts and realizations went through her mind while she was still sitting across from him and looking into his eyes.

Right then, that feeling came over her for the second time that day. Like she was watching this whole scene, instead of living it. Now, it was over. She had lost again. She was in a state of shock. Not because she was facing another in a seemingly endless series of setbacks. But because she never really thought she would ever find her husband and make him pay for what he had done. Then, after the letter she received telling her where to find him and the support she got from officer Frank Malzone, she had allowed herself to become somewhat optimistic. For it all to come to such an abrupt end like this. Because of another unforeseen act of deceit, was too much for her.

As her husband's lawyers were gathering their paperwork and placing them back into their briefcases, Carmela came back to the reality of the moment. She looked at her husband for the last time and put her rosary beads into her pocketbook. Then she got up from her chair as a hush came over the room. She hung her pocketbook over her shoulder. Nobody knew what to expect. Then she looked at Sgt. Russo and said, "I will not come back here tomorrow morning to find out what I already know!" Then she picked up the chair she was sitting on and swung it as hard as she could. Everybody in the room watched in shock as the chair slammed against the side of Alfonso's head. The force of the blow knocked him back against the wall and onto the floor. The room fell silent as everybody tried to absorb what had just happened. Then, chaos gripped the room. Now everybody was out of control. Trying to figure out what to do first. Everybody except Carmela. She just dropped the chair and walked out. It was the ultimate personification of her personality. Sensing the hopelessness of the situation, she did the only thing she could do. Knowing that it was hopeless legally, she had to do something. So she did. She needed some type of closure. And she decided this would be it. And who could blame her? She knew it was over now. And as she walked down the stairs and out of the Police station, she stopped and took a deep breath, then exhaled. As though she had just digested the whole situation for the last time and spit out the disappointing outcome. And she felt good about herself because she had finally confronted the man. And even though things didn't turn out the way she had hoped, she was satisfied. She was used to things not working out right for her. She was always able to draw strength from adversity. And this was no different. She would go on and move forward. As she stood on the sidewalk, Frank Malzone walked up behind her and put his hand on her shoulder. She turned to face him and he said, "I'm sorry Senora. I wish I could have done a better job for you. You deserved a better outcome to all of this. And don't worry about what you did in that room. I talked to Sgt. Russo and you don't have anything to worry about." As he looked at her, he knew she was still very upset. He watched as her emotions shifted from anger to concern about what might happen next. Then he said, "Carmela, what you did upstairs won't help you. But I'm happy I was there to see you do it. I was shocked to hear how he set you up and took advantage of your trust in him. So I can't even imagine how you must have felt. But I don't want you to worry. You've been through more than enough. I can't do anything about what happened to you in the past. I thought I could but that has all changed now. And I'm sick over it. But I can do something about what will happen to you from now on. And I will. We have ways of dealing with situations like this. Legally, we can't do anything anymore. And I think you know that. For that I am truly sorry. Sgt. Russo is a friend of mine and he will work with me on this. I promise. You will never have to worry about anything ever again, when it comes to that bastard. For someone like you, who has already been through unimaginable heartbreak, we make exceptions.

Jack Ryan stood in the back of the room and waited. He watched as Sgt. Russo tended to Alfonso. As he stood there, Alfonso was going on and on about how he was going to make Carmela pay for what she had done to him. After a few minutes, Jack Ryan and Sgt. Russo made eye contact. Without saying a word, they both knew what had to be done. By now, they were both sick of Alfonso's shit. Sgt. Russo told Alfonso's lawyer that there was paperwork to be filled out before he could be released. Then he opened the door and told him to go into his office, across the hall. As they started to walk out of the room he said, "Have a seat by my desk. I'll be there in a minute." They walked out and he closed the door behind them. Then he looked at Alfonso and said, "Jack and I have been friends for more than twenty years. Pay attention to what he has to say to you. When you hear him, you hear me." Then he walked out of the room. The door slammed shut behind him. Now, Jack and Alfonso were alone in the room.

When Alfonso turned to look at him, Jack was smiling at him. Alfonso said, "What's going on here? I want my lawyer." Jack said, "Shut the fuck up and listen to me. Right now, time stands still for you. You don't have a lawyer or anything else. All you have is me. I'm your judge and jury. You don't walk out of this room until I say so. We all know what you've done to your wife and your children. Legally, you're in the clear. You have nothing to worry about as far as the law is concerned. But this isn't about the law. This is about you and me. We have ways of dealing with scumbags like you that have nothing to do with the law. So now I'm going to tell you how the rest of your life is going to play out. And I don't care if you believe me or not. I'm gonna be on your ass every day. If Carmela ever sees your face or hears your voice again, you will have to deal with me. And I'm not talking about if you try to bring charges against her for what she did today. I mean if she even sees or hears from you again, ever. I'll make you my main priority. Let me make it even clearer for you. Just in case you might be as stupid as I think you are. If that happens, I will take you out. If you enter her life again in any way, you're a dead man. I almost hope you do. Because anybody that could cause as much pain and suffering on his own family deserves to die. And believe me, you will. You'll just disappear. You'll become another dead guy that nobody gives a fuck about." Alfonso looked at him and said, "You can't do that. You're a police officer." Jack walked toward him and started to laugh. He reached under his left arm and pulled out his service revolver. He pressed the barrel of the gun against the side of Alfonso's head and said, "Don't ever tell me what I can or can't do. Like I said, I hope you do try to cause trouble for your wife. I would love to blow your fucking head off." While the gun was still pressed against the side of Alfonso's head, Jack leaned down to his ear and said, "Don't make me wait too long."

The door opened again and Sgt. Russo walked in with Alfonso's lawyer. Alfonso just sat there looking at Jack Ryan. Then his lawyer said, "Alfonso, is there a problem?" Alfonso said, "No, I'm fine. Can we go now?"

His lawyer said, "Yes, we're finished here. Let's go downstairs. Then I'll drive you home." Alfonso got up and walked toward the door. Sgt. Russo held the door open for them. Right before they walked out of the room, Alfonso turned and looked at Jack Ryan. Jack looked back and winked at him. Then they walked out. Sgt. Russo pushed the door closed behind them. Then he looked at Jack and said, "How did that work out?" Jack said, "Exactly the way I wanted it to. Thanks for taking him out of the room." Sgt. Russo said, "Whatever it takes, brother. You better go touch base with Frank. Let me know if there is anything else I can do. And tell Carmela if she ever needs me, I'm here." Jack thanked him and went downstairs to find Frank.

Carmela was sitting in the front seat of the car with Frank Malzone, when Jack walked out of the building. Jack opened the door and sat in the back seat. Frank looked at him through the rear view mirror and said, "Is everything taken care of?" Jack said, "Yes sir. No problem." Carmela said, "I'm sorry for all the trouble I caused for the both of you. And thank you again for trying to help. And now, I have to get back to my daughter." Frank said, "Carmela, I'm sorry we couldn't do more. If you ever need anything all you have to do is call." Carmela thanked them again and started to get out of the car. Frank said, "Carmela, I'll drive you home." She looked at him and said, "You've done enough already. I'll take a taxi." Then before she got out of the car she looked at him and said, "God bless you and I will always remember you, policeman." Then she smiled at him and got of the car. It was a smile that he would remember for the rest of his life. They watched her as she stood in the street and waited for a cab. A few minutes later, a cab pulled over to let her in. As she was getting into the cab, Frank got out of his car. He stood there and watched, as the cab made its way uptown. He watched until the cab disappeared into traffic and he couldn't see it anymore. He was lost in thought. He had never met anyone like her. A woman who got stronger whenever her situation worsened. It bothered him that he couldn't do more for her. He was still standing there when Jack Ryan got out of the car. Jack put his hand on Frank's shoulder and said, "Don't beat yourself up. You did everything you could do." Frank looked at him and said, "Yeah, maybe. But it wasn't enough, was it? I'll never forget this one, partner. And I don't think I will ever be able to get that woman out of my mind. She's just so unbelievable. After everything she went through, she deserved so much more."

As Frank and Jack stood on the sidewalk in front of the police station, Carmela's taxi was bringing her back to her daughter and their struggle. Frank knew he couldn't do anything else for her. And that ate away at him. He tried to put it out of his mind and chalk it up to another case he had no control over. But he was not able to. Carmela had left her mark on him. He thought about how she looked. Waving to him as her taxi pulled away. So, that's where it ended for him, so to speak. But there was no end for Carmela. Just another beginning. And he knew that, too. Because endings and beginnings always came down to the same thing for her. The start of another challenge.

The immigration identification card for Donato Genelli

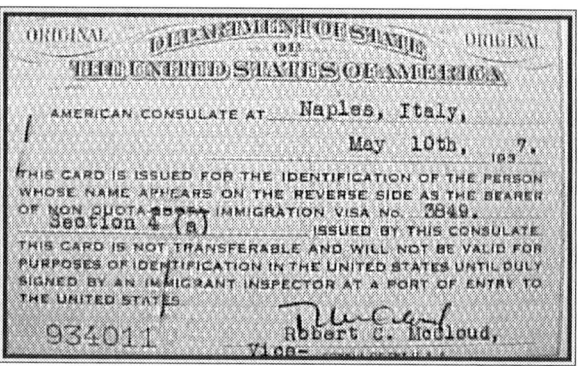

    Carmela's taxi pulled up in front of her apartment building. She paid the driver and got out of the car. She stood on the sidewalk, looking up at the building. Then she took a deep breath and exhaled. Like she was letting go of everything that had gone on earlier that day. She knew she had to put that all behind her before she saw her daughter. Once she had done that she walked up the steps and into the building. She walked through the hallway and started up the three flights of stairs. Every step she took seemed to distance her from all the pain she had just been through. By the time she got to the apartment of the friend that was caring for her daughter, she was exhausted. Mentally and physically. She knocked on the door and waited. When the door opened she could see her daughter sitting by the window. She thanked the woman and walked inside. Carmela stood there frozen in time as her daughter ran to her and jumped into her arms. She wrapped her arms around her daughter and held her tight. At that moment, she put Alfonso out of her mind for the last time.

Frank Malzone never saw Carmela again. And Carmela never saw or heard from Alfonso after that last day. Until the day she learned from a friend in the neighborhood that he had died from a ruptured appendix at the age of thirty-six.

* * * * *

Eventually, Carmela was able to put away enough money to send for her sons. But by then eight years had passed. Donato was now 16 years old and Anthony was 11. Carmela's son Donato, bore most of the responsibility of providing for the family. He did this by working at any and all jobs he could find. Mostly, he worked as an apprentice tailor, but also worked at a florist. He delivered flowers throughout the five boroughs of New York. The subways were his only means of transportation, of course.

As time went by and the years passed Donato was drafted to fight in the Second World War and years later Anthony was also called to serve his new country. Carmela remained in the city and did what was necessary to raise her daughter and pray for the well being of her two sons. Donato was already overseas in the Army and Anthony was to be stationed somewhere in the states in a few months. Being in the Army and fighting for his country seemed just another in the seemingly endless and constant tests of character of Donato, now 22 years old. He would survive the war and return home but not before being wounded during the ally's invasion at Normandy. He would come home with two souvenirs from the war, bullet fragments that were dug out of his right knee, and the Purple Heart.

Donato and Delores Genelli were married in 1948. It was a great marriage and family to come. They had two children, both boys, Joseph and Anthony. Donato Genelli lucked into a job in New Jersey. He worked for Interstate Motor Freight run by the very powerful Teamsters Union. It was a job that offered stability, good pay and benefits.

Chapter 4

Pasquale Pia

Pasquale Pia was an unbelievable character. I say this about him with the utmost respect. This was a man who did nothing but give himself to a family in need. To this day I have a portrait of him hanging in my kitchen. When my grandmother passed away, I took his portrait from her apartment. It was done by an artist from the neighborhood. It captured his personality perfectly. He was sitting in his work clothes and cap, and he had his trademark Italian cigar hanging out of his mouth. A Di Nobili, how perfect.

He spent the better part of his life becoming the backbone of a family he had tried to help. I have never known anyone quite like him. On Sunday, he would come home from his grueling days work and spend the rest of the day playing with his

From left to right: Anthony Genelli, Carmela Genelli, Pasquale Pia and Mary Genelli.

wife's grandchildren. We were lucky enough to be those grandchildren. We would wait for him to come home. He would ring the bell downstairs and let us know he was home. Then he would climb the stairs to the fourth floor apartment. We would stand in the hallway looking down the flights of stairs. Four stories down until we could see his hand on the banister. Slowly making his way up the stairs. When he finally got to the fourth floor, we would all run to him and jump into his arms. As we ran to him he would have to put down the bags of fresh fruit and toys he bought for us.

Once inside the apartment he would spend time with all of us. When he walked through the door he'd always say, "Hi ya gang". Then he would start passing out all the things he brought home for all the kids. Toys... balloons... fresh fruit... you name it. And he would have a handful of change for each of us. Then he would get down on the floor and wrestle with all of us. He'd be on his knees and one by one, we'd all climb on his back. This man, who had just broken his ass working would come home and still do this for the kids. Not his kids, the grandchildren of the woman he had come to love.

My memory of Pasquale, the man who would become the only grandfather I have ever known is vivid. As a kid growing up in the Bronx, we'd look forward to going to grandma's every Sunday. More than five decades after her children were taken from her, she was still in the same apartment. Her children and now, her grandchildren were there every Sunday. This, as much as anything else was a reflection of her personality.

On Sunday's, we were there from morning till night, with me and my brother Joey, there were seven grandchildren. Grandpa worked seven days a week. He would get home around five or six after breaking his ass all day.

He maintained seven apartment buildings on the West Side. It was brutal work. In those days there were no oil furnaces. Every building was heated by coal. Everyday he would shovel hundreds of pounds of coal for each building, and then the ashes from all the coal had to be shoveled out of the furnaces, brought up to the street to be picked up. It was unbelievable. And in the winter, he had to clear the snow away from all the buildings first. Just to be able to bring the coal in and ashes out to the street.

Pasquale became the only grandfather my brother and I ever knew. My mother's father died when my brother was two years old and before I was born. And, obviously we never met the bastard who kidnapped my father. This was probably a good thing because with the personality I had developed by the time I was a teenager, there's a good chance I would have hit him with a baseball bat for what he put my family through. This would not have been right either, but I wasn't exactly known for doing the right thing in those days. Anyway, Pasquale was our grandfather in every way, and to us he was "Gramps". That was all we every called him.

As I got older and found out he was never even related to us, it blew me away. I loved him so much. When I learned the truth, I loved him even more. It just amazed me that this man who had given so much of himself to our entire family, wasn't even related to us. As a kid, I always wondered how he could work as hard as he did and still do what he did for us. All those Sundays, after he broke his ass all day working, he would still stop off on his way home, to shop for all the things he knew we loved. He always made time for the kids. And then, spent the rest of the day playing with all of us. He never thought of himself. I admired him for that. I just figured he did all theses things because we were his grandchildren. That was the only way it made any sense to me. I mean, nobody could blame this man if all he did after working seven days a week was go to sleep when he got home, or even just relax. But he never did. I remember times when my grandmother would yell at him to stop playing with us and get some rest. He just ignored her and kept playing with us. He was really something. When I found out years later, that he wasn't our real grandfather I was dumbfounded. To me, it just magnified all the things he did for us. But even more than that, all the things he did for my father, my uncle and my grandmother. If it wasn't for

Carmela Genelli and Anthony Genelli (the author)

Donato Genelli

him, there's no telling how all of our lives would have turned out. Soon after, the modest West Side neighborhood we lived in was scheduled for demolition in order to make room for the construction of the Lincoln Center complex.

Donato moved his family to the Bronx. The neighborhood was to become known as the "Little Italy" of the Bronx. Although there were other ethnic groups in the area, it was the Italian population that dictated the tone and the atmosphere. It was very safe.

Delores and Donato Genelli

It was on these streets that Joey and Anthony enjoyed the best years of their youth. There were good schools; the family was strong and very close. They were both also very active in sports, football and baseball especially. There were neighborhood leagues that were very competitive with baseball; they organized leagues throughout the sandlots of the Bronx. Both boys were very good and it was Joey that went on to winning two MVP trophies back to back on two different teams and tryouts at Yankee Stadium.

* * * * *

I was twelve years old when Grandpa died. The year was 1966. I remember my mother waking me up to tell me what had happened. She woke me and my brother Joey up because we had to drive downtown to my grandmother's house. I can picture the whole scene to this day. I was standing by the kitchen table with my brother. I can't remember if my father was there or not. My mother was holding both of our hands. She started talking about Grandpa. All the things he did for all of us. Then, every couple of minutes, she would stop and hug us both. We knew that it couldn't be good news. She started to cry a little. She knew we loved him so much. She looked into both of our eyes and told us that Grandpa had passed away. It was my first experience with death, and I remember it to this day. At the time, I thought it was the worst thing that could happen. I couldn't even imagine going to grandma's house and not wait for him to come up the stairs after work. I didn't want to know what that was like. It was the first time my life was changed by a death in the family. I had no way of knowing that six months later, my mother would be gone too.

We dealt with grandpa's funeral, like most people do, first the shock, then the responsibility of making arrangements for the funeral, and finally, the loss.

During the same year my cousin AnnMarie also passed away. She was only ten years old. She had been suffering for years and was eventually overcome by her illness. Her mother Mary was my father's sister. She was also my mother's closest friend. To me and my brother, she was LaLa. At some point when we were kids, that became her name, LaLa. To this day, that's all I've ever called her. She was then and still is now my favorite person in the family. I don't have the words to explain what she means to me. After my mother died, she was the only person who even came close to filling that void for me. She was always there for me. And she did this for my brother and me while she was suffering from the loss of her own daughter. I can't even imagine how she did that. Like I said, I don't have the words to do her justice. I love her.

Dolores Genelli, the mother of Donato's two sons died of Lupus. Joey was 18 years old and Anthony was 13. So that was 1967 for me. The year that changed my life forever. I lost my little cousin AnnMarie, Grandpa and then my mother. I have never been the same since. The same as what? I have no fucking idea, but everything was different after that year. Losing two people in your immediate family was very difficult. But being 13 years old didn't help either. But the loss of my mother during that same year was devastating. I didn't care about anything after that. I just figured, if this could happen, anything could happen. And whatever the consequences were for me not going to school or not going home at night or not doing whatever the fuck it was

Dolores Genelli

that I was supposed to be doing, it could never be as bad as losing my mother. And, I couldn't care less who understood or who didn't understand. And believe me, most people didn't. But to even try to explain how little that meant to me, would suggest that I thought about it and I didn't.

Donato, Joe and Anthony went on with their lives somehow, with great difficulty at first, in the face of their incredible loss. The credit going without any doubt to Donato, who had to somehow go on with his life with the unenviable task of raising two boys and continuing his very demanding job as a truck driver and dockman with the teamsters. It is very crucial to understand the difference between being a widower as opposed to being divorced. Donato and Delores were very happy together and were only just beginning their lives and setting up a future together by laying the foundation for their family. Joey and Anthony, now at an age when parents could start thinking ahead.

Coming to grips with the fact that your wife of 18 years suddenly and very unexpectedly was gone. (She was in the hospital for only four or five moths beginning with a simple physical examination and culminating with death by a very unusual and rare disease) is very hard to imagine let alone deal with. Compounded by raising two children and continuing with work that was physically demanding. This accomplishment in no way suggests that the situation wasn't incredibly difficult. Donato's character would show itself years later by the boys he managed to raise. Both eventually growing into responsible hard-working adults. Joey was quiet, consistent, dependable and fiercely loyal to the family. The latter being a quality shared evenly by his brother Anthony and obviously his father. He also was a major factor in the long awaited maturing of his brother. With Donato working nights in New Jersey, Joey was counted on to guide his younger brother.

Anthony on the other hand, was quite different in personality. While sharing the same fierce family loyalty, Anthony was less responsible, and in the long run, would unknowingly and unintentionally become another test of strength of character of his father and brother.

Anthony grew up and strayed from the family slightly. Just enough to be influenced by the significantly wilder and less responsible crowd he began to hang out with. He would often react defensively and somewhat hostile to any advice offered by his family or anyone else concerned with the overall good of the family. In contrast with which Joey progressed in his life, Anthony was consistent in one way and that was remaining the visible, controversial figure in a family with more that it's share of problems.

But there was always LaLa. No matter how much trouble I was in or what I had done wrong, she was always there for me and she never judged me. I knew I could always go and stay at her house in New Jersey for as long as I wanted. And I did that pretty often in those days. It was the only place I felt normal. She knew me better than anybody and probably still does. She could look inside me and get inside my head, which in those days was a pretty scary place to be. And she did this without criticizing me. Nobody else did that. It was something I really needed and made me feel like I was still okay. I knew she didn't approve of my behavior, but she never put me down for it. She would always talk to me and try to understand why I was doing what I was doing. I couldn't tell her of course, because I didn't know either. But she would ask instead of condemn. I loved that about her. That, plus she fed me all day long. And she could cook like nobody else. I would stay a week or two at a time and then leave. Although we never really solved any of my problems or figured out why I was so weird in those days, she stuck a cork in the biggest hole of my life. A little bit at a time, with every visit to her house, she helped fill a void that was tearing me apart. She could never replace my mother, both of us knew that, but she was the only one trying. She was also the only one who knew my real problem. She is one of a kind. For all she has been through, for all she did for me back then and what she is still doing for me today, and now for bringing that same special love to my own children, I could never thank her enough. And no one could every replace her in my life. Nobody, but my mother.

Joey graduated high school with honors. He excelled in language. That language, not surprisingly, was Italian. With the help of a teacher who would later become a close friend of the family, Mrs. Rasari took interest in the life and development of the oldest son of a family that had endured the jolt and despair of losing a parent. A parent is a huge understatement in describing the mother of this family.

She was very strong in personality and will. Moreover, she was the backbone and driving force behind Donato. The difficulty in describing the contribution she provided for the family is only another tribute to the woman herself. It is hard to comprehend how close this family would have become had she lived, had it not been deprived of the special emotional and loving bond she could have and unquestionably would have provided.

Carmela Genelli, the way the family always remembered her at the stove on 78th Street in Manhattan, New York

The Genelli family went on through all the obstacles that would have easily destroyed a family without the special bond they had. A bond that began with the foundation that was built by and sustained with the great love, strength and determination of both parents.

Joey applied himself in the computer industry. Then a very young industry, but obviously the wave of the future. He applied himself with the same consistent and responsible values with which he had previously shown in school using every bit of the knowledge acquired in a very ordinary course taught in computer operating and some programming. A course another person without the drive he developed, would have used and settled for a job operating computers. A respectable job, nothing any other individual could not achieve. Instead, he absorbed every useful bit of information that enabled him to become one of the very best in the field; fluent in the five of seven different computer languages.

Anthony completed grammar school and was, with good intentions, force-fed into going to catholic high school in Mount Vernon, NY. The school, Mt. Saint Michael, was a very respectable, but also very strict school run by the Marist Order of Catholic Brothers.

This particular order of brothers was very successful in molding and guiding the young lives of thousands of students. However, neither Anthony nor the school were quite ready for each other. The result was three years of turmoil and emotionally straining times in the life of a young boy with more than his share of problems already.

This was a boy who was completely unreceptive to the help and advice of his family. Given that fact, one could expect revolt towards these brothers who tried in vain to shape his life. His disdain for these (strangers) grew stronger with each year at the school. Failing scholastically, he was asked to leave at the end of each year. Only the efforts of his father gained him an opportunity to return by speaking to the school's principal. Continuing for the three years mentioned until the inevitable and gratefully acceptable departure that was attained.

For his final year, Anthony enrolled at DeWitt Clinton High School in the Bronx. The same school his brother had graduated from.

During the three years at Mt. St. Michael, it was a virtual production to cut classes. By needing a phone call from a parent that day and a note the next day for one day's absence or a doctor's note for three day's absence, Anthony had his work cut out for him. It never even slowed him down. He would make the call himself saying he was his brother, and his father was working. Also writing the note and forging his father's signature. For three days out, he would simply use a prescription pad from a local doctor and forge his signature. Sometimes it worked, sometimes it didn't. He never really cared one way or the other. But it became a ritual of daily defiance towards the brothers at the school. An authority he considered a joke.

By contrast, DeWitt Clinton was the complete opposite. It was a public high school and Anthony was free to come and go as he pleased.

Exactly what he was doing the last three years only without all the notes and phone calls. He gradually went less and less until he finally stopped going altogether. It was then that the streets took full control.

Chapter 5

Joe Genelli

It was 1971 and neighborhoods were exploding with emotions. There were all kinds of different factors separating each one of them. There were the typical guido types that dominated the area, and the wise guy wannabes who were always just a sideshow. Most of the guys we hung out with had no use for them. They were very rowdy and would jump at any chance to kick the shit of out anybody.

We were completely different. We played ball, baseball, football and handball. We were good and we held the area championship for football. JoJo's Candy Store was our sponsor. We also were very involved in drugs. We never thought of it as any kind of deterrent to what we were doing, just a way of bringing our game to another level. All the time forming a very strong bond between us.

We were very strong willed and confident in our ability both athletically and mentally. It was a strength that challenged everything that was going on around us. A strength that served as a kind of anticulture. It was something that Anthony was drawn to. It allowed him to be himself but still stay apart from what was expected of him. Whatever the hell that was. P.S. 32 schoolyard, The Circle and most notably, JoJo's Candy Store were home now.

Our problems were everybody's and everybody's problems were ours. We looked out for each other. There were always plenty of problems especially from Ruthra Avenue. They were too rowdy for us and we were never rowdy enough for them. They were assholes. They never cared for our love of music and sports. Thankfully, they had distractions. The annual summertime attempt of infiltration by black people into the neighborhood was more than enough to keep them busy. The neighborhood was a very close-knit place. There were a lot of different kinds of characters, but they all felt the same way about the streets they called their own.

It wasn't at all unusual to witness confrontations. I mean beatings. The very distinct sound of somebody's head hitting the concrete or the sound of someone's fist making contact with the face happened for a lot of reasons, but mainly these things centered around black and Puerto Rican people trying to move into the neighborhood.

Summertime was usually the time when most of these things came to a head. School was out, not that many people went, but everybody was around in the summer, and it was hot in more ways than one. One of the borderlines or boundaries of the neighborhood on the south side was 182nd St. which was the address of St. Martin of Tours Elementary School. The school most of us went to when we were younger. About ten blocks to the north was Borough University. Borough Road was the northern boundary, east was the Bronx Zoo and to the west was the Grand Concourse and Yankee Stadium. This was our world, and it was here that our lives took shape.

After my mother died in 1967, I had learned how to separate parts of my life and apply them where need be. It was really strange after my father got married again. Especially since his new wife's kids were good friends of mine, and I saw them every day in the neighborhood. Then all of a sudden, we all lived in the same house. Well, anyway, I would have to write a whole other book to cover that subject.

* * * * *

My stepsister started dating a guy named Rocco. He was the quarterback of a rival neighborhood's football team of course. Anyway, Rocco's mother had worked with my mother right up until she went in the hospital and passed away. They both became big parts of my life for a while anyway. Life kind of throws you these curveballs every once in a while just to see if you're paying attention I think. I kind of liked the idea of having somebody around that knew my mother.

In 1972, Joe Genelli married Tora Capriati. Joey was then and still is my best friend. He is my big brother in every possible sense of the word.

Back in those days, I was too stupid to realize all he did for me. I was too busy being a jerk. But he stood behind me and was always there when I needed him. I don't know how he put up with me. Today, 28 years later, we're still best friends. And we're together all the time. I'm just not a jerk anymore.

The wedding of Joe and Tora Genelli. Anthony Genelli, best man, standing to the right of the groom.

Back in 1972, Joey asked me to be his best man at the wedding. Of course, I said yes but I was nobody's idea of a best man in those days. I was 18 years old and completely nuts. I was still living at home, but it was a difficult time for all of us. It was five years after my mother died, and my father had remarried, which was fine. He had been through so much and I really wanted him to be happy. My problem was I didn't know how to live without my mother being around and I still don't.

So now, we're all living together, my father, brother and me with my stepmother and her two kids, Jackie and Debbie. Somehow, we're all still a family to this day. We all went through a lot, but Jackie and I were the same age and dealing with a lot of the same problems. I was living without my mother and he was living without his father. We were in the same classes at school, hung out with the same people on the street and lived in the same house. We became very close. My brother Joey was five years older than we were. At that age, five years was a big gap. At that time, because of our age, I spent a lot more time with Jackie than my brother. We were good kids with a lot of problems, but we were really nuts. We did whatever we wanted to do no matter what. We took advantage of every situation. My brother's bachelor party was a prime example.

The best man usually organized and pays for the bachelor party. But I was the best man, so there was no way that was going to happen. Not because I wouldn't do that for my brother, but at that time, I couldn't afford something like that. I don't remember who set it up, but it really doesn't matter. The party was at a topless bar in the Bronx. When me and Jackie showed up, the whole party changed a little bit. It was Saturday night and we hadn't been home since Thursday. When we walked in and saw the dancers, it was like ringing the dinner bell. We looked at each other and went straight to the bar.

We got a drink and went over to the dance floor. All the guys were already there. It was a circular dance floor with chairs around the whole thing. There were two empty chairs across the bar from where my brother Joey was. I told Jackie to grab the seats and went to say hello to Joey. I gave him a hug, he looked at me and said, "Where the fuck have you been", I said, "It don't matter, where are the broads?" He said, "The first one will be right out, try not to make a spectacle of yourself." I said, "I'll try, you just make sure you get a blow job tonight." He told me not to do anything stupid and I went back over to sit with Jackie.

The first girl came out and got up on the dance floor. She was a nice looking Puerto Rican girl with long legs. She started to work the room. The usual shit, coming on to the guys who couldn't handle it. She did her thing for the guys, one by one as she made her way around the bar. Jackie and I watched and waited for her to get to where we were sitting. Joey was keeping an eye on us. My brother was really cool and a couple of guys he worked with were okay too. But all the other guys were chumps. The dancer was sticking her tits in their faces, and they were backing away. I couldn't believe it. Jackie and me were already trying to figure out how we were going to get laid. We couldn't wait for her to get over to where we were sitting. When she got to the guy next to us, we were ready. She went through her routine and the guy was petrified. It was pathetic. These guys were five and ten years older than us and they had no idea what to do.

When she came over to where I was sitting, Jackie and me stood up on our chairs and took our pants off. She said. "You guys are crazy, wait till I'm on my break." I said, "Okay, no problem, but don't think we're going to be satisfied with the bullshit you're feeding these guys." She said, "If you're looking for some action, we could go down to the basement on my next break." Jackie said, "What the fuck do you thing we're looking for, directions to the zoo?" She said, "Okay, but it's going to cost you $20 for a blow job and $50 for whatever else you want to do." I told her no problem. She told us to meet her in the basement after her next set. I said, "We'll be there, just make sure you don't forget us while you're taking advantage of the patsies at the bar." She laughed and said, "How old are you guys anyway?" Jackie said, "Don't worry about how old we are, we got more experience than any of these guys." She said, okay and went over to the guys next to us.

Jackie looked at me and said, "At least we got something lined up." We both laughed and went back over to the bar. We had a couple of beers at the bar and watched what was going on. We hadn't slept in two days. Between that and the beers, we were starting to get a little fucked up. We were already bored with the party. Most of the guys were assholes. They were intimidated by the dancers. We were trying to figure out a way to get them into the basement. Jackie said, "You got any money? I got enough for a blow job." I said, "You take care of yourself, I got an idea."

I was a real nut in those days. I had no shame. There is nothing I wouldn't do to get what I needed. I started talking to some of the people my brother worked with. Then I talked to his boss, who was also there. I gave them all the same bullshit story. I told them I had a chance to have sex with one of the dancers, but I was a couple of dollars short and asked each one of them if I could borrow a couple of dollars. They all got a kick out of what I was trying to do and thought it was funny. I made the rounds and they all started to hand me a few dollars. In a few minutes, I had more than enough to get what I wanted. I spotted the girl I wanted and walked over to her. She was dancing for a couple of other guys so I stopped at the bar. As I watched her, I had a couple of shots of scotch. Now I'm pretty fucked up. The two guys she was with were hopeless. They had no clue. I walked over to them and said, "When you're done with these two clowns, I'm ready." The three of them looked at me and one of the guys said, "Who are you?" I said, "It don't matter who I am, what matters is that I'm trying to have sex with this girl and you guys are just trying to survive being near her." I'm not sure if that made any sense to these guys, but I really didn't give a fuck. I had found a way to come up with the money I needed, which wasn't easy. There was no way I was going to let these two assholes get in my way. She walked over to me and said, "Are you always this reckless or is it just when you're horny?" I said, "I don't know, nobody ever asked me that before." While I was talking to her, the other two guys got up and walked away. She said, "I guess I'm not going to be able to get rid of you tonight so why don't you go downstairs?" I told her if she wanted to get rid of me, I'd go and find another girl. I was tired of talking about it and asked her, "Is that what you want?" She said, "You're unbelievable, no, that's not what I want." I said, "So why don't you tell me what you do want?" She said, "I want you to take me downstairs."

She said her name was Delia not because I asked. Her name was the last thing on my mind. She asked what my name was. I told her it was Johnny. When we were done in the basement, I wanted to go back upstairs and disappear into the crowd. I didn't want her to know my name. It might not matter, but you never know. Even though I was just a kid, I already knew there was no way of knowing how a girl would act after you had sex with her. Any girl, even a girl that was working a room, if she was going to be looking for anyone, I wanted it to be a guy named Johnny.

When we got downstairs, my brother Jackie was down there with one of the other dancers. It was just an empty room with a cement floor. But we made the most of it. We were both on the floor banging these two girls. The floor was cold and hard, but we managed to have some fun. When we were done, Jackie and I went back upstairs.

I found my brother and went over and gave him a hug. He said, "I haven't seen you for awhile, I don't know if that's good or bad." I said, "Is that any way to greet your brother? Did you get a blowjob yet? If not, I can hook you up." He said, "Now I know I don't want to know where you've been." I said, "Don't worry about where I've been. There's four or five girls walking around her that can be had. It ain't right that I get some action, and you don't." He looked at me and said, "Don't worry about me. You think I need you to tell me what to do?" That was my brother. Joey was always a step ahead of me and everybody else. You just never realized it. He had such a way about him. He was always so calm and laid back that nobody ever noticed what he was doing. I loved that about him. I felt stupid for thinking he needed me to set him up but only for a second. I was always happy to be wrong about that. I expected him to be smarter than me, and it was rare that he wasn't. That's the way I liked it. I always wanted to be more like him. Even though I knew I never would be.

That was always the difference between us. To this day, it's still the same. It's not that Joey wasn't as nuts as we were, he was, but most people never noticed. I always did. We were brothers and had been through a lot together. We had the same blood running through our veins. We went about out lives differently, but we were the same. It took a long time before we both realized that, but as the years passed, it was obvious. We were always close, but as we got older, we became even closer. As I've said, he was five years older than I was. When my mother died, we were at different stages of our lives. He was dealing with that loss as an 18 year old kid, while I did the same at 13. At that age, five years is a big difference. As we got older, it meant less and less. And now, it doesn't mean anything. But back then it did. I don't know how he dealt with not having our mother around, and I'm sure he doesn't know how I did either. We never really talked about it. It doesn't matter. We both knew we were dealing with the same pain. We had lost our mother forever. It's very difficult to explain. We had nothing but great memories of her and the love she gave us, but there would be no more for the rest of our lives. How fucked up is that?

As bad as we felt, we knew it was nothing compared to what our father was going through. She was our mother, but she was his wife. They loved each other before we were even born. I don't know how he did it. He had already been through so much in his life, and now this, and through it all, he was still able to be the kind of father he was to us. Where the fuck did he get the strength to do that?

* * * * *

Today, 33 years later, I'm still learning about my father. Now I have a wife and three children of my own and knowing how I feel about the woman who gave birth to my children this gave me a whole new perspective of what my father had been through, and how hard it must have been for him. It was a tough time for all of us, but like I said, it had to be tougher for my father. I couldn't have had a better role model. If I could be anything like him, that would be enough for me.

Left to right: Joe, Donato and Anthony Genelli in our Bronx kitchen.

Left to right: Joe, Donato, and Anthony Genelli

Donato Genelli

Chapter 6

Anthony Genelli

Rocco's cousin Niko was a person that during the time that I knew him and was around him, exposed me to the most fascinating, exciting and potentially dangerous experiences that I've ever had. I know that really sounds like an exaggeration, but believe me, it's not.

Niko had a constant companion named Dante. He was only about six feet, six inches tall and 250 lbs. and spent time in Vietnam with the Green Beret, which was the rumor anyway. If you looked at him, you'd believe it. The best way to describe Niko is that he was the only person that Dante was kind of afraid of. That's all you really need to know about Niko. We knew he was connected but to what extent, we didn't know. It really didn't matter.

I was about 18 or 19 and had just gotten my first apartment. It was right across Borough Road from Borough University. There aren't many things that didn't go on in that apartment. I knew a girl around that time that used to pay the rent sometimes. Sometimes Rocco would pay it, or Niko, and sometimes I would even pay it. Sometimes nobody paid it, but it didn't matter. Something could always be "worked out".

One night at the apartment, I answered the door, and it was this guy James Ruffo looking for Rocco. He was pissed off about something and decided to take it out on me. I tried to tell him it had nothing to do with me, but he didn't want to hear it. He was a big guy, and I didn't want to deal with him especially since I didn't even know what the problem was. He started to wreck the place, and when I tried to stop him, he smacked me around a little bit and then left. On the way out the door, he kicked over my TV and stereo then put his foot through the TV screen. I was a little shaken up. I went out to use the pay phone at White Castle because I didn't have a phone in the apartment. When I came out of the building, Dante was pulling up and asked me where I was going. He saw that something was wrong and asked me what the problem was. When I told him what happened, he said, "Go back upstairs and wait there." In about 15 minutes he came back with Niko.

Niko wasn't the type of person to waste a lot of time. He asked me what happened and then I quickly explained, which was a big mistake. I told him I knew where the guy lived and what bar he and his brother hung out in. I was still pretty shaken up so I wasn't really thinking about what they might do. There was no way I could have anticipated what happened next. Niko was the kind of guy that took things personally. Being that he would hang out at my apartment once in a while and that this guy came to my house looking for his cousin, this really pissed him off. After listening to me for a couple of minutes, he said, "Let's go."

We went downstairs, and he opened the trunk of his Cadillac. He pulled out a machine gun. I'll never forget it. It was a silver machine gun. He held it up, screwed the silencer to the end of the barrel then threw it back in the trunk and said, "Get in." As we drove down Pelham Parkway, music blasting on the radio, he asked me how to get to this guy's house. Right then, I started to panic a little bit. I mean, he wasn't exactly going to talk to the guy. Although about a half-hour before, I hated the guy who slapped me around and wrecked my apartment, I didn't really want to stand there and watch him get blown away. I started to make believe I wasn't sure where he lived, even though I knew Niko and Dante both knew I was full of shit.

Anyway, I reluctantly showed them where he lived. Now I'm walking up to the front door. It was a big house on Eastchester Road. I had no idea what to say or do if he answered the door. His brother answered the door, thank God and asked me what was wrong. He could see the car in front of the house and I'm sure he didn't think these guys were there selling Boy Scout cookies. I told him what happened and asked him where I could find his brother. He said he didn't know where he was. I went back to the car, got in and took a deep breath figuring that was it. Niko looked at me through the rearview mirror and said, "Where's the bar?" We drove the couple of blocks to the bar and I walked in with Niko and Dante behind me.

The bar on Eastchester Road sponsored the football team these guys were on. The place was packed. As we came through the front door, I walked to the bar with Niko. Dante stayed by the front door covering it completely with the butt of a sawed off shotgun sticking out of his belt. As the bartender walked towards us, Niko put his 45 caliber automatic on the bar. "Stoli, rocks", he said. I swear time must have stopped because I could picture this whole scene to this day.

The bartender asked, "Is there a problem?" as the whole place started to notice something was going on. Niko asked him if he knew James Ruffo. The guy said, "Why, what's wrong?" Niko just smiled at him and said, as he looked from the bartender then to everybody else in the place. "You tell him, that him and everybody he knows is in a lot of fucking trouble." By this time, all you could hear was the music on the jukebox as everybody now was paying attention. Nobody made a move. I broke the silence by telling Niko I was going to wait in the car. I walked out of the bar, past Dante, completely amazed at what I just saw. Niko wanted to finish his drink.

As I sat in the car outside, I saw somebody running out the back door of the bar and into the street in front of me. It had started to snow and it was hard to see. As he passed in front of me, I could see who it was. It was him, James, the guy we were looking for. He started running down Eastchester Road. Then Niko runs out the front door of the bar and into the street. This scene I will never forget. Niko pulling the 45 caliber in the middle of the street, snow coming down, firing one shot after another as the guy ran away and disappeared into the night. Right then, it became obvious to me, and I'm sure Niko knew too. That's why he stayed in the bar. As soon as we left the guy's house, his brother must have called the bar to warn him we were coming. It made perfect sense. But of course, like I said, Niko had already thought of that.

A couple of days later, Niko showed up at my apartment around midnight, which wasn't unusual. He had a really good-looking woman with him, but that wasn't any surprise either. They sat down at the kitchen table with me and Niko asked me how I was doing. I said I was okay, and he said, "Any problems after we stopped at that bar?"

I said, "No, and I'm sure there won't be any".

He said "How do you know?" and without waiting for an answer, he said, "This is Gina, I brought her here for you, you don't mind right?"

What was I going to say? I told him I had to work in the morning. He said, "So you go in late, she's going to stay here tonight." I knew there was no point in arguing with him. By now, I was able to read his moods. I also knew there was something else on his mind.

We had a couple of beers and played some cards. We always played cards when he was there. I never asked any questions. I just waited. I started making some small talk with

Gina. I figured if she was going to spend the night, I should at least talk to her a little. As I'm talking to her, I kept an eye on Niko. She was a nice person and very good looking, but, she was pretty stupid; not a bad combination. As I'm thinking this, I hear Niko say, "I found out who his father is." I said, "Whose father?" He said, "The guy we were looking for the other day. We'll pay him a visit tomorrow when you get home from work." What was I going to say? I was still thinking about what I was going to do with Gina.

Niko finished his beer and said, "I gotta go take care of some things, I'll be back in an hour or two. Have a good time." He said he'd take Gina home when he got back.

After he left, I was already worrying about what was going to happen the next day. I didn't really have much time to think about it though because I still had Gina sitting at my kitchen table; not to mention getting up for work in the morning. I decided to at least enjoy the next couple of hours. I knew she would do whatever I told her to do.

Before I had time to think of something, she said, "Why don't we do it on the table?" I thought for a second and said, "Why not?" I remember thinking an hour ago I was getting ready for bed. Now I'm having sex on my kitchen table with somebody I've never seen before. That's the way things were happening for me in those days.

We made love on the table and I actually enjoyed it. It was a little uncomfortable and the table was cold, but she was hot and after a while, I think the table even warmed up a little. Anyway, every time I ate at the table after that, it was a little different. Niko must have picked her up early because by the time I got up, she was gone. She left me a note on the table with her phone number to call her whenever I wanted. I got dressed and went to work already wondering what was going to happen that night.

Somehow, I got through the day at work. Needless to say, I couldn't concentrate on anything. I couldn't wait for the day to be over, but at the same time, I hated the thought of what was going to happen later on. Whatever was going to happen, I just wanted to get it over with. As it turned out, I didn't have to wait to long. I took the subway up to the Bronx. I got off on the Grand Concourse and walked down Borough Road to my apartment. When I got to my building I saw the Eldorado parked right in front. I took a deep breath and went upstairs. I didn't really know what to expect. The thing about Niko was if he said he was going to do something, you knew he would. What you never knew though, was how far he would go.

I opened the door to my apartment and walked into the living room. Niko was at the table with Dante. They had a big spread of Chinese food. Niko said, "Hey Anthony, just in time, sit down and have something to eat." It always amazed me how matter of fact he was in situations like this. I was scared shit and he was having a good time. I sat down at the table with them. I was starving and started eating. I figured what the hell; I might as well eat. There was no way I was going to stop him from doing whatever he was going to do. As I'm eating, Niko asked me if I had a good time with Gina last night. I said, "Yeah, thanks." Even though that felt like so long ago.

I was surprised that I could eat at all in that situation. I was looking around the room and I could see the 45caliber handgun on the TV set. On top of the refrigerator, there was a sawed off shotgun and leaning against the closet door was the machine gun I had come to know so well. We finished eating and I cleaned up a little. Niko said, "Let's have a drink and go straighten out this problem, finish it." I said, "Are you sure it's necessary, I think the point has been made." He started laughing and said, "Did I ask you if it was necessary?" That was the end of my input. I gave Niko and Dante stoli on the rocks. I pick up a bottle of Dewar's and drank from the bottle. I figured I would need it. On the way out of the apartment, Niko grabbed the 45 and Dante picked up the shotgun off the refrigerator. Niko picked up the machine gun and put it under one of the cushions of the couch. I guess he didn't think he'd need it. For some reason, that made me feel better.

We walked down to the car and drove to Prospect Ave. I was nervous but not afraid. I felt bad for this guy's father, whoever he was because he had no idea what was about to happen. I wasn't afraid because I was sure that nobody in the club would be able to stop Niko and Dante. On the other hand, I couldn't imagine things going smoothly, it wasn't like we were walking into a Boy Scout camp. These guys were older than Niko and had their own set of connections. Plus, it was a private club and nobody was allowed to just walk in.

Of course, none of these things meant anything to Niko. We pulled up and parked right in front of the club. We got out of the car and I followed them to the front door. Niko opened the door and we walked in. Before the door closed behind us, some guy stepped in front of Niko and asked, "You got some business here?" Niko smiled at him and said, "Get the fuck out of my way." As the guy backed away, Niko said, "Whose James Ruffo's father?" One of the guys playing cards at a table stood up and said, "He's my kid, what do you want?" Niko walked over to him and said, "Your son wrecked my friend's apartment and smacked him around. I'm here to stand up for him." The guy said, "Maybe he had a reason for doing that, I'll talk to him about it." I was standing by the front door with Dante and I could just feel something was about to happen. Niko walked over to the television by the bar, picked up a barstool and smashed it into the screen. Then he said, "When you talk to him, tell him now he owes us both a TV." One of the guys in the corner picked up a baseball bat and started towards Niko. Dante grabbed him, picked him up and threw him over the bar. The guy hit the wall behind the bar and dropped to the floor. It was unbelievable. The sound of bottles being smashed by this guy flying against the wall. Then Niko said, "Don't make us have to hurt everybody in here." Then he walked over to the guy's father and said. "You see this kid (as he was pointing to me) If anybody fucks with him because of what we did her today, this will seem like a good day to you." If you want to come after somebody, come after me, I'll be in the neighborhood."

The guy said, "Okay, okay, relax; there's no need for all this. I'll straighten it out, calm down." Niko said, "That's all I want, the only reason this happened it because of what your son did. Don't try and lay blame anywhere else."

Niko looked at me and said, "Anthony, you ready to leave?" I was shocked and said, "Yeah, sure let's go." We started to walk out and when we got to the door, Niko turned around and said, "Remember what I said about this kid here." He put his arm around me and said, "If anything happens to him, even if it seems like a coincidence, I'm going to blame you."

One of the things about Niko was that you never had to wonder what he meant. Whenever he got involved, he made sure there was no misunderstanding. This was no different. I knew he liked me and looked out for me. But I also knew he loved this type of thing.

We got into his car and drove away. I was in the back seat, and I could see him look at me through the rearview mirror. He said, "Anthony, you look worried, don't worry about nothing. They're scared shit of you now." Then Dante said, "Yeah, if anything, they'll come after us now." And that was the other factor. They knew it, but I'm not sure if they were aware that I knew it too. But I did. This guy's father in the club and probably the guy Dante threw over the bar were connected in their own way. But they wouldn't be looking for me after this. They would be looking for them. But like I said, Niko knew that before he even decided to go there, he just didn't care. I looked back at him through the mirror and said, "I'm not worried, Niko. I'm hungry." They both busted out laughing. Dante said, "He's pretty funny, this fucking kid." I wasn't trying to be funny. I just wanted to change the subject. By now, I knew when it was possible to redirect his attention. It didn't always work. But it was always worth a try. This time it did. Niko said, "You hungry Dante?" "Yeah, I could eat." They decided to go to Sergio's. I was relieved. The place was only a couple of blocks from my apartment, and I could walk home from there. I was dying to go home and relax if that was possible. The only problem with that idea was that I knew the machine gun was still under the cushions of my couch. I figured I would deal with that later.

We got to Sergio's and went inside. We walked up to the bar and ordered a round of drinks. It didn't take long for the manager to come over to Niko and ask him if he felt like eating something. Niko said, "Yeah, we're all hungry. Whatever you think is the best thing on the menu, three orders. Run a tab and make sure nobody pays it but me."

I hung out at the bar and had a beer. Thank God there was a Yankee game on. The food came, and we all ate. I was getting used to eating in these situations. After a while Niko came over and asked me if I was okay. I said I was and that I was going to head home in a couple of minutes. He said okay and told me he would pick up the machine gun tomorrow unless I needed it for something. I told him I didn't think I would and then I thanked him for everything. He said, "No problem, let me know if you need anything."

After a while, I slipped out of the bar and walked home. It was about nine o'clock, and I couldn't wait to go home to an empty apartment and just relax. I got home, grabbed a beer and watched the rest of the Yankee game. I was sitting on the couch thinking about what went on. I thought about going to work in the morning and somebody asking me what I did last night. I would tell them that me and a couple of guys I know walked into a low-level Mafia hangout and threw somebody over the bar. Then we threatened everybody else in there and left. After that, we went to another place and had dinner. Then I'd ask, "What did you do last night?" Of course I could never tell anybody that, but that's what I did last night. I don't know how many times I've said this already, but you can't make this stuff up, you really can't.

I was really enjoying sitting on the couch by myself and watching the ballgame. It was the first time I was able to relax in a couple of days. I knew that at any time the bell could ring, and it could be Niko and who knew who else, but I just didn't give a fuck at that point. I was just in a zone. Every once in a while I would look over at the end of the couch and think about the machine gun under the cushion. I had to laugh. I mean, how fucking unbelievable was this?

After the Yankee game was over, I put the news on and started getting ready for bed. As I'm watching the news, I realized that nothing on the news that night even came close to what I just went through. I decided to have another beer and watch the rest of the news. I wasn't worried about anything anymore. There was no way anybody was going to fuck with me now. So I decided to just enjoy that fact for awhile. I was just hoping Niko wouldn't show up; not tonight. I was too relaxed. I really loved the guy for all the things he was doing for me, but just being around him took so much out of me.

The news was over, and I cleaned up the rest of the Chinese food that was still all over the kitchen. Then I walked over to the couch. I knew I was going to do this sooner or later. I lifted the cushion and pulled out the machine gun. I just wanted to see what it felt like to hold it. It was heavier than I thought. As I'm holding it, I realized it was probably loaded and ready go to. That scared the shit out of me. I gently lifted the cushion of the couch and slid it back under it. I shut the TV off and went to sleep.

* * * * *

The next day at work was even stranger than the day before. But at least I didn't have to worry about what was going to happen after I got home that day. I still never knew what would be going on at the apartment when I got there. But at least, I hoped, that whole situation was over with. Even though I knew that, with Niko nothing was ever over.

I got home after work and nobody was there. The first thing I did was look under the cushion of the couch. The machine gun was gone. For a second I thought, most people check the mail when they get home, I was checking for a machine gun. I figured Niko must have picked it up. I guess I knew, if I thought about it, it was a pretty strange way to be living. Everything else in my life around that time was pretty strange anyway. I figured what the fuck. I knew it wasn't normal, but what the hell was normal anyway? The weirdest thing about all of this is that it's all true.

You can't make this stuff up. I mean you either live through this kind of thing or you don't and even if you do, its kind of hard to believe especially since I was pretty much still just a kid and this was pretty powerful stuff.

I was working at New York Hospital Cornell University in the medical library. I'd work the three to eleven shift so by the time I got back to the apartment at night, anything could be happening there. Rocco had a set of keys and sometimes he would be hanging out when I got there.

One night in August right around my birthday, Niko decided to give me a birthday present. He left a beautiful 35year old woman at my apartment for three days. Seriously, it was really strange at first but then, I mean, how bad could that be? She was beautiful and she was crazy about Niko and would do anything he told her to do. All we really did for about three days was eat, drink, play cards and have sex. Not always in that order, but that's all we did. Sometimes Niko would stop by and be with her for a while, but that was okay. I mean it's not like I was going to complain. Her name was Gloria and I'll never forget her.

Anthony Genelli

Chapter 7

The neighborhood was pretty wild around this time. There were a lot of things going on. Oak Tree Park served as kind of one of the boundaries of the neighborhood on the south side. The area was almost all black and Puerto Rican, which was okay as long as they stayed there.

The Circle was a couple of blocks away. That is where we would usually hang out. JoJo's Candy Store was about a half a block away and whenever we got thrown out of there, we would usually wind up in the park. When I say the park, what I'm talking about is a few benches and a couple of concrete tables. Jo-Jo didn't take any shit from anybody. Every once in a while she'd get sick of us since she saw us just about every day.

There was a motorcycle gang called the The Nomads, who had a clubhouse right near Oak Tree Park. Almost all of them were black and Puerto Rican. Once in a while they would cruise into the neighborhood just to see how far they could go. You could just feel the tension as they went by. They rigged their bikes to be extra loud just to piss people off, and it was only a matter of time before something would happen.

There were a lot of people hanging around JoJo's and the park one night when all of a sudden you could hear the bikes. Sure enough, they started cruising around the corner, but this time, they came right down in front of the candy store. They were glaring at everybody just daring people to do something about it. Somebody yelled something as they went by, which wasn't unusual, only this time they stopped and a couple of them got off their bikes right by The Circle. There were a lot of people hanging out in the park. My sister, Debbie was one of them and a guy named Bobby, who was living at Niko's mother's house at the time, was there too. They started pushing people around and a fight broke out. Luckily Debbie wasn't hurt, but Bobby caught a pretty good beating. He had a gun on him that fell out of his pocket while they were kicking him in the ribs. They took the gun, smacked a few other people around then got back on their bikes and left. Nobody really got hurt that badly; only Bobby was pretty messed up. Somebody took him home and helped him out. It wasn't until the next day that we found out the gun Bobby had belonged to Niko. Anyone who knew Niko knew that as soon as he found out he was going to go and get it back. What I learned about Niko was that he loved situations like this.

The Nomads were feeling pretty good about themselves that day. They went back to their clubhouse about three blocks away and had a good time bragging about what they had done. Because not only had they smacked around a neighborhood guy, but they had actually gone into the neighborhood to do it.

You could hear the music blasting from their hangout a block away. They had no way of knowing the problem they had just caused for themselves. Before people had even stopped talking about what had happened, Niko was on his way to their clubhouse. He knew very little about The Nomads. All he knew was that they came into his neighborhood and caused problems for people he cared about. It wasn't about the gun they took. That just justified in his mind whatever he decided to do. One of the things that always amazed me about Niko was that when things like this happened, he never got a bunch of guys together. He always went alone or with Dante. He just showed up when people least expected it. And you better be ready to deal with him, which nobody ever was. The Nomads were no different.

We all knew that Niko was nuts, but this was really something. It took balls to do something like this. All Niko knew, or managed to find out about The Nomads was that their "leader" or whatever you wanted to call him was a guy named Carlos, a black guy. The police wanted Carlos for various things, including murder, in a couple of states. I wasn't there personally to see this happen, but I knew somebody who was. No matter, because by the next day, everybody knew what had happened.

Niko pulled up in front of their club, got out with Dante, walked up to the front door and kicked it open. Once inside, Niko asked, "Which one of you assholes is Carlos?"

"Who the fuck are you?" was the response he got from the guy standing in the corner. "I guess you're Carlos", Niko said. With that Niko walked up to him, pushed him against the wall, in one motion and actually lifted him up on the wall while sticking the barrel of his 45 up the guy's nose. "Where's my gun?" Niko asked. Nobody made a move probably because Dante was there. Carlos motioned to one of his guys to get the gun. Somebody gave it to Niko, and he put it in his pocket. All this went on while the 45 was still a half inch up Carlos's nose. Dante walked up to the biggest guy he could find in the place and broke his nose with one shot. Not another word was spoken. They just walked out of the place, got into their car and left. That was that. The Nomads never came into the neighborhood again. In fact, they even moved their club a few blocks away.

Chapter 8

It was business as usual in the neighborhood. People went about their business, and you couldn't help but feel good about what had recently happened. Niko's reputation continued to grow, and my being around him, especially with him being at my apartment as often as he was, was something special. Not that he was what you would call a role model or anything like that, but for a kid my age it was pretty impressive. I never abused or took advantage of it though, and it's important to point out that if you ever went to him with a problem, the first thing he would ask was if you were at fault in any way. If you were, you were on your own, but if you had done no wrong, he would help you. If you weren't a jerky wiseass kid, which I wasn't, you had it made. By this time, word had gotten out around the neighborhood of my involvement with Niko and things began to change a little bit. A lot of the wise guys in the area that normally would break my balls or try to take advantage of me started treating me as if they wanted to be my friend. It was obvious why, I just ignored them. They couldn't touch me now and I just as soon left it at that. I had no desire to want to have anything to do with them anyway.

Niko was pretty funny sometimes, or as funny as somebody like him could be. The neighborhood was almost all Italian in those days, but there were a few Puerto Rican families living there; very few.

One of those families lived on Beaumont Avenue, right next to the building I lived in. The father was the super of the building. There were three brothers in the family. There was Danny, Willie and Edgar. Willie was a real good guy. Danny was weird, and I think Edgar was a fag or something. I was pretty friendly with Willie and we would hang out sometimes. Even though it was an unpopular thing to do, but he was a good guy.

Anyway, it was around this time that Niko had bought one of the bars on the outskirts of the neighborhood. Well, who knew if he actually bought it or not. Took over one of the bars is probably a better way to put it. Whatever, it was his now. It was called Badlands. Why, I don't know. It became a major hangout. Niko was in and out all the time and Dante would actually tend bar once in a while. It was wild. There were always a lot of women in there. They were there for one reason, Niko. He was that kind of guy.

Anyway, I walked into the bar one night and saw Niko by the cash register. I walked over to say hello, and he said, "I was hoping you would come in tonight." I remember wondering why would be he hoping I would come in.

I said, "Yeah, why?" He looked at me and said, "You know a spic named Willie?"

I said, "Yeah, why?" I wasn't surprised anymore about the things he knew, and I was thinking, now what?"

He said, "He came in here looking for you and asked where you were."

I said, "Yeah, he's a good guy. He lives on my block." He said, "You sure?" I said, "Yeah, I'm sure, why?"

He said, "Okay, I didn't know why he was looking for you. We got him in the back room." I said, "What did you do to him."

He said, "Nothing, I just wanted to find out if you knew him, and why he was looking for you."

I said, "How long has he been back there?" He said, "Who gives a fuck, go get him if you want. Dante's back there stocking beer and keeping an eye on him." We looked at each other for a second and he just started laughing.

He said, "What's the matter with you. You think I'm gonna let some Puerto Rican come in here looking for you and not find out what's going on?"

I walked in the back room, not knowing what to expect. There was Willie, sitting on one of the refrigerators they kept the beer in. When he saw me, he said, "Anthony, thank God man!" And there was Dante saying, "You know this guy?" I said, "Yeah, he's okay." He said, "Good, get him the fuck out of here He's getting on my nerves." I walked Willie out the back door and told him I was sorry for what happened. He said "Anthony, what the fuck happened, man? I didn't do nothing." I told him it was a misunderstanding and apologized again. I said, "I'll see you later, I gotta go back inside."

I went back into the bar, sad down and had a beer. I was thinking about what had happened. Niko was talking to some people, of course. To him, this was nothing what had just happened. A minute or two later he came back over to where I was sitting.

He said, "How's Willie?" I looked at him and just started laughing. He said, "What are you laughing at?" I said, "You." He smiled, then smacked me in the back of the head and walked away. It was his way of saying I'm watching your back. I never really understood why he did things like that for me. I guess he just took a liking to me. It's not like I was going to complain or anything, but it was a pretty unusual situation, to say the least.

Obviously, I never knew what was going to happen at my apartment in those days. I tried to go about my daily life, go to work, come home, but there was nothing normal about it. I never knew who would be at my apartment when I got home from work. I never knew when Niko would ring the bell in the middle of the night. The only thing I did know for sure was that when Niko would show up in the middle of the night, he would always have women with him; at least one, sometimes two or three. Now, at first you might think, well, how bad could that be?

But you have to ask yourself when was the last time you were sound asleep and the bell rang at two or three in the morning. After that, you have to think about somebody like Niko coming in your front door with a couple of women. Then picture him pulling out a 45 caliber handgun, putting it down on the table and asking you which woman you want. Then maybe you could imagine what I was feeling. Maybe!

Niko had a very dynamic personality. He was a guy with a big heart. But he was nuts! He was very generous, but he was ruthless if you crossed him or caused a problem for someone he liked. I was amazed by him and some of the things he would do. He also scared me. The bigger the problem, the more he liked it.

He was somebody you couldn't help liking. You always had a good time whenever he was around. He could strike fear into anybody at the drop of a hat. I mean anybody. There was a shylock in the neighborhood; his name was Donnie Barbato. I had borrowed money from him for some reason and was unable to pay him back. It wasn't a lot of money, maybe $20 or $40. In those days, that was big money to me. I was still a kid. I was also very irresponsible. As a matter of fact, I probably had no intention of paying him back when I borrowed it. That's the way I was then, who knows why.

Anyway, this guy Donnie hung out at JoJo's Candy Store where we all hung out. He had a reputation as a tough guy and would smack people around to get his money. Anyway, I started avoiding the candy store and The Circle, which was right across the street and where we usually were when we weren't in the candy store.

After a couple of days, people started to notice I wasn't around, and it was pretty obvious why because the loan shark was asking people where I was too. In those days, I would cause these really stupid problems for myself and then try and figure out how to get out of them. Why? I have no idea. Looking back, I actually think I enjoyed the excitement. That, plus the fact that I really didn't give a fuck. Whatever it was, I was in this situation now and things began to snowball.

It wasn't long before my stepsister, Debbie, heard about what was going on and being that she was going out with Rocco, who was Niko's cousin; it wasn't surprising that Niko heard about it. Soon after, which was something I had never even thought of because, at that time, I didn't even know Niko, but he knew who I was through Debbie and Rocco. Like I said, this was before I even knew him. Before he ever hung out at my apartment and before all the situations I've already talked about.

Debbie told me to go to JoJo's Candy Store, To the Circle or wherever else I wanted to go because everything had been taken care of. I was a little embarrassed that she knew what had happened, but I didn't ask any questions.

The next day, I walked down 182nd St. to JoJo's like I normally would. I was pretty nervous because I still didn't have the money I owed. I could see people hanging out in front of the candy store. I couldn't tell who was there, but I figured "what the fuck". As I got closer, I noticed Donnie's car right in front and I though, here we go.

I was about to walk in when Donnie walked out right in front of me. He said, "Hey Anthony, where have you been?" I haven't seen you in a couple of days, is everything all right; can I do anything for you?" I was pretty shocked, and I said, "No, I'm okay, how you doing." He said, "Good, good, let me know if there's anything you need." I said, "You know, I feel a little bad about the $20 I owe you." He said, "What $20, I don't give a fuck about that, don't worry about it." Right then I knew Niko was involved. There's no way this guy would be talking to me like that if he wasn't worried about something. I said, "Okay, Donnie, thanks." I walked away from him towards The Circle, which was a half block away. As I'm walking toward the park, I see Niko and Dante sitting at one of the tables in the park. Now it all makes sense. Niko had already gotten to this guy. I shouldn't have been surprised, but I was. Every time I thought somebody was pretty big in the neighborhood, Niko was bigger. Not only that, he thought the whole thing was funny. He loved punking people out no matter who they were. Obviously, I was relieved that I didn't have to worry about this guy or the money I owed him, but my relief was short lived once I realized the mood Niko was in.

He was the kind of guy that could always help you no matter how hopeless you thought the situation was. You never knew how far he would go or what he would do. Your idea of solving a problem was never the same has his.

I sat down with him and Dante at the table. We had a couple of beers and hung out for awhile. I loved listening to him talk. His mind was all over the place. He was involved with everything. Things were actually pretty normal for about an hour, then Niko started getting bored. You could just tell with him. That's when I would get nervous around him.

He finished the last of his beer, threw the bottle into the garbage can and leaned back on the bench. Then out of nowhere, he stood up and said, "Let's go kick Donnie Barbato's ass." I said, "What? For what, everything's okay with him. I just talked to him." He said, "I want to make sure he got the message, Dante, you ready?" I looked at Dante and he just shrugged his shoulders and said, "I don't give a fuck, let's go." I said, "Come on Niko, you don't have to do that, everything's okay."

He said, "I know I don't have to do that, but I'm bored." What else are we gonna do? You want me to get some broads and bring them to you apartment?" I said, "Yeah that sounds good, let's do that." I really didn't care if he got the girls or not, I was just trying to distract him. I was learning how and more importantly, when to do that with him. Sometimes it worked, sometimes it didn't, but it was always worth a try. He looked at me and said, "You sure, I know he's in the candy store, I'll go in there, drag him out and fuck him up. You can hit him to, if you want." I said, "I'm sure, really. Why don't you see if you can get some girls?" He said, "See if I can? How many you want?" He was laughing now, and I was hoping that was the end of it. He said, "Okay, go to the apartment and wait there for me. You need a ride?" I said, "No, its okay, I'll walk." I got up to leave, and I thought, thank God, I started walking home. I didn't even want to turn around in case he might change his mind.

As I'm walking home, I'm thinking what a relief. Now, the worst that can happen is there'll be a couple of beautiful women at my house when I get there, which was great of course, but at least, I didn't have to watch him beat the shit out of this guy or worse. You never knew what he would do, or how far he would go.

I got to my apartment building and didn't see his car so I went upstairs. In about a half-hour the bell rang. I buzzed to let him in, not knowing what to expect. I opened the door and looked down the hall. I could see Niko coming up the stairs. Dante wasn't with him. He had a girl with him. I didn't recognize her, but she looked pretty attractive. He got to the front door and said, "Hey Anthony, I brought you a present." He walked in the door with her and said, "Let's go in the kitchen and have a beer, she's gonna go in the bedroom and change." We walked into the kitchen and sat at the table. Before he sat down, he pulled a 45caliber automatic out of his belt and put it on the table. I remember thinking he probably doesn't know it, but this was Donnie Barbato's lucky night.

I got us a beer and Niko said, "Let's play some cards." I got a deck of cards out of the kitchen draw. All the time wondering what kind of night I was headed for. We were playing poker for about 10 or 15 minutes when I heard the bedroom door open. I tried to be cool about the whole thing, but I was pretty nervous. I had no idea what was going to happen or what my role in the whole thing was going to be.

She walked into the kitchen and sat down at the table with us. "Deal me in," she said. I knew I was staring at her, but I couldn't help it. All she had on was a bra and panties. They were all lace and covering nothing. Her name was Gina, and she was better looking than I thought. I'm thinking, okay, this isn't so bad no matter what happens. As I'm thinking, she says. "Niko told me it was my job to make you happy tonight. And I always do what Niko tells me to do." I said, "That's great, and I'll do anything I can to help." They both started to laugh, and I actually relaxed a little bit.

We played a couple of hands then Niko said, "Here's the deal, if I win a hand or if Anthony wins a hand, you have to take something off." She says, "Okay that sounds good to me." I'm thinking, she's only got two things on!

She dealt the cards and lit a cigarette. I looked at my hand and saw that I had three queens. I was really getting turned on by her now. We all pulled our next cards, and I saw I got another queen. Niko called, and I threw down my four queens. She looked at me and smiled. Then she put her hands behind her back and dropped her bra.

Now, at some point, I have to mention that I'm 19 years old when this was happening. At that age, you like to think that you're all grown up and you can handle things, but to be honest, I was pretty nervous. Right at that point, I was wondering what was going to happen next, and how I was going to handle it. Needless to say, I won the next hand too. She stood up and took her panties off then sat back down. As soon as she sat down, Niko downed the rest of his beer and said, "I gotta go." Now I'm petrified. "What do you mean?" I said. He said, "I gotta take care of a couple of things in the neighborhood, I'll see you around." Like a dope, I said, "What about Gina?" "What about her?" he asked. "You don't like her?" "Yeah, I like her." He said, "So?" Then he grabbed his keys and his .45 and was out the door. A minute later, he opened the door and said, "She lives a couple of blocks away, so when you're done, she can walk home. Have fun."

The door closed again, and he was gone. Now I'm sitting there with this naked woman, who I've never seen before, at my kitchen table. It wasn't the worst thing that ever happened to me, but it was strange. I didn't want to seem like a wimp and just sit there. If, for no other reason that I didn't want to have Niko breaking my balls for a week, I said, "We'll play one more hand, whoever wins decides what we do." "Sounds good to me," she said.

She won and she decided. I guess it was great. I really don't remember. I woke up in the morning and she was gone. Either we had some fun and she left, or she was bored and left. I guess she had fun, though, because if she didn't, I never would have heard the end of it from Niko. Anyway, from what I remember, I had a good time. It didn't really matter, she'd be back and if she wasn't, it would be somebody else. That's the way it was in those days. Things were just falling into my lap because of Niko. It's impossible to grow up in a neighborhood like we did and not have it affect your personality in some way. It's not something you're aware of at first, but then you look back at the way you handle certain situations that come up in your life, it's obvious.

Chapter 9

If I had stayed in the neighborhood, I don't think I would ever have noticed, but after living in New Jersey for the past 12 years, it's more than obvious. I never felt like I was different than anybody else, and I always respected other people. Growing up in the neighborhood, I had learned to treat people the way you would want to be treated. It was as simple as that. At least, I thought it was. I always got along with everybody. Whenever I ran into problems, it was always for the same reason and that was when people tried to treat you like shit. I just could never deal with it. I grew up on the street, like a lot of other people I knew. It wasn't the best way to grow up, I'm sure, but you grew up fast. You learn how to read people, at a very young age. It was one of the few benefits of being in a situation like that. You learn to trust, only yourself. You develop an instinct about people and situations that can only come from being on the street. Nobody can tell you about it and you can't read about it somewhere. You have to live it. I developed a kind of reactionary personality. I gave what I got. In my mind, respect was earned. You didn't just get it. I reacted to whatever was in front of me. I gave people the same respect they gave me. No matter who it was. I believed it was fair whether it was people on the street, friends, people you worked with or people you worked for. Everybody.

By the time I was in my 20's, I was at the point where I could deal with people in any situation. No matter who they were. I could talk to people I knew or people I had just met and after five to ten minutes, I'd know what they were all about see right through them. Not because I thought I was hot shit or anything like that, I never thought I was anything special. It just came so easy. It was just one of the things you developed growing up the way I did. The combinations of that kind of experience and the personality I had in those days would sometimes cause me problems. For whatever reason, I never learned how to hide what I was thinking. I'm not saying I was proud of it, I'm just saying that's the way I was. Sometimes it would cause trouble for me, but for the most part, it helped me. There was always some asshole trying to take advantage of you.

The attitude I had at that time was the only thing they respected. Of course, this didn't go over big with my family or whatever authority figures I was dealing with at that time. But, what the fuck, I was always in trouble for something back then. It might as well be for something that was helping me on the street.

It was right around this time that I experienced a situation I never expected. I was at a point where I wasn't surprised at anything Niko did, or so I thought. I couldn't help but wonder about his relationship with Dante. I knew he was Niko's right hand man because that was obvious. Why that was, I didn't know. I new there must have been a good reason though, there had to be. To me, he seemed to be just as crazy as Niko was and he was so big. He towered over Niko and everybody else, but there was no questions who called the shots. Nobody challenged Niko and that included Dante.

I came home from work and had dinner at my apartment. It was Friday night, and I didn't feel like sitting in my apartment. I took a walk to "Badlands", Niko's bar. I didn't have a car in those days so I couldn't go far anyway. I also new If I went there, I could drink for free. Niko made sure every bartender knew I would never see a check. If I did, it would be their ass.

I got to the bar and went inside. It was pretty crowded, but I was able to get a spot at the bar. I wasn't shocked, but it was unusual. I looked around for Niko, but didn't see him. Dante hadn't seen me yet. He was busy with the two women at the other end of the bar. I was surprised that there wasn't a bartender back there. Dante was doing shots with his lady friends when I noticed there were a few people waiting for drinks. As I'm thinking this Dante looks over and sees me sitting there. He yelled out "Hey, Anthony, how the fuck you doin? You want a beer?"

I said, "Yeah, sure." He grabs me a beer and brings it over to me walking right past everybody else waiting for a drink. He puts down my beer and reaches over the bar to give me a hug. He lifts me up from my barstool, kisses me on the cheek and says, "You need anything all you gotta do is say so." Then he puts me back down and goes back over to the woman he was talking to. While he had me in a bear hug, I realized he was wasted. People were trying to get his attention, to get another drink, but they were afraid. Nobody wanted to piss him off. Whenever somebody would try to get his attention, he would say, "Relax, I'll be right there, calm the fuck down." Me and the two girls he was talking to were the only ones being served.

I had a couple of beers and watched as Dante eventually got to some of the customers. I couldn't help thinking that none of this would be happening if Niko was here. I figured what the fuck; this had nothing to do with me. So I sipped my beer and kept an eye on Dante. The mood he was in, I thought there was a good chance he might hit somebody. As I'm watching him, I'm thinking there's never a dull moment. Then I realized that one of the girls he was talking to looked familiar to me. I couldn't place her at first, then it hit me. It was Gina, the girl I had sex with on my kitchen table. It was weird. To think that this was only the second time I had seen her ever and we had already had sex. That was pretty strange, but what wasn't? I was still looking at her when she looked right at me. She smiled, picked up her drink and started walking over to where I was sitting. Now I'm thinking here we go. What kind of night is this going to be? I just sat there and thought, now what? She came up behind me and put her arm around my neck. Then she leaned over, stuck her tongue in my ear and said, "Remember me?" I turned around to face her and said, "Who could forget?" she said, "That's a great answer, why don't we hang out tonight?" I said, "We'll see, can I buy you a drink." She said, "Sure, I'm in good company." I couldn't believe I said that to her, but I wanted to buy some time.

Obviously, I had forgotten about watching what Dante was up to so I never saw him hit this guy. It was the sound of the guy getting hit that got my attention. He was only a couple of feet away from me, but I was looking the other way at Gina. It was an awful cracking sound, followed by the sound of him hitting the floor which was all he was able to do after he got hit. To me, it sounded like a broken nose, and when they picked the guy up to take him outside, it looked that way too. What can I say, when you grow up in the neighborhood, you get to know what sounds like what.

As they're carrying the guy outside, Niko walked through the front door, which I though was the worst possible thing that could happen right then. Niko looked at the guy and said, "What the fuck is this? One of the guys that were carrying him said, "Dante hit him." The bar was pretty crowded, and the music was also loud. So this whole scene had pretty much gone unnoticed, believe it or not. But anyone at the bar with any real connection to Niko had to be worried. I was one of those people. I didn't now when or how, but I was sure the whole night was about to change. I was just hoping that when it did, it would have nothing to do with me. I knew Niko was going to be pissed off about what was going on.

I was pretty nervous when I saw Niko walk into the bar, but that was nothing compared to how I felt when he walked towards where I was sitting. Gina was sitting on the stool to my right. There was a big guy with an even bigger mouth on my left. I was thinking that I should have stayed home and watched the Yankee game. For a second, I though maybe he was going to walk past me and sit somewhere else. That's when I felt him slap me on the back and say, "The girl on our right ain't bad." "But this big mouth, fat fuck on your left has got to go." I busted out laughing for a couple of reasons. First, because it was so funny, and secondly, the guy had to hear him say it. That was one of the amazing things about Niko. Everybody remembers a time in their life when they wanted to just say what they were thinking. Niko did that all the time. I loved that about him.

Right then, the guy turned around and said, "Who you calling a fat fuck?" Niko leaned over, picked up the guy's check and tore it up. Then he said, "Your drinks are on me, go sit some place else." The guy looked at him for a few seconds and said, "Why should I?" Niko moved toward him. There were only a couple of inches between them, face to face. Niko looked into his eyes and said, "Because five minutes from now, you're either gonna be having a beer in another seat or spittin up blood. We already know you're a fat fuck, so now we just have to find out if you're a stupid fat fuck." Now a couple of things are going through my mind. Obviously, Niko was in some fucking mood. I also thought he was going to make an example of this guy. Partly because he was gearing up for the next situation. Which would be dealing with Dante, which was what I was really worried about anyway. The guy turned away from Niko, took his money off the bar and said, "I'll move to another seat, no hard feelings, okay?" Niko didn't even acknowledge the question. He just sat down in the guy's seat.

So now I have Gina on my right and Niko on my left. I look over at Niko, and I see his gun in his shoulder holster. I looked at him in the eye and said, "You know, you really need to calm down a little bit." He smiled at me and said, "I don't remember asking you what I need to do." Dante brought me another beer and gave Niko a stoli on the rocks then went to take care of some new customers. Niko sipped his drink and asked me, "What's he doing behind the bar?" I said, "I don't know, he was back there when I got here." He said, "Never mind, I'll find out."

By now, I had forgotten about Gina. So much had happened since she had come over. She grabbed my arm and said, "Watch my stuff; I'm going to the lady's room." When Dante came back over to us, Niko said, "What are you doing behind the fucking bar? What happened to the bartender?" Dante told him that he sent him home because he didn't like his attitude. Niko looked at him and said, "Yeah, well, maybe I don't like your fucking attitude. You're drinking behind the bar and not taking care of the customers. On top of that, you're smacking people around. You think you're in your house? You're in my bar; you understand what I'm saying? Whatever happens in this place happens because I allow it. That goes for anybody who walks through that fucking door. And that includes you! So if you don't agree with that or understand it, I'm sitting right here."

So much for me not having anything to do with what was going to happen that night. In all the situations I had been through with the two of them, they were always on the same side. This was weird, not to mention tense. Nobody there wanted to be around if the two of them went at it; especially me. As I sat there, I was hoping Dante would back down because I knew Niko wouldn't. I was beginning to understand why Niko was doing this and why Dante was so loyal to him. He had to be able to punk out Dante. It was the only way to keep everything in place. Niko would never settle for anything less. It was a pretty simple theory, but one that could only be carried out by somebody with balls; somebody who could be fearless and calm. At the same time, somebody that made you feel like you were better off not fucking with him. That was Niko.

So I sat there, next to Niko, and waited for Dante's reaction. He downed the rest of his drink, looked at Niko and said, "I didn't mean any disrespect. Maybe I'm a little fucked up, but it was nothing that was ever directed at you." Niko said, "That's all I wanted to know. Now that was your last drink tonight. If you want to drink, you do it on this side of the bar." Then he said, "You okay to work the rest of the night? If not, I'll put Anthony behind the bar." I said, "Me, I'm not going to work tonight." He said, "Come on, you wouldn't take five hundred to finish out the night?" Then Dante said, "I'm okay, I'll get some coffee and finish the night." Niko said, "Okay, no problem. See, wasn't that easy? Now we can all relax and have a fucking drink."

Everybody started to loosen up a little and the night went on. Niko slapped the back of my head and asked me why I had money on the bar. I looked at him and said, "Hey, this ain't Dante you're fucking with here, I don't back down." We both started laughing, and I was just happy that things turned out the way they did. Then he took out his wallet, pulled out two, hundred dollar bills and stuffed them in my shirt pocket. He said, "That's for almost having to work tonight." I told him he didn't have to do that. He said. "When I need you to tell me what I have to do, I'll let you know. I'll say Anthony, what should I do? Help me please, I'm scared." I said, "You know, some day that attitude of yours is gonna get you in trouble." He said, "It already has. It don't matter. The only thing that matters is that you can get out of the trouble you get yourself into, and be able to handle whatever kind of shit somebody throws your way. Remember that, never get involved with anything you can't control. That's it. And if you do, all you gotta do is call me."

Obviously, this was good advice. He was right and as usual, he was trying to help me, but I couldn't help finding it funny. He was giving me advice he believed in. I knew that, but he never did things that way. Not because he didn't believe in what he was telling me. That's what was so funny to me. It's just that he never felt there was a situation he couldn't control, but that was him, and he could never understand why he made me laugh. He would look at me and say, "What's so fucking funny?" I'd look back at him and say, "Who gives a fuck, don't you have enough things to worry about? You gotta wonder why I'm laughing too?" For some reason, I could talk to him that way. Why, I had no idea. I can't remember how or when it happened. Somewhere along the line, I had become that close to him. I could break his balls about anything, and I did no matter how serious or dangerous the situation was. And at that time, everything was usually serious or dangerous.

Being able to be that way with him was the reason I was able to handle what I was going through at that time. I don't know if Niko knew that or not. Knowing him, he probably did. From what I remember, he got a kick out of the way I would fuck with him, or thought it was funny. It was one of the other. Otherwise, I would never have been able to do it. I knew that for sure.

By now the bar had started to empty out a little bit. Dante was on his third cappuccino and starting to get bored. I was thinking that this would be a pretty good time to leave. I slapped Niko on the back and told him I was going home. He said, "You taking Gina with you? She's hot for you." I told him I didn't think so. "It's okay, I'm just gonna get some sleep tonight." He said, "It don't have to be Gina, you want one of the other girls?" I said, "No, really, I'm just gonna go." He said, "Finish your beer, and I'll give you a ride."

I couldn't believe it. This was exactly what I was trying to avoid. Now that he was going to drive me home, everybody would know I was leaving. I should have just left without saying anything, but I knew that either the next time I saw Niko or even worse, as I was walking out, I would hear him say, "What, you can't say good night?" It was either deal with him now or deal with him later. So, as I'm sitting there thinking that I should have left, here comes Gina. She sat down next to me and said, "When are we leaving?" I said, "What do you mean, who's we?" She said, "If I'm sitting here with you, and I say we, that must mean me and you." One of the funny things about the neighborhood that usually goes unnoticed is that the girls talked the same way the guys did, and if you thought about it, why shouldn't they. But for some reason, it was always funny; anyway, I told her maybe next time. I said, "Besides, Niko said he'd give me a ride." Meanwhile, I didn't even want a fucking ride home in the first place. Then she said, "Listen, he just told me to take you home. He said you were tired and wanted to get some sleep. He told me to stay at your place tonight because you might want me I the morning." I said, "That's really nice of you to do that." Then she leaned over, put her hand down my pants and said, "Or you might wake up in the middle of the night with a hard on." Even though I really wasn't in the mood for anything weird going on at my apartment that night, she did have a point. If I was sure I would only be dealing with her all night, I wouldn't mind, but I knew if I brought her home, there was a chance Niko would stop by later, or even worse, he might stop by with Dante and a few other girls. I'd have people at my apartment for the rest of the weekend, and no one can imagine or understand what that's like unless you've done it. I had done it, more than enough times, so I knew how things would play out.

So I walked over to Niko. He was talking to some guy at the bar. He had his back to me so he didn't see me coming. As I got closer, I could hear their conversation. The guy was trying to explain why he didn't have the money he owed him. When I got there, I put my arm around Niko and said, "Sorry to interrupt." He turned around and said, "Don't worry about it; I'm tired of this guy's bullshit excuses anyway." I said, "I just wanted to thank you for Gina." He looked at me said, "And what?"

Even when I thought I knew what I was going to say to him, he still made me nervous. I said, "What do you mean, and what?" He said, "You got something else on your mind, I know you. Just tell me." I told him I didn't mind going home with Gina, but I really didn't want to have all kinds of people at the apartment. I just didn't want you to think I was ungrateful or anything like that. He said, "I understand, I'm not welcome at your apartment, right?" I said, "You see how you are?" You know that's not how I feel." He said, "I'm breaking your balls a little bit, that's all. Don't worry about it, go home with Gina and have a good time. I'll make sure nobody bothers you, ok?" We both started to laugh, and I said, "Give me a hug, you fucking nut." He stood up and grabbed me; we slapped each other on the back. I had forgotten all about the guy he was talking to before I came over. When we looked over at him, he was just sitting there looking at the two of us. Niko said, "Hey Anthony, should I believe this fucking asshole?" I said, "I don't know, Niko, I'd say give him a break, but that's probably because it ain't my money, and I'm getting laid tonight, so you can't go by me."

I walked back over to where Gina was sitting. She said, "Let's have one more drink and leave." I said, "How about we just finish what we got and have a drink at my place." I felt a lot better about going home now that I didn't have to worry about anybody showing up there later. Besides, by now I knew there was no way I was going to get out of the bar without Gina. As we were finishing up our drinks, Niko walked by with the guy he was talking with a minute ago. They were behind us by the front door. Before the guy left, he thanked Niko for giving him more time to pay him. I turned around to say good night to the guy. I felt bad for him. Then Niko said, "I'll tell you what I'm gonna do. You owe me how much, two grand? I'm knocking off three hundred from that. Now you owe me seventeen hundred from that. You see this kid here? His name is Anthony, and he's a friend of mine. He said I should give you a break so you can thank him for that. In return, I want you to keep an eye out for him. If he ever needs anything, and I ain't around, you take care of it. How's that?" The guy said, "Sure, no problem, thank you." Then he came over to me and told me his name was Joe Falcone. He said if there was anything I needed, I should stop by the Canbrelling Ave Lounge and ask for him. I thanked him and he thanked Niko again. Then he left.

I looked at Niko and said, "You're really fuckin' something, you know that? What the fuck was that all about? He told me that this guy, Joe Falcone, was a good guy with a bad gambling habit. He told me that all this guy's money was used for two things, gambling and taking care of his mother. He lived with his mother ever since his father died. Niko said the guy always owed him money and would never really be able to pay him so he would lend him money, and if he ever needed the guys help for anything, he could count on him. Then he said, "Besides, I can't be fucking everywhere. Now you got some insurance if I ain't around." I told him I appreciated what he did for me. He said, "Don't worry about it, and don't ever hesitate to go see Joe at the Canbrelling Ave Lounge. I'm talking about if I ain't around. He's a good guy. He takes care of his mother, plus he knows if he doesn't help you, he's gonna have to answer to me." Right then I thought, so that was it. Niko had a soft spot for people who did the right thing especially when they did it for family. He would never admit it, but that didn't matter. It was that aspect of his personality that I respected and admired the most.

I couldn't help wondering about this guy Joe Falcone. In all the time I'd been with Niko, it was the first time he said something like that to me. He had never told me to go to anybody else before. I knew there had to be a good reason. I knew he was loyal to Niko and would never cross him, but there were a lot of people that fell into that category. I had to know. I looked at Niko and said, "So why him?" He said, "What do you mean, why him?" I said, "You've never told me to go to anybody but you. For you to tell me to go see him if I was in trouble, there must be a good reason."

He said, "He's loyal to me, and he's a good guy." I said, "What else?" He said, "He's a tough motherfucker with balls, and I know he'd be able to handle things for you if you needed him. I said, "How tough?" He said, "What the fuck is wrong with you? He can fight, and he can punch. If he hits somebody, they're gonna go down." I said, "How do you know that?" He said, "Okay, you pain in the fucking ass. Years ago, we were both boxing in the golden gloves. We had both beaten everybody in our weight class. Then we fought each other for the golden glove title that year. It was a three round bout. He knocked me down twice in the first round. I had never been knocked on my ass before that night, and I was down twice in the first round. I knocked him out in the third round and was the golden glove champ that year, but it was the toughest fight I have ever been in both in the ring or on the street. Nobody ever hit me that hard." I just looked at him. He said, "You satisfied now, you prick?" I said, "Yeah, that's a great story." He said, "I never told anybody about that and you never will either." I said, "Of course not, thanks for letting me in on that." I finished my drink and grabbed my jacket from the back of the barstool. I looked at Niko and said, "Wow, I feel really weird now." He lit a cigarette and said, "Yeah, what's your problem?" I said, "I don't know, I thought I knew you. Now I find out that you've been knocked on your ass twice in the first round of a fight. How's that supposed to make me feel?" He started laughing and said, "I don't know, but I do know how you're gonna feel if you don't get the fuck out of here. Don't you have to go get laid or something?" Now we were both laughing. I loved breaking his balls like that.

Meanwhile, Gina was sitting there through this whole conversation waiting to leave. I stood up and put my jacket on. I looked at her and said, "You ready to go?" She said "Am I ready to go? Yeah, I'm ready. I just need a minute to dry my eyes after listening to that love scene between you two."

We all laughed for a minute, then Niko said, "Gina that was your first and last wise crack of the night. Now go drive my buddy home and do what you gotta do. Make sure he falls asleep with a smile on his face." She said, "He'll be smiling before that." Niko said, "Good, now the two of you get the fuck out of here. I have to close up and get out of here myself."

We left the bar and walked to her car. She told me that if I felt like driving, she would give me a blowjob on the way. I said, "Why don't you drive and just think about blowing me?" We got in the car and drove to my house. We parked the car and went upstairs. We walked into my apartment and sat at the kitchen table. We had a couple of beers and then she started to take her clothes off. In no time, she was sitting naked across the table from me. She said, "What are you gonna do to me tonight?" I said, "What do you want me to do?" And that was that. There's no need to get into what went on, it was just another good night.

By now word had spread through the neighborhood that I was part of Niko's inner circle. It didn't matter if that was really true or not. What mattered was that was the word on the street. I could feel it wherever I went. I never acted any differently, but everybody else did. It was very inconspicuous, but it was there. And that was more than enough for me. I took pride in the fact that I never abused it in any way.

During the next few days, I did nothing. I went to work, and then I went home. I decided to make a serious effort to keep myself away from any problems. Things actually went smoothly for a while. This gave me a chance to reflect on what was going on in my life at that point. I had plenty to think about. I didn't realize it at first, but after awhile, I noticed that I hadn't paid the rent in a long time. I wasn't sure if it was being paid or if Niko had gotten to the landlord. Something must have happened because the guy who owned the building was a real pain in the ass. He was always knocking on my door looking for the rent, even before it was due. Now, he never did. He was still always around, knocking on people's doors. He just never came to mine anymore. Whenever I saw him in the building, he just avoided me completely, which was fine with me. I hated the fucking guy. I just figured it was one less thing I had to worry about.

It's almost impossible to explain how I was feeling during this time of my life. Obviously, it was difficult to deal with. Being 19 years old didn't help either. At that age, you think you know everything, but in reality what you really know is nothing. I couldn't really talk to anybody about what was going on because it was so weird. If I told my father or my brother, they would just worry about me even more, and it would solve nothing. The last thing I wanted to do was cause either of them any more problems. Especially if no good would come out of it. So I was pretty much on my own with this, which was fine. I loved them both so much and nothing was more important than that.

During this time, another strange thing started happening. About once a week, I started getting meat deliveries from the Hunt's Point Meat Packing Company. Steaks, chops, chicken, you name it. It kept coming, more that I could ever use. Whenever I asked the delivery guy, he would just tell me he was told to drop off the meat and never collect payment. I figured Niko must have set this up so I just kept my mouth shut.

Chapter 10

Knowing Niko and being around him in those days will always be special to me. Not just for the obvious reasons, as I've said before, he had a big heart. I know about that, first hand. I'm sure the problems I had in those days, which he made disappear, were no big deal and that's really the whole point. He didn't have to do any of those things for me. But he did.

I never really understood why, but that didn't matter either. He also looked out for the rest of my family and who knows how many other people. When there was trouble in the neighborhood, he made sure we were protected. I'm not sure that I ever really thanked him enough for what he did. Maybe someday I'll get a chance to do that. He deserves to hear it. It's been almost 25 years since I've seen him. It's hard to believe, but everybody's life goes on. During the past year, I've been going into the neighborhood about once a week talking to people here and there as I came across them.

One night my brother Joey and me stopped in at Giovanni's on Ruthra Ave. I knew Gino Vallenti owned the place so I figured we might run into some people there. We had a couple of beers and took in the atmosphere, which is always interesting in the neighborhood. My brother and I both thought the bartender looked familiar. We made some small talk and left.

I started going into the neighborhood once a week after that, usually with my brother Joey, and sometimes by myself. After I did my shopping and had something to eat (you always had to do that when you were in the neighborhood, just because it would be stupid not to) I would always stop at Giovanni's. It was right on Ruthra Avenue and it was the best place to run into people. If not in the restaurant, everybody shopped on Ruthra Ave.

The second time Joey and I went to Giovanni's, we started talking to Pete, the bartender. He looked familiar to us, and we looked familiar to him. Once we started talking, we found out we knew a lot of the same people. As I said, Gino Vallenti owned the restaurant, and he would stop in often. Seeing him was amazing to me. It was like stepping into my past. In fact, everybody that came into the place looked familiar to some extent. That's when I first though that if I had any chance of finding Niko again, this was a good place to start. I never really thought I would see him again, but after talking to Pete for a couple of weeks it was the first time I actually started to think I would.

It felt great to be back in the neighborhood. I mean, over the years, I always ate and shopped there, but I never hung out there like I was now. I really enjoyed it. Sitting at the bar and talking to Pete was really interesting. He was the kind of guy that knew everybody. After a while, my brother and I became regulars at the bar. We got to know the restaurant staff and some of the regular customers.

I started talking to Pete about Niko. I wanted to find out if he knew him, and more importantly, if he ever saw him around. I wasn't surprised to hear that he knew him, but I was shocked when he told me that he saw him once in a while on Ruthra Ave. I never expected that. After I heard that, I was in the neighborhood every Tuesday night. It was an unbelievable feeling to be writing about my family's history and then my own experiences in the neighborhood. While I'm doing that, I find out that it's possible I might be able to connect with Niko again. It would be like stepping into my past instead of just writing about it. I gave Pete my phone number and told him to give it to Niko the next time he saw him. I knew it was a long shot, but I figured what the fuck?

I had been in touch with "Diana" ever since Jean Marie's funeral. She knew about me trying to find out anything I could about Niko. After about six months of going to the neighborhood every week, I hadn't really found out anything about where he was. I had a feeling that being around this neighborhood, as often as I was, was the best chance he might hear that somebody was asking about him.   That wouldn't surprise me at all. Somehow, he would know.

Right around this time, I got a call from Diana. She told me that a friend of her brother's knew one of Niko's kids. This guy's friend was married to Niko's daughter. When I heard that, I started laughing. Diana asked me what I was laughing at. I told her that just the thought of having Niko as a father-in-law was funny to me. I said, "Now there's a marriage that's going to last. " We both laughed, but seriously, this news really got me excited. I asked her to have this person get word to Niko that I wanted to contact him and to ask him if that would be okay. She said she would. Before we hung up, I told her to make sure she didn't mention anything about the story I was writing. If anybody was going to tell Niko what I was doing, it was going to be me

He was very smart, and I always knew he had a big heart. Even though he always tried to downplay that part of himself, I had firsthand experience with that side of him. I never forgot it.

It was about two weeks later, when Diana called me again. During that time, I thought about him a lot. About all the things that went on when I was around him back in those days. I was excited about the possibility of getting in touch with him again, but I was nervous about it too. He wasn't exactly your average guy. And although 25 years had gone by since I had seen him, I didn't expect him to be much different from what I remembered. I know there are exceptions, but generally, I don't believe people change that much. Especially somebody like Niko. He was always sure of himself and what to do. And like I said, he was smart. He knew what he was doing all the time and always in control. In other words, I didn't expect him to be working for the post office or something like that.

Anyway, when I talked to Diana that day, she told me that her friend had talked to Niko. I couldn't believe it. She said, "Anthony, you got the green light." Niko said he remembered you and it would be okay to call him." Then she said, "You got a pen, he left this number for you." I wrote down the number and thanked her. She said, "Anthony, good luck. I know how much this means to you." She was right of course. I thanked her again and hung up the phone.

Now I'm walking around my house from room to room thinking about what I just heard. Things were happening so fast. I had to get ready for work and drop my kids off at my mother-in-law's house. Things I did every day, but I just couldn't focus on anything. What I was doing and what I was thinking about were worlds apart. I dropped the kids off and left for work. The ride to my job gave me time to think, I was really excited. Now, I had to call him. I figured, at least, he knew I was going to call. It was better than just calling him out of nowhere, but it still made me nervous as hell. Even so, I couldn't shake the feeling that things were all falling into place. Almost like after all this time, this was supposed to happen. After all, this is what I wanted. Maybe I just never expected to get this far. Who knows?

I decided to wait a couple of days before calling Niko. I needed to think about what I would say to him. I figured I would call him on my day off at the end of the week. In a way, I was thinking I would need a day off after talking to him.

The next day, I made the call. I was nervous and didn't know what to expect. I dialed the number and a woman answered the phone. I said hello and asked if Niko was there. She said he wasn't home and asked who was calling. I explained who I was and said it had been over 20 years since I had talked to Niko, but I had gotten a message that it was okay to call him. She said, "Oh, is this Anthony from the neighborhood?" I was relieved and said, "Yeah, that's right, is he home? She told me that he was at a friend's house, but she would tell him that I had called. We made some small talk, and I said I would call him back the next day. She was very nice. She said she was Niko's wife, and her name was Gerri. She was also from the neighborhood so we talked about that for awhile. I don't know why, but I was surprised at how well this was all going. I thanked her and said I would call back. We said goodbye, and I hung up the phone. Even though I didn't get to talk to him, I felt good about the phone call.

The next day, I called again. Gerri answered and said he was across the street at work. She explained that the business they had was right across the street from their house. She said "Hold on, I'll put you on the three-way intercom". I waited on the phone as she connected the call.

Now I was really nervous. Then I heard Gerri say, "Anthony, are you there?" I said, "Yeah, I'm here." Then she said, "Niko, pick up the phone." Then I heard his voice for the first time since 1976. "Yeah, it's me, what is it?" Hearing his voice again after all those years brought back a flood of memories. I said, "Niko, it's Anthony, you remember me?" Then I heard him say, "I can't hear nothing, I'm coming over there." Then his wife told me to hold on, he'd be here in a minute. I asked her what was going on, and she said, "He has to hang up the phone there, walk across the street and pick up this phone. He'll be here in a minute." I said, "Oh, that should put him in a great mood." She said, "Don't worry, you know him, he's got a short fuse." I said, "That's good news. When I knew him, he didn't even have a fuse."

We both laughed and she said hold on. He'd be here in a minute. I waited for him to pick up the phone. I was so nervous thinking about what I would say to him. While I'm thinking this, I hear, "Yeah, I got it, who's this?" I said, "Niko, it's Anthony Genelli from the neighborhood. You remember me?" He said, "Yeah I remember the apartment on Lorrilard Place, right?" I said, "Yeah, that's right." I really couldn't believe I was talking to him. I said, "It's got to be 20 years." He said, "It's more than that. What have you been doing?" I told him I was living in New Jersey. I was married and had two kids and one on the way. He said, "So, you've been busy." We both laughed, and I said, "Yeah, I guess so." I told him I would really like to see him. Would it be okay?" He said, "That's easy, come to the coffee shop on Crosby Ave." I said, "That's great, when?"

"How do we set this up?" But before I was even finished saying that he said, "You just tell me." I told him I was off on Tuesdays and Thursdays and asked him if next Tuesday would be okay. He said, "What time?" I said, "What's good for you?" He said, "Don't worry about what's good for me, give me a time." I said I could be in the neighborhood around one in the afternoon. He said, "I'll be there, call me if anything changes." And he was gone; just like that. I hung up the phone and sat down at the kitchen table. From the kitchen table, I could see the lake, which was frozen solid this time of year. It struck me how different my life was now. The contrast between the time I spent with Niko in those days and what I was looking at out of my window was unbelievable. I'm not sure how long I sat there. It felt like a long time, but I'm sure it wasn't. The thing about growing up in the neighborhood was that you experienced so much there. Even at a young age, by the time you were 20 years old you probably had to deal with more intense situations than most people would in a lifetime. It was almost as though I was living another life now; a life so completely different from what I was familiar with. I had no complaints, though. At this point in my life, I had a great wife, two beautiful kids and one on the way. Somehow, I had to balance that with what I was doing now. I wasn't sure how, but I knew I would. I had all the support I needed. Thank God for my wife, Barbara. I believe that she is much more than I ever deserved.

* * * * *

So now I'm set to meet Niko. I found out that the coffee shop was an after hours joint at night. I also learned that the club it turned into after hours was run by Niko's son, Carlo. The last time I saw his son, he was about five years old. So it was weird to think of him doing that now. It was weird, but not surprising. When I though about it, his son was running a place like that. Having Niko for a father would be invaluable. For whatever reason whether it was for advice, connections or protection. Who could be better?

Anyway, that Tuesday came when I was supposed to meet him. Believe it or not, there was a snowstorm that day. It started snowing the night before and didn't stop until Tuesday afternoon. I was lying in bed that morning when the phone rang and woke me up. My wife had already left for work, and I heard my son answer the phone. I could hear him say, "My father is sleeping." Then I heard him say, "Okay, I'll tell him when he gets up." I got out of bed and went into the bathroom to wash my face. I called out to my son, "Danny, who was that on the phone?" I figured it was my wife calling to make sure he was up for school. Danny yelled back to me, "I don't know, some guy named Niko. He said to tell you he couldn't make it today because he was snowed in." I went out to the living room and saw that there was about a foot of snow outside. I looked at my son, sitting there watching TV as if nothing had happened. And I thought about how strange it was that he had just talked to Niko.

    I called Niko back, and when he answered the phone, I said, "Niko, it's Anthony." He said, "I'm fucking buried." There's snow all over the fucking place." I said, "I can't believe it, 25 years, and it's gotta snow today." He laughed and said, "Don't worry about nothing, we're gonna hook up." Then he said, "Call me when all this shit melts." I said I would and then he told me he would be going to Atlantic City at the end of the week. After that he said he was going to Florida for a day or two with his son. I said, "Okay, I'll call you in a couple of weeks then." Now he was getting impatient. I could just tell. It was just like when I knew him back then. He said, "What's a couple of weeks, I'll be home by Sunday night. I can't stay any place too long. I get fucking aggravated." I said, "Okay, I'll call you Sunday or Monday." He said, "That sounds good, I'll talk to you then." Then we hung up, and I just had to laugh. I was glad to hear him sound the same as he always did. I'm not sure why. Honestly though, once I thought about it, I guess I always hoped he would still be that way. I couldn't imagine him being anything different from what I remembered. But a lot of time had gone by. We're talking about 25 years here. But once I heard his voice and actually talked to him a couple of times, I knew he hadn't changed much.

    I talked to Niko that Sunday night and left it with him that I would meet him in the neighborhood the following Thursday. So much was going on with him, which wasn't surprising. And with my work schedule and Barbara being pregnant, it's not surprising that this meeting got screwed up too. Niko told me that if I didn't hear from him, he would be there on Thursday. What I didn't know, but found out later, was that while he was out of town, his wife had misplaced my phone number. He had wanted to call me to tell me he couldn't be there on Thursday. Anyway, I didn't know this so I went to the Bronx that day.

    I was really excited at the thought of seeing him. I got to the neighborhood around noon. I parked on Crosby Avenue where the after hours joint was. I sat in my car and looked at the place for a few minutes. I started to get really nervous and realized that if I didn't just walk into the place right then, I never would. It was a typical neighborhood hangout. The windows were painted black so there was no way of seeing inside. I had no way of knowing what I would be walking into. I decided to just do it. Somehow I knew that once whoever was in there knew I was there to see Niko, things would take care of themselves. I got out of my car and walked up to the front door. I grabbed the door handle and pulled the door open.

When I walked in all eyes were on me. There were a few guys playing cards at a table and a couple of older guys drinking espresso at the bar. I knew if I acted like I was supposed to be there, everything would be fine. I walked up to the bar and said, "Is Niko around?" One of the guys looked at me, took a sip of his espresso and said, "No, he ain't here." I looked at him and said, "You know who I'm talking about?" He said, "Yeah, I know who you're talking about, he ain't here." I said, "Okay, thanks. Do me a favor, if he comes in tell him, Anthony stopped by to see him." and then I walked out. It was very tense, but I expected it to be. As a matter of fact, I would have been disappointed if it wasn't.

I went back to my car and called Niko's house on my cell phone. His wife answered and asked me where I was. I told her I was in the neighborhood. She said, "oh my God, he's gonna kill me."

Then she told me that while they were away, Niko wanted to call me to tell me he couldn't be there on Thursday, but she couldn't find my phone number. I told her not to worry about it. I'll just meet him another time. She told me I should give him a call at his office and gave me his phone number. I dialed the number, and he picked up the phone. I said, "Niko, it's Anthony." He said, "Where are you?" I said, "I'm where I'm supposed to be, where are you?" He told me he wanted to call me, but didn't have my phone number. I said, "It's no big deal, I wanted to meet my brother in the neighborhood anyway." He said, "This is unfuckingbelievable. I'll be there tomorrow, what about you?" I told him I was working the next day and couldn't be there. He said, "I don't fucking believe this." I told him it didn't matter because I was just happy to be in contact with him after all this time. He said, "Yeah, I know. Just give me a call when you know you're gonna be in the neighborhood." I said, "Okay, maybe you'll show up next time." He said, "You getting fucking smart with me?" I said, "Of course I am, I can't do it in person, I gotta do it on the phone." He laughed and said, "Now you're starting to make sense again." Then he hung up the phone.

I met my brother that night and went to see Pete at Giovanni's. We hung out at the bar for a while and took in the atmosphere. There was one thing you could always count on in the neighborhood, especially on Ruthra Avenue, and that was atmosphere. It was the heart and soul of the neighborhood.

It was during that time that I was able to work on my story from a different viewpoint; one I had never expected. Even though I had spent the last year going to the neighborhood about once a week for this very reason. Hoping to run into some people and kind of fine tune what I was writing about, I never thought I would be able to accomplish what I had. Being there as often as I was. I was able to see some of the people I had written about. And being in touch with Niko on a regular basis was so much more than I had ever hoped for. I still hadn't actually gotten to see him, but that didn't matter. I knew that it was going to happen soon. To be honest, I was so nervous about seeing him, I didn't mind waiting. I needed time to get myself ready for that. He was that kind of person.

Chapter 11

There was so much going on in my life, it was hard to concentrate on anything. My wife, Barbara was still working in the city. My son, Danny, was 11 years old and involved with every sport you could thing of. My daughter, Maria, was almost two years old; enough said. I was also having major work done on my house, new doors, windows, floors plus what I was involved with in the neighborhood, and I was bartending at night. It was nuts.

I had three or four guys working on the house during the day. I had a landscaper taking down seven or eight trees on my property. Because of all the work going on at my house, I had to reschedule the doctor's appointment I had for the following week. I was going to have a vasectomy so we couldn't have any more kids. My son is inside keeping an eye on my daughter while I'm filling the dumpster outside. I'm standing in the dumpster when my cell phone rings. It was my wife calling from her job in Manhattan. I answered the phone, and Barbara said, "I know you're busy, but I have to talk to you." I said, "Busy ain't the word, what's up." She said, "I have to tell you something, but I don't know how to tell you." The tone of her voice made me nervous. I said, "Don't tell me something like that, what's wrong? Just tell me." She said, "I just found out I'm pregnant." I'm standing in the dumpster looking at all the guys working on my house and everything seemed to spin around once and stop. I said, "Yeah, but I got the appointment." She said, "It doesn't matter now." Then I said, "Well, we can't have this baby." And then there was complete silence on the line. Right at that moment, I realized two things. I was going to have another child and I was ashamed at myself for thinking about ending the pregnancy. I was just so shocked. We waited ten years after my son was born before we had our daughter because I didn't want to have one right after the other. Now, ten years later, that's exactly what we would be doing. The reason I felt that way in the first place was because I know what it takes to take care of a baby all day long, every day. My wife went back to work in the city when my son was six months old. Not because she wanted to, she was making more money than I was when we had him. So,

I quit my job to be home with the baby. Once I got the hang of that, I began tending bar at night, which I'm still doing now, 14 years later. It's worth mentioning that my wife, Barbara, is not the kind of woman that would rather work than be home with our children. She had a great job and had been with the same people for almost 20 years. Both of us had a special relationship with the two guys she worked for. One of them was my daughter's godfather. Both of them were very generous and just great people to know. But if it wasn't for the fact that I was able to be home during the day, she would have quit anyway. Knowing that the kids would be with me was the only way she could keep working. It was a brutal schedule for both of us. We had identical responsibilities at opposite ends of the day. Barbara worked in Manhattan during the day and took care of the kids at night. I took care of the kids during the day and worked at night. It was extremely difficult on the both of us. This didn't leave much time for us, but the kids would always be with their mother or their father. The security and stability that gave them was more than enough to justify our sacrifices. There's nothing easy about creating the best possible situation for your kids, but there's no excuse for not doing all you can. Luckily, we both felt that way. The bottom line was always the same. The kids would benefit. That's it. Nothing else mattered, nothing that you could live with.

The thing about devoting your life to your children is that as hard as it is, it makes you feel good about yourself. To me, it made all the bullshit you had to deal with worthwhile. All the things everybody has to go through to get by, your job, the bills, your boss, the asshole next door, whatever. You knew you were doing it for them. And there's no better reason. I was grateful for that. I felt lucky because my wife and my kids provided a purpose in my life and I hadn't had that for so long.

I believe that having that kind of stability in my life was the reason I was able to write about my past. There were alot of scary things lurking around back there. I don't think I could have done it if I wasn't happy about where my life was now. I felt like

I was ready for anything. And I would have to be. Because now, my present and future were about to catch up with my past.

I couldn't forget her. She was beautiful. Also, I was 19 and she was 30 something, and she left a lasting impression on me of course. I couldn't show this in front of Niko, he would just break my balls. To him, she was just another woman. To me, she was the best-looking woman I had ever seen. Every once in a while, he would stop by. You never knew when or what time. He would always have at least one woman with him, sometimes two or three. I was always disappointed when Gloria wasn't with him. Not that the other women were unattractive or anything like that, I just never got over my three days with Gloria as a birthday present.

Obviously, Niko was a real character. He used to love getting me involved in situations with him. Hunts Point in the Bronx was an area where everything went on legal and otherwise. His influence was there too.

One night we took a ride there. I had no idea what was going to happen but that was nothing new either. We pulled up in front of this bar. He told me to wait in the car, and he would be right out. I was a little nervous because it was an all black area, but this didn't seem to bother him.

There was a bunch of black guys hanging out in front of the bar. Niko walked past them and disappeared in to the bar. After awhile, I started to worry. Here I am, sitting in a car in this neighborhood with no idea what he went in there for. I could tell they weren't exactly thrilled to see him. After a couple of minutes, he came out of the bar. He literally pushed a couple of people out of the way on his way back to the car. When he got in, he handed me a couple of rolls of cash all hundreds. He told me to count it as we drove away. I stopped counting at $8,000 and looked at him. He was laughing. He said, "Never mind counting the rest, they know better than to short me. Let's go get something to eat." I didn't know what was going on. I was just happy to be getting out of there. I found out later that they paid him so much every week to stay in business.

We went back to Sergio's Restaurant on 17th St. and hung out while the food just kept on coming. Everybody in the place seemed to cater to him. People kept coming over to him to make sure he had everything he wanted. He told me to make sure that if I had any problems with anything that I would come to him first no matter how serious I thought they were. After a couple of weeks went by, Niko stopped by and asked me if I had heard anything about this guy James Ruffo. This was the guy he had shot at on Eastchester Road that night. I told him no. I said I wasn't worried about it because I was sure the guy had gotten the message. He said, "That's not good enough, let's take a ride."

We went to the Canbrelling Ave Lounge Bar and he talked to a few people. We were hanging out for awhile when he told me to write this guy's name down on a piece of paper. I was pretty naive at the time so I did. Partly because I just didn't want to disagree with him about anything. It just wasn't worth it. After I wrote his name down on a piece of paper, he slid it down on the bar to this guy standing next to us. The guy picked it up and put it in his pocket without saying a word.

Right then, it started to hit me what was going on, but it was way too late to stop anything. I started to feel really badly about what might happen to this guy. But it was too late. The guy we gave his name to was somebody you would never want to deal with under any circumstances let alone having him look at you.

As time went by, I tried to forget about the whole situation, but it wasn't easy. It didn't help that I never saw the guy again. In a way, I could understand that he wouldn't want to come near me, but I couldn't help wondering why I never even saw him around anywhere him, his brother or any of the guys he knew. In a way, I was happy because that's what I wanted, but on the other hand, I felt kind of badly because I didn't really know what actually happened to him. Anyway, this was the way things were happening for me around this time. I couldn't really complain, but it did make me a little nervous.

My apartment was right off Borough Road and right around the corner from Bartlet High School, which by this time was mostly black and Puerto Rican. I was walking back to the apartment one night and there were a bunch of Puerto Rican guys heading straight for me. They were drinking and carrying bottles of beer with them. As they got closer to me, they started breaking my balls a little bit. I tried to cross the street to avoid them, but they cut me off and started fucking with me. Nothing serious, just verbal abuse and laughing. They said maybe I should be careful where I was walking. I said, "Yeah, okay." and kept walking. A couple of them broke off from the pack and started following me. I walked a little faster and they did too. About a half a block later, they started throwing beer bottles at me. I started to run, which was a bad move, but what else could I do since I was alone. As I turned the corner, I saw this guy I knew, Frankie Labatta, sitting in his Mustang. They must have seen him too because they turned and went back the other way. Somebody was with him in the car, but I couldn't tell who. I got to my building and went upstairs.

The next day I went to work and had to stay a little later then usual so I didn't see anybody when I came home. The day after that, I found out that the guys who chased me had a basement clubhouse in the apartment building that my brother Jackie lived in. They were all Puerto Rican guys, and they used to hang out in front of his building. He overheard some things and put two and two together.

A couple of more days went by and I was sitting at the bar at Sergio's. Niko walked in and sat down next to me at the bar. We said hello, and the bartender brought us a couple of beers. Niko told the bartender to tear up my tab and then he said to me, "I told you not pay for anything in this place." I know", I said, "but I don't like to take advantage." I started watching the Yankee game on the television when I heard him say, "So how come you didn't tell me what happened the other night when you were walking home?" I shouldn't have been surprised, but I was. I said nothing happened, and it was no big deal. I really didn't want to get him involved because he was the kind of guy that had two speeds, neutral and overdrive. He said, "I'll decide what's a big deal and what's not. Finish your beer and let's take a ride." I tried to talk him out of it, but it was no use. He said, "I found out where they hang out, this will only take a minute."

I walked out of the bar with him to his El Dorado. As we got in, I could see the machine gun under his leather jacket on the back seat. I was really getting tired of seeing that thing. It was only a couple of blocks away. As we came down the block where the building was, I could see a bunch of guys hanging out on the stoop in front. As we got closer, he floored the gas pedal and jumped the curb. They all scattered. We came to a screeching stop right in front of them. Now they were really pissed off, but that all changed when they saw him lean over the seat to pick up the machine gun. Niko really knew how to make an entrance; you had to give him that.

We got out of the car and walked toward them. Niko just let the machine gun hang down on his side. He said, "Anybody in that fucking club downstairs?" They said nobody was down there and he said to me, "Let's go see."

We got to the door and it was locked. He kicked the door once and then again. It flew open hanging on one of its hinges. There was nobody inside, thank God. We walked back to the car and they were all staring at him. I was standing on the passenger side. He opened the door on the driver's side and threw the machine gun in the back seat. Before we got in, he said, "Pay attention assholes." He pointed at me and said, "When you see this guy, you see me." Then we got in and drove off the sidewalk back onto the street and left.

We drove a couple of blocks back to Sergio's and went inside. It was like we never left. My beer was still on the bar, and Niko was saying hello to people and joking around as if nothing had happened. He sat down next to me and said, "Let me tell you something, if you let these lowlifes get away with shit like that, you're just asking for trouble. It's bad enough that they're in this neighborhood at all, my mother lives here. If you do nothing, it's the same thing as telling them to do whatever they want." He was right; of course, it's just that I really couldn't concentrate yet. My head was still buzzing from what just happened. I don't mid saying that my hands were trembling a little bit.

    A couple of days later, I was hanging out at home when the bell rang. I went to the door, and it was my brother Jackie. With him were two or three Puerto Rican guys. I remember thinking, now what? Jackie said that they were here to apologize to me for the other night. They didn't mean anything, and they were a little drunk and got out of hand. I said, "Yeah, whatever. I just wanted the whole thing to be over with. They told me they just wanted to make sure I knew that they had no problem with me. They said they were sorry the whole thing happened in the first place. I knew they were only there because what we had done. I told them it was okay and not to worry about it. They left and Jackie and I hung out for awhile talking about what had happened. Niko's point had been made, again.

* * * * *

    I have to say that I was really enjoying the neighborhood right around then. I mean, my problems were disappearing all around me. The best part about it all was that they were all problems that I didn't cause. I didn't deserve the things that were happening. I guess that was the whole point. In a way, I couldn't understand why I was lucky enough to have this kind of backup, but on the other hand, I was loving it. It was a balance I couldn't really understand, but was forced to deal with. It's not that I was ungrateful, but just overwhelmed. It was a nice problem to have. I just had to be really careful not to take advantage of the situation I was in.

Chapter 12

I was working at Cornell University in Manhattan, of all places, and right across the street from the circulation desk of the medical library where I worked every night was Olin Hall, the dormitory for all the nursing students at New York Hospital. They all had to pass right in front of me every night to study and do their research for their classes. They also had to check out whatever books or materials they needed through me. Sometimes things just work out right. I got to meet a lot of the nursing students in the couple of years that I worked there. The year was 1976 and that was the year I met Malory Collins. We would spend the next four years together. She was the kind of woman that at first you couldn't believe was interested in you, and I couldn't know then, but she would cause me the biggest heartbreak of my life. Looking back now, 22 years later, I guess it was worth it.

Malory and I went through a lot in the four years we were together. We were completely different people; in every way you could imagine, which I'm sure was part of the attraction. She was from Syracuse, NY, I was from the Bronx. She was a nursing student at Cornell University in NYC. She had her whole life and career planned out for her by her asshole parents. I was working at the medical library of Cornell Medical College. I had nothing planned and no idea what the fuck I was doing. She was serious about her career and was brought up to always have an eye on her future. I wasn't serious about anything, and the only thing I had my eye on at that time was her. We would stay at her apartment in the nurse's dorm on the nights I had to work. When I was off, she would come up to the Bronx and stay at my place. This went on for about a year until she finally just moved in with me.

At some point during the first year, we lived together. She had to go up to Maine to work in a hospital up there as part of her training. We weren't happy about it, but it had to be done. She had to spend three months here. I hated to see her go, and it was tough to say goodbye.

During the first month she was there, she wrote to me every other day. It was 1976 and believe it or not I didn't have a phone in my apartment. I couldn't afford it. In those days, you needed some kind of credit history to get a phone. I wasn't even paying the rent on a regular basis. Sometime during the second month she was up there, I got a letter from her that was about five or six pages long. She wrote to me all the time, but it was always pretty short. You know the usual, how's everything, I miss you, do you miss me, that kind of thing. So when I saw all those pages, I knew something was wrong. It was either that, or I was getting dumped. As I read the letter I realized that there was something wrong. She had been assigned to a patient that had a drug problem. It wasn't her only patient, but this was the one she was having the problem with.

The girl was in her 20's. She was hospitalized because she had been beaten. Her boyfriend who was also in a drug program had beaten her. So, I'm thinking, okay, she feels bad for this girl. I can understand that. Malory was a very kind and understanding person, which is why she took up nursing in the first place. Anyway, she goes on to tell me that the boyfriend came to the hospital everyday to see this girl. Obviously, he was an asshole junkie, but Malory always looked for the good in a person. Then she tells me that for the past few days this guy has been making comments to her right in front of his girlfriend. Talking about what a nice body she had and that he had a thing for nurses. Now I'm really starting to get worked up. The next few lines I read put me right over the edge. She said that this guy lived in the same apartment complex that her and the other nursing students lived in and that he was always hanging around when she got home from work.

Now I'm done. I had all the information I needed. I read the rest of the letter without really comprehending anything. Something about her saying, "But please don't worry, I'll be fine." Women have a way of always coming out with something stupid in a situation like that.

It was about one o'clock in the morning when I read the letter. I copied down the return address on the envelope and put it in my wallet. I had just gotten home from my job in the city, but I was furious now I knew this was a bad situation. I also knew that it had to be a day or two since she wrote the letter. Who knew what this lowlife was up to by now? I decided to go to Maine that night. I was sure of three things. Malory was afraid, I was worried and this guy would never be expecting me to show up. I wanted to give him something else to think about.

I started to pack, which was a joke, because I didn't even have a suitcase or anything. I had never been anywhere else before. I looked around the apartment and saw my guitar in its case in the corner of the room. I took the guitar out and used the case to pack a few things. I put an extra pair of jeans and a couple of sweatshirts in the case. There wasn't much room for anything else. Then I stuffed in a baseball bat and an old pair of brass knuckles that I had from who knows where. I had about $150.00 on me and figured that would be enough. I put on my leather jacket, and I was ready to go. I didn't really now what to expect once I got there, but I knew I had to go. What else could I do? I didn't know anything about this guy that was bothering Malory. Maybe just showing up would solve the problem. Maybe not. If worse came to worse, I could always just beat the fuck out of him and be on the next bus out of town. At least then I would know he would be in no condition to bother her.

  I left my apartment and walked back the eight blocks to the train station I had just come home from. It was about 1:30 in the morning and I would take the train downtown to the Port Authority and see what bus I could get to take to Maine. There was no time to tell anybody what I was doing or where I was going. It was the middle of the night, not that I gave that much thought, anyway. That's the way I was in those days. I just did things and worried about them later if I had to. I got to the Port Authority about 2 o'clock and check the schedule board for a bus to Maine. I saw that there was one leaving at 2:30am. It would get me to Maine about 7pm. I would be on the bus for about 15 hours. I wouldn't have a chance to call my job, but I didn't give a shit about that anyway. I didn't leave word at the hospital for Malory that I was coming either. I didn't want her to know. I knew she would panic if she knew I was coming, and I didn't want her to let anybody now especially this asshole. The best thing I had going for me was the element of surprise and I wanted to keep that for as long as I possibly could.

  I bought a six pack of beer and waited for the bus. I was pretty tired already, but I wanted to make sure I would sleep on the bus. I knew the ride would suck, and I would be bored to death so the longer I slept the better. By now, I had gotten the bus's schedule and it was going to make about a million fucking stops before I got there.

  I downed my fourth beer just as the bus was pulling up. I gave the driver my ticket and found a seat in the back of the bus. I fell asleep hoping nobody would be sitting next to me when I woke up, no such luck. The first thing I saw when I woke up was the sun coming through the window. The second thing I saw was the faggot sitting next to me. I looked at my watch and saw that I had only been sleeping about 3 hours. I had 12 hours to go before we hit Maine. As I'm thinking this, I hear the fag say,

"Did you have a nice rest?" I looked at him and said, "If you don't change your seat at the next stop, I will beat you until somebody drags me off of you." Then I took the baseball bat out of the guitar case and put it next to me. While I was doing that, he moved to another seat. I had enough things on my mind. There was no way I was going to sit next to a fag for 12 hours. The bus ride seemed to go on forever. I couldn't believe how many little shit towns there were or that people actually lived there. The bus stopped in every one of them. It was brutal. I hadn't even gotten there yet, and I was already depressed about making the trip back. Somehow, time went by. It was about 5:30 p.m. when the bus pulled into Bangor, Maine. I had managed to get through the rest of the bus ride with only a couple of people sitting next to me off and on. Although they were boring, none of them were as annoying as the faggot I had started out with.

I got off the bus and walked around the town for a couple of minutes. I still had to take the ferry to get to Bar Harbor where Malory worked, but at least I was finally off the bus. As I'm walking, I realize there's a cop car cruising along side me. I look over and the cop asked me what I was doing in Maine. I said I was visiting my girlfriend who was working at the hospital on the island. He said, "Stay out of trouble." Then he drove off. I guess I shouldn't have been surprised. I didn't exactly blend in up there. I was wearing a leather jacket and carrying a guitar case. I was just happy that he didn't ask me what was in the case. Between the bus ride, the fag on the bus, the cop following me, I was really starting to get pissed off. I decided to take it all out on the junkie that was bothering Malory. I walked over to the dock where the ferry looked like it was ready to leave. After a few minutes, I got my ticket and got on.

The ferry took about a half hour to reach Bar Harbor. The ride over gave me time to wonder what the fuck I was doing in Maine. Which, of course, really didn't matter because now I was there. The ferry docked and I got off. I grabbed a cab to the hospital where Malory was working, then called her from a payphone. She was surprised to hear my voice. When I told her I was calling from the lobby, she was in shock. I told her to meet me in the lobby and hung up the phone.

I went over to the gift shop to see if I could get a New York paper. Forget about that. As I'm walking out of the gift shop, the elevator door opens in the lobby. Malory sees me and comes running over. She gives me a big hug and kiss and says, "What are you doing here, are you crazy?" I said, "I came to make sure you were okay and to straighten out the asshole who's bothering you." She said, "I can't believe you came all the way up here because you were worried about me." I said, "Yeah, well believe it. Where is this fucking guy?" She gives me another hug and says, "This is great. How long can you stay?" Then before I could answer her, she says, "We could have a drink when I get off tonight, and we could have dinner tomorrow night because I'm off." I grabbed her face in both of my hands, looked into her eyes and said, "Calm down, we can do whatever you want to do after I do what I came up here to do." She kissed me on the lips and said, "You're so sweet, but I found a way to avoid him." I've been going in through the back entrance to my apartment so I don't have to pass his door to go home." He really hasn't had the chance to bother me." I started laughing because she sounded so naive. I told her that after I go and see him, he's not going to bother you ever again whether he has a chance to or not. So I asked her again, "Where is this guy, where can I find him right now?" She said her shift was over at 7:30, and we could go to her place after that. I said, "Okay, that's fine."

It's was almost 6:30 so I told her to go upstairs and finish up her shift. I wanted to get something to eat. I told her to meet me in the cafeteria when she was done. I knew the food would suck, but I was starving. I had a disgusting cheeseburger and waited for her to come down. Between the bus ride, the cops and the food at the cafeteria, I was in a real bad mood. It was the perfect time for me to confront this guy.

Malory and Anthony

Malory came down about 7:30 pm and we went out to her car. It took us about 15 minutes to get to her place. She was real nervous and didn't say much on the way, which was fine with me. I wanted to concentrate on what I was going to do. I told her not to worry. I said, "In a few minutes, we'll be in your apartment and you'll never have to worry about this guy again." She said, "I'm afraid." I said, "I know you are, that's why I came here." I told her to walk to her door and go inside. I would be watching. I could see this idiot sitting on a beach chair, drinking a beer. I knew it was him before Malory said, "That's him." I said, "Okay, just do what I told you to do. Don't come out of the apartment no matter what you hear."

Malory did exactly what I told her to do. When she got close to her door, I could hear this guy start the usual verbal abuse. Then I heard him say, "You look good baby. You look better than last night. You think going in the back way is gonna stop me from checking you out, no way."

He was still looking at her doorway when I got to him. He never heard me coming. I got his attention by slapping the beer bottle out of his hand. He looked up and said, "Hey, that's my beer." When I got a good look at him, I knew this was going to be easy. I grabbed both ends of the baseball bat and jammed it under his chin. He was screaming now. I pushed him up against the wall with the bat. He couldn't move and could hardly breathe. I held him against the building and said, "I just spent 15 hours on a bus form New York City to see you. I'm in a real bad fucking mood. Malory is my girlfriend, and I'm going to spend a couple of days with her. Then I'm going back to the city. If she ever mentions your name to me again, I'm going to come back and open your fucking head like a melon. Do you understand what I'm telling you?" His eyes were bulging out and his face was turning red. He said, as best he could, "Yeah, I understand. Please don't kill me." I pulled the bat back and he dropped to the floor. I looked at him and said, "Don't do anything stupid." He said, "I swear I won't, please let me go." I walked over to Malory's door while he picked up his things and went inside his apartment. I knocked on her door, and she let me in.

I closed the door behind me and locked it. I turned around and Malory was just starring at me. She said, "Are you all right?" I said, "Yeah, why?" She said, "Because I heard screaming, that's why!" I told her that I wasn't the one screaming so she shouldn't worry. She went into the kitchen and got me a beer. As she handed it to me she said, "You really are a nut. You know that?" I told her that sometimes that's what it takes. I felt that if I didn't do anything, eventually, this guy would have hurt her. I was sure of it, and now I was sure he wouldn't.

I stayed with her for two days. I never saw the guy again. I told Malory not to worry. I was pretty confident this guy had gotten the message. I was really dreading the ride home. Malory managed to get me a few valium for the ride so I could sleep. It helped a little. The ride still sucked.

Malory wrote to me twice a week after my visit. For the next three weeks, she only saw the guy twice even though he practically lived next door. Both times, she said, he didn't even look at her. She left Maine after that without incident. Anyway, that was that. When she was done with whatever the fuck she went up there for she came home and moved back in with me. We picked up right where we left off. We were pretty happy together, or so I thought. Toward the end of our fourth year together, Malory rocked my world and shook my confidence in myself. Something nobody had ever been able to do.

I came back from work one night and the apartment was empty. To make things worse, I had just come from the dentist and my face was all swollen. I'm trying to call her name with my swollen face and I could hear a kind of echo in the apartment. All her stuff was gone, and our new car that my father had co-signed the loan for was also gone. Within a matter of minutes, I had gone from living with a dynamite looking girl in the Bronx, with a new car parked outside, to living alone in an apartment in the Bronx with no transportation. The very next day, I was forced to get up and take the train to work, not to mention being emotionally destroyed for about a year after that. What I didn't know then, but do know now, is that there is no point in trying to understand why somebody does something like that. It's just a complete waste of time. Naturally, everybody thought I had done something to cause this to happen. We were together four years and had spent all the holidays with my family and everything. It just didn't make any sense.

Anyway, life goes on. I couldn't sleep in our bedroom for months afterward. I was drinking excessively just so I could fall asleep on the couch in the living room. My father would meet me at the train station when I came home from work for awhile just to make sure I wasn't going completely nuts. Looking back, though, I think after having to deal with my mother dying, it somehow helped me to deal with abrupt changes in my life. Not that it was easy or anything like that, but I had learned early in my life that there were things that were going to happen that you had no control over. You have to move on no matter how unfair things seemed to be.

Chapter 13

The neighborhood was a place where you couldn't help but develop a personality all your own. There were so may influences all around you, it couldn't be helped. As early as grammar school. A lot of things happened there. It was kind of strict. We had to deal with the nuns in school and of course, they meant well, but, it set the stage for many laughs.

One of the nuns we had to teach Geography was really funny. Not that she meant to be, of course, but she was. Her nickname in the school was "Nifty". I really don't remember why, but it fit. She was very old and she couldn't see too well. She had very thick glasses and a really goofy face. Looking back, we were pretty mean to her, but that doesn't mean it wasn't funny. Every time she turned to write something on the blackboard, almost half the class would shoot spitballs that would stick all over the blackboard where she was writing. By the time she turned around, we would all be looking at our books. The next time she turned around there would be paper airplanes flying all around the room. The funniest thing, though, was every day when class would start; she would set an alarm clock on her desk for when the class would be over because she couldn't see the clock on the wall. Each class would last an hour. She would set the clock for an hour, and after about 15 minutes while she was writing something on the blackboard, one of us would reset the clock to go off in about two minutes. When it went off, she would get all her stuff together and leave for the next class not knowing what had happened. She would come back with the principal, and we would be in trouble. We were always in trouble. It was really funny.

Then there were the more serious and more dangerous nuns. That would be Sister Francis Marie and another nun known only as "Deadeye". She was really scary. She could be seen any day walking down the hallway swinging her oversized rosary beads around her hands until they would snap to a stop across her knuckles. She got her nickname because she could spot anybody doing something they weren't supposed to be doing and in one quick motion, slap them across the mouth almost without moving any other part of her huge body. Things were different back then. There was nothing unusual about a nun whacking somebody in the mouth and continuing on with the class as if nothing had happened. Sister Francis Marie was famous for that kind of move. One day she caught a kid named Steven Borrello laughing with some other kid while she was lecturing about something. She walked down the aisle he was sitting in and he had no idea she was coming or what hit him, and she backhanded him across the nose and blood started pouring down his face. She threw her handkerchief in his face and said, "Here, you won't die." I mentioned his name because Steven Borrello was an honor student. The message wasn't lost on us, we understood. We were good students, but by no stretch of anybody's imagination were we honor students. We figured if an honor student could get nailed like that; there was no telling what would happen to us. This leads us to Sister Angela, the principal of the school. She looked like a big fat penguin in linen. If you got to see her, you were really in trouble, unfortunately, we got to see her often.

I realize I may sound mean or insensitive in describing the nuns and brothers that I've had to deal with in these schools, but my lack of respect for them is a direct result of their behavior towards me.

Everyday after lunch we had a recess period of about a half hour that was spent in the gym. It was a wild place where a lot of frustration was released. You could shoot baskets, play games, throw some moves on the girls or just hang out. This time of day always came to an end the same exact way every day. Sister Angela would make her way to the middle of the gym with a large cowbell that she would ring at the end of every recess, which meant that everybody had to stop whatever they were doing and take their seats on the bleachers. From there, we would line up by class and head back to the classrooms. Only this particular recess period would end the way no other had ended before, and I'm pretty sure the way none had ended since.

Sister Angela started ringing the bell and everybody started to stop what they were doing. The basketballs were bouncing to a stop all around the gym, but this time one of the side doors to the gym was left open and one of the older guys in the neighborhood, Tommy Boy, sneaked in and grabbed one of the basketballs. In one quick motion, before anyone even knew he was there, he grabbed one of the basketballs and threw it half the length of the gym right at her. This all took place in a matter of seconds. As the bell was ringing, all you could hear was the bell and the sound of the balls bouncing to a stop. Everybody just sat there and watched as the basketball was heading right for her. She was the only one who didn't know what was about to happen. We all just froze and watched. The sound of the basketball hitting her right in the side of her head was a sound I will never forget. Sister Angela, the basketball and the cowbell all went in different directions. Her nun's habit was knocked almost completely off as she lay there on the gym floor. We were in shock as the rest of the school staff ran to help her. Tommy Boy was gone before the ball hit her so naturally we were all suspects. Nobody could admit to doing it so we all had to stay after school for weeks as punishment. It was one of the most unbelievable things I have ever seen. We felt bad for her, but it was so funny. With all the beatings we got from the nuns, it was almost like a blow from all of us not to tell who had really thrown the basketball.

* * * * *

Summertime in the neighborhood was really something. We had all day long, and there still wasn't enough time to do all the things you could do. We played ball all day long. A lot of us were supposed to go to summer school, but we never went to that either. It always kind of amazed me how they expected to get us to go to school in the summer when they couldn't get us to go any other time of the year. We played stickball in the street and handball in the schoolyard. We even had the balls to play in the schoolyard of the school we were supposed to be in.

Then there were all the neighborhood games like ringalevio, buckbuck, hot peas and butter, spud and munkfreeze. The latter being one of the strangest. I'm not sure how it started, but everyone had to freeze or not move. Whoever moved had ten seconds to count to ten and yell "munkfreeze" while everybody else kicked the shit out of him. It wasn't the most common game in this city, but for some reason we had fun.

We had Orchard Beach and City Island as our recreation areas. We also had the New York Botanical Gardens and The Bronx Zoo as our playgrounds. Every summer there were three or four feasts that were celebrated on 18th St. That's where the unlimited food and spirit of the neighborhood was on display. This was really the heart and soul of the neighborhood. We would come back from the beach and just walk through the feast at night, and it seemed the days just went on forever. It was our own little world, and we were proud of it.

Then we had the club, which was a four room apartment in the basement of one of the apartment buildings on Beaumont Ave. This was our home away from home. The only way to describe the club is that there wasn't much that didn't go on down there. We were there all the time. All we did was hang out, listen to music and try and get one of the girls in the back room. We had an old phonograph player, and the only two albums we had were The Beatles, Sgt. Pepper and Cream, Wheels of Fire. They were on all the time. The club was nothing fancy. All the walls were painted black and whoever felt like painting or drawing something on them just did. The artwork was pretty amazing. It was in the basement so there were no windows or any outside light. It was more like a cave than anything else. Life, such as it was, went on for me. There were so many things going on that I think that helped me underneath all the distractions. I was very angry about what had happened to my mother. I really didn't care about anybody's idea of what I should be doing. Nothing could bring her back to me. I guess that was pretty selfish. After all, it wasn't just me who was dealing with the loss. I should have though more about my father and my brother, who were going through the same thing and worrying about me. But I didn't, no excuses, I just didn't. I loved them so much and I still do. Thank God for them. What I didn't know then, but am sure of now, is that it was the love we all shared as a family and the help of God that I was able to go through all of this and still wind up with everything I have now. To just turn out to be a decent person, this was always important to me. I think of my mother all the time and no matter what we were going through, it could never compare to what she had to go through with her illness and then to leave us. I would never let myself feel sorry for myself. I think I got that strength from her and my father and brother. She was only 40 years old, and the love for her and the strength we all got from her is just another compliment to the woman.

Chapter 14

The 70's were coming to a close. It was after Malory had left me, and I was pretty screwed up. A good friend of mine, Louis Trofe, was moving to California. He was working with his brother-in-law and they were going into the refrigeration business out there.

After he had been out there about a year, he started putting the idea into my head about moving out there. By now, he had started his own business and he offered me an opportunity to go out there, live with him and his family and try and make a fresh start for myself. It was very generous of him, but that's the way he was. We had gone through a lot together in the neighborhood and he was trying to help me out, give me another direction to go in. It sounded pretty good too. I just couldn't see myself living anywhere but here, let alone California of all places. It just didn't seem real to me, but Louis convinced me that it was not only real but also real profitable.

I knew it was probably a good idea. There was nothing keeping me from trying it, but in the back of my mind, I already knew that the only thing that would stop me would be leaving my family. I had never been away from my father and brother. After my mother died, we had become even closer, if that was even possible.

What it all came down to was that if I asked myself why I wouldn't go, I mean, besides the fact that I would miss everybody; there was no reason not to go. I had a place to live, a job and a real good friend to live with, so I decided to go.

It was a real emotional time for me and especially for my father and brother. I had never been away from home and especially because nobody, including me, knew how long I would be gone for. The only thing I knew was that I had to try it.

What was interesting in the weeks before I left was that I found out how much people cared about me. It was really something. It was a great feeling, but at the same time, it made it even harder to leave. By the time the day came that I was actually leaving, I was an emotional wreck. A bunch of people came to the airport with me. Close friends, and of course my brother Joe. I had to get on a shuttle bus to the plane, and right up until the door closed, all I did was stare at my brother. For the whole ride to the plane, I just sat there and cried. I couldn't stop.

When I got to California, my friend Louie met me at the airport. From the minute I landed, he and his wife Marilyn bent over backwards to make me feel at home. It really helped, for a while anyway. The fact of the matter was that I wasn't at home and it was only a matter of time before that fact was just too much to bear.

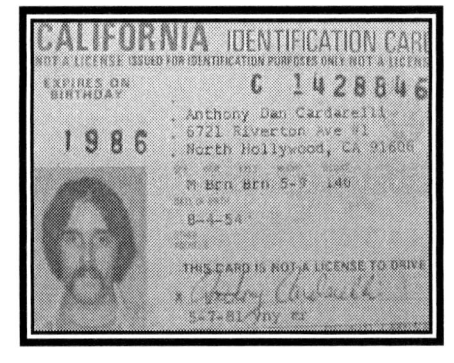

Life in California was really weird. Nobody was from there. Everybody that I met there was from some place else. Nothing about growing up in Manhattan and the Bronx could prepare you for California. I was used to neighborhoods and great food. In California, there were no neighborhoods and the food sucked. Of course, the weather was great, but after a while it was like "now what". And, 90 degrees and a Christmas tree did nothing for me. You know, New Years Eve: "let's go to the beach". Forget it... it was really strange.

I remember one day, it was the day before payday. I was starving and I pulled into this place that said, "Italian Hero's". As I pulled up in front of the place, there was an Oriental guy flipping pizza dough in the window. I couldn't believe it. I mean, you don't even keep this guy in the back or something. You have him right in the front window like there's nothing wrong with it. That's all I needed to know about California.

I had a few girlfriends while I was out there. It was really easy to meet them because if you were from the East Coast, you were interesting or different. If you were Italian and from the East Coast, especially New York City, you had it made. They thought I had a great accent. I found this hard to believe. I thought they were the ones with the accent. I used to tell them, "You're the ones with the accent". When Columbus discovered America, he didn't land on the West Coast and go east. He landed in New York. "You're the ones who talk funny"! They had no clue. The girls were great out there, but guys couldn't stand me. They were jealous. Not that I was any big deal, but I was just different and that caused some problems. But, hey everything had its price.

I was in California for about seven or eight months when I started hanging out with a girl. Her name was Wendy. She had a son about three or four years old. I wound up living with her in her apartment. She had a great body and she wanted me to eventually support her and her kid. I just wanted to get laid.

Anyway, the holidays were coming around, and I was planning to go back home for a visit. The problem was by now I was really getting sick of California. I wasn't working with Louie anymore, which was one of the reasons I was even out there in the first place. His business got a little slow, and his wife was pretty sick. In and out of hospitals and they weren't sure what was wrong with her, but it was pretty serious. With all that going on, plus I was really homesick; I never thought I would miss New York so much. I knew I would miss my family and friends but I never thought about missing where I was from.

I went home around Christmas time. My brother and a couple of guys met me at the airport along with my friend, John Donovich. I became close friends with John while working at City Plaza, which was an apartment complex in the City that was managed by my other good friend Rocco. That's where we were going to end up that night. I got off the plane with my only piece of luggage, a pool cue, which gives you an idea of my state of mind in those days.

I had kind of half decided that maybe it wouldn't be too bad if I just stayed in New York while I was on the plane, but that wouldn't be so easy since I was living with this girl in California. When I met the guys at the airport and especially when I saw my brother Joe and hugged him, it was all over.

We went into the city and ate in an Italian restaurant. After that we partied at City Plaza with Rocco. It was Christmas time in the city and if that doesn't explain what I was feeling, nothing will. There was no way I was going back and that's the way I did things back them. I decided something and did it, then I worried about it later. Well, I really didn't worry about it at all; I just did it. Man, did it feel good to be back. I didn't know what to do first. I still hadn't even seen my father yet. I couldn't wait. My mind was racing. I was still excited about visiting for the holidays. But the idea of staying really had me going nuts. I was standing outside on the deck, up on the 34th floor in Rocco's apartment at the City Plaza looking out at New York City all lit up at Christmas time. I was home and I remember thinking how did I ever leave here. I knew one thing, I wouldn't leave again. All this happened in just a few hours in the city. All I know was the feeling I had to stay was stronger than any feeling I ever had to go.

My California experience was really weird. I was there for nine months but it felt like five years. I was born in New York City and raised in the Bronx. I had never been anywhere else. All of my friends were either born in the Bronx or had moved there from the city just like me. To us, everybody else was an asshole until proven otherwise. Right or wrong, that's how we felt. There were a lot of assholes in California. Nobody was from there. Everybody I met out there had come from someplace else. There was no feeling of belonging. It was completely opposite from the way I grew up. As I said, it didn't take long for me to run into problems out there. I had no problems with the women and nothing but trouble with the guys out there. I couldn't care less. My attitude was fuck them and what they thought.

While I was living with this girl Wendy, a situation began to develop. She had an ex-boyfriend I didn't know about. I found out later that he used to beat her up on a regular basis. I walked her to her apartment and she started telling me about him. I said, "Fuck him, if he causes any trouble I'll deal with it." She said, "My next door neighbor is having a party tonight and I know she's going to invite him. He's been asking about me and I'm a little nervous. If he comes to the party I know he's gonna get drunk and come over here. He knows that you've been staying here and he's probably going to start some trouble." I said, "That's fucking great. You got any more good news for me? When does this party start?" She said, "It already has and I know he's here because I saw his car in the parking lot." I said, "What the fuck is wrong with you? How long have you known about this party?" She said, "About a week. I couldn't decide when would be the right time to tell you." I said, "So you figured you'd tell me the night of the party when he was already here?" She said, "I'm sorry, I was afraid to tell you. He's a big guy and he's always drunk. I know he's going to start trouble."

I couldn't believe what I was hearing. I just walked in from work and heard all of this. I wasn't sure what I should do. I didn't know this guy, so I didn't know if he was a punk or a real threat. The only thing I could do was wait and find out for myself. What else could I do? I had to stay with her. We had a four year old kid sleeping in the other room. We couldn't leave. I told Wendy to bring me the bottle of scotch and sat down at the kitchen table. She asked me what I was going to do and I told her I wasn't sure yet. I wouldn't know until I saw this guy for myself. I wanted to see how big he was. That was my first concern. After that, I'd be looking for two other things. I wanted to know if he could be intimidated and if he was drunk. If he was big, I was hoping he was drunk. If he wasn't big, I didn't give a fuck. A big guy that was drunk couldn't be intimidated. But he could be taken advantage of. If he wasn't big he was going to get hurt whether he was drunk or not. I had to see him before I would know what I was dealing with.

I sat at the table and drank some scotch. I could hear the music blasting from the party next door. I sat there, read the newspaper and kept drinking. Wendy asked me if I wanted something to eat. I told her I was in no fucking mood to eat. I just wanted to get this thing over with. I was really pissed off about being forced into something like this with no warning. But I didn't have time to be pissed off. I had to figure out what I was going to do when this jerk showed up.

About twenty minutes later somebody started pounding on the door. I was sure it was him. Then I heard him. He was really loud. He said, "Wendy, open the door, I know you're in there. I just want to talk to you." Wendy said, "That him Tony. What are we going to do? I'm so afraid. My son is sleeping in his room." I drank the rest of the scotch in my glass and said, "Don't worry about it. Open the door." She said, "What are you going to do?" He started banging on the door again and calling her name. I said, "Listen to me, just open the door. It'll be OK."

She went to the door and opened it. He came inside and said, "That's better." Then he put his arms around her and hugged her, lifting her off her feet. She said. "Put me down, you're hurting me." I just watched. I wanted to size him up. See what I was dealing with. He was tall, but not big. He put her down and sat on the couch. I was sitting at the table across the room. Wendy was still standing where he put her down. She was by the front door, between me and him. He kept talking to her like I wasn't even there. Which was fine with me. I wasn't going to say anything until I had to. But he was so loud; I knew it was coming soon.

Wendy was scared shit. She said, "Why don't I get you guys a beer." Then she walked into the kitchen. Now we were looking right at each other. As I looked at him, I thought he was drunk, loud and stupid. I was willing to gamble he had no balls. Like I said, he was drunk and talking way too loud. He looked at me and yelled across the room at her, "Hey baby, is this guy your new friend?" I looked at him and said, "Why don't you lower your fucking voice, her kid is sleeping in his room." He said, "Hey Wendy, your friend ain't being nice to me." I said, "I'm nice to people and animals, you're somewhere in between." Now he was really pissed off, but he wasn't sure of himself. Wendy brought us a beer and asked him not to start any trouble. I grabbed the bottle of scotch and started to laugh. He said, "Wendy, I don't think your friend knows what kind of guy I am." I took the top off and drank from the bottle. I put the top back on and said, "Hey fuckface, I don't give a fuck what kind of guy you are. I grew up in the Bronx and had some problems. I had to move out to California for awhile until things got straightened out. You think I give a fuck about you?"

Wendy walked over to me and said, "Tony, calm down. He doesn't mean any harm He's just had a little too much to drink." I took another sip from the bottle and said, "Hey, I understand that can happen to anybody. I'm ready to drop the whole thing if he is. I'm not looking for any trouble."

I was setting him up for the last move. He hadn't said a word since I went off on him. I wanted him to feel comfortable. I figured he still had one stupid move left. Then he said, "I wasn't looking for trouble either man, you got me all wrong." I said, "Maybe you're right." Let's go out on the terrace and finish our beer. I don't want to wake up her kid." He said OK and we went outside.

Wendy lived on the second floor. In California all the apartment complexes were the same. There was a swimming pool in the middle and the apartments were around the pool. There was a ground floor and one or two floors above. Every apartment had a balcony over the pool area. Wendy's balcony was about ten or twelve feel high. When we got outside, I kept a close eye on him. I was sure he was going to try to surprise me. I could just feel it. He was pretty fucked up and that could only help. Plus, he was a stupid fuck. He would tip me off. I would make my move right before he made his.

He held his beer up toward me and said, "Cheers!", then he gulped down the entire can. He crushed the can in his hand and threw it off the balcony. Then he said, "So you're from New York City?" I said, "Yeah that's right, where you from?" He said, "I'm from Iowa." I looked at him and said, "Iowa, that must suck. I didn't think anybody was from there." Now he was getting worked up again. He said, "You fucking New Yorkers are a real pain in the ass. You think you're smarter than everybody else, don't you?" I said, "No not everybody, but somebody from Iowa, yeah. The smart money would be on the New York guy." Now he was ready. He started screaming. "Fuck you, asshole." Then he came towards me. He pulled his arm back to throw a punch. I kicked him right in the fucking balls. He screamed and backed up holding his balls. I walked over and pushed him over the balcony. I heard him hit the ground. I looked over the side and saw him laying there. He landed face down on the tiles by the pool. He must have hit the tree first because his foot was still stuck on one of the branches about two feet off the ground. What a fucking idiot. I turned around and started to walk back inside. Wendy came running out onto the balcony. She said, "What happened? I heard a noise?" I said, "Iowa lost." Then I went inside the apartment. She said, "What does that mean, Iowa lost? Where did he go?" I said, "Gravity man, gravity. I gotta go. I'll be back later." As I was leaving, I heard her scream. I guess she figured it out. I wanted to see how he was, not that I gave a fuck. I was sick of this guy. I didn't want this to happen but if somebody was going to get hurt, it wasn't going to be me. I figured if he was dead, nobody would ever see me again. I would just disappear. If he wasn't, he wouldn't bother her again.

When I got downstairs, there was a crowd around him. He was lying on his back and somebody had gotten his foot out of the tree. I got a little closer. I could see that he was bleeding from the mouth and it looked like his nose was broken. I didn't want to be bothered but this was the perfect chance to make sure this was over. I couldn't pass it up. I walked over and pushed my way past the crowd around him. I knelt down next to him, lifted his head up and said.

"What the fuck happened to you man?" I felt bad for him, he looked really fucked up. He said, "I'm hurt real bad man." I looked over at a woman standing in the doorway of her apartment. I said, "Call an ambulance." She grabbed the phone off the wall and started dialing. I put his head back down and said, "Don't worry, you're going to be ok. We're going to get you some help. Just relax." He said, "Why are you doing this for me?" I could hear the ambulance now getting closer and closer. I wiped the blood off his nose and mouth so he could breathe. I said, "Can you hear me?" he said, "Yes, I can." I said, "You know who Wendy is?" he said, "Yeah." I could see the paramedics coming through the front gates. I said, "If Wendy ever sees your face again, you'll wish you had died tonight." Then I got up and walked away.

I went back to the apartment. I walked inside and saw Wendy standing on the balcony. I walked over to her and said, "Hey, what's going on, man?" She said, "Are you out of your mind? You could have killed him." I said, "Yeah well, I didn't. Now he's all fucked up and scared shit too. You should be thanking me. He's never gonna bother you again." She said, "Yeah, I know, but you didn't have to throw him off the balcony." I said, "Why don't you shut the fuck up. At this point, I'm sick of you and him. I come home from work and get hit with all this shit. You got a short memory. Twenty minutes ago you're saying Tony, what am I gonna do? He's gonna come over here. My kid is sleeping in his room. I'm afraid, what should I do. Now everything is taken care of and you want to start breaking my balls?" She said, "I'm sorry, I'm just afraid that he is gonna come back and try to get even." I said, "He ain't coming back. He knows if he comes back he's dead." She said, "You would kill him?" I said, "Listen to me because this is the last sentence of this whole fucking conversation. It don't matter what I would do. The only thing that matters is what he believes right now. He's got all the information he needs. Trust me, he ain't coming back."

I went back inside and poured myself a glass of scotch. Wendy walked in behind me. As I sipped from the glass, she put her arms around me from behind. She hugged me and said, "Thanks for taking care of me tonight." I stood there and said, "That's the first thing you've said all night that makes any sense." She laughed and said, "You really are a crazy bastard when you have to be, aren't you?" I said, "Congratulations, you made sense twice in a row." I turned around and grabbed her face with both hands. I said, "Listen to me; you got nothing to worry about now. He ain't gonna bother you again. Relax and take care of your kid." She said, "You're not leaving are you?" His friends are here too. They might come over here." I said, "His friends are all chumps. They saw what I did to him. They were all downstairs. I looked at them all in the eye. Not one of them even looked back. They wanted nothings to do with me. You got nothing to worry about. I'm gonna go get a steak. The restaurant is two blocks away. I'm gonna order my meal and call you while I'm waiting for it. If there is a problem, I'll be here in two minutes. Besides, there's a good chance that somebody called the cops. If they show up and ask any questions, you never saw me before. Just tell them I came over here from the party next door. Everything is gonna be OK. The hard part is over. That asshole is gonna spend the night in the hospital. And the next idiot that causes a problem is gonna wind up there too." She said, "OK, but you're gonna come back here later right? I want you to stay with me. I don't want to be alone tonight." I said, "Yeah, don't worry about it. I'm coming back."

I had my steak and went back to the apartment. I stayed there for three or four days. I wanted to make sure she was ok. During that time, Wendy tried to convince me to move in with her. She brought it up everyday. She told me that she would take care of all the bills. It wouldn't cost me anything. She just wanted me to be there. I told her I'd think about it and let her know.

It wasn't a bad deal. I didn't really give a fuck about the money because I wasn't paying the rent at my apartment either.

I figured if I stayed at her place, I would at least be getting laid on a regular basis. But like everything else, there was a downside involved. She had a four year old kid. I wasn't crazy about having her kid around all the time. Plus, the kid was a pain in the ass. It wasn't his fault. He was living with his mother. Any kid who grew up without a father's influence would lack discipline. I understood it, but I didn't want to have to deal with it on a regular basis.

After a few more days of that shit, I figured fuck it. I decided to move in. I was getting sick of being in California and didn't think I'd be out there much longer anyway. I didn't tell Wendy that, but I could see it coming. I told her I'd start bringing my stuff over, not that I had that much. She was really excited. I felt bad, but what could I do? She wanted me around and she was going to pay the bills. But she wanted me around long term for her and her kid. No matter what she was saying now, sooner or later that pressure would end the relationship. That's what single mothers are looking for. No matter what they say. I couldn't blame her but I wasn't going to do that.

John Donovich, my buddy

In a couple of days, I had all my stuff there. I figured we might as well enjoy whatever time we had left. Things were going better than I expected and we were pretty happy for awhile. It was about three weeks after I had moved in when I saw him sitting by the pool. I was having a beer, sitting on the balcony of the apartment. The same balcony I threw him off of a month ago. I laughed and thought to myself, what a fucking idiot. I wasn't happy about seeing him because I was in no mood for another fucking problem. Which I knew had to happen. Him coming back here told me that. A couple of things were going through my mind right away. I wasn't worried about him, he was a punk. I knew he didn't have the balls to come back unless he had help and if he had help, he definitely had a plan. Without thinking about it and before I got up from the chair, I decided to move back to New York. If I stayed in California, I would be going through this kind of shit over and over. If it wasn't this asshole, it would be another one. I sat there looking at him while I finished my beer. My mind was made up. I was already excited about going back home. I decided that before I left for New York, I was gonna make an example of this guy. For that, I was going to need some help. I got up, went back inside and called John Donovich.

    It had been about eight months since I talked to him. We wrote a couple of times but it ain't the same. When he answered the phone I said, "Hey, what's going on man?" He said, "Who's this?" I said, "Who's this? Who the fuck do you think this is?" He said, "I don't know. It sounds like somebody that's living on the wrong side of the fucking country." I said, "You got that right man. How the fuck have you been?" He said, "I'm good. How about you?" I said, "I'm OK, I'm sick of being out here. I'm coming back home." He said, "It's about fucking time. You don't belong out there. When are you planning to leave?" I said, "I'm not sure. I got a problem I need to take care of out here." He said, "Yeah? You need any help." I said, "That's why I'm calling. I don't know if you're working or not but can you get away for a couple of days?" He said, "Don't worry about if I'm working or not. Are you ok?" I said, "I got a situation out here that I don't think I can handle by myself." He said, "What do you want me to do?" That was it. That's what I loved about John. For whatever reason we were exactly the same when it came to things like this. It was the reason we became friends and stayed friends, no matter what. I said, "Can you fly out here by the end of the week and stay for a few days?" He said, "Yeah, no problem, what are we gonna do?" I said, "I'll explain when you get here. In a nutshell, what we're gonna do is something like this. We'll hang out and go to the beach. We'll spend a couple of days with some girls I know. Then we'll beat the fuck out of some assholes and go home. Like we always do. How's that sound?" Before I finished talking, John was laughing on the phone. Then he said, "Sounds like a perfect vacation." I said, "I got some cash, I can probably pay for half or your trip." He said, "Fuck that. You're giving me a place to stay and you're providing the entertainment and activities. I'll take care of my airfare. You set it up and tell me what day I'm leaving". I said, "OK, thanks man. I'll call you in a day or two, but figure on leaving by the end of the week. I'm looking forward to seeing you." He said, "No problem. I'll talk to you soon."

I hung up the phone and thought about my next move. Setting things up with John was exactly as easy as I thought it would be. Now I had to tell Wendy that I'd be gone in a couple of weeks. That would be anything but easy. Unless I didn't tell her. It was a tough call. It sounded fucked up but if I didn't tell her, we could at least enjoy the time we had left. If I did tell her every day would be a pain in the ass. I had enough to think about. I was going to need a clear head. I had to concentrate on setting up a plan. First, to deal with this asshole who just showed up again. I didn't know what his plan was or even if he had one. I didn't think he did. But either way, I didn't want anything to go down until John got here. On top of all that, when John got here he'd be staying with us. The last thing I needed was to be arguing with Wendy through the whole thing. I decided not to tell her. I went into the kitchen and got myself a beer. I walked out onto the balcony and looked down at the pool. The asshole was still sitting there. I laughed to myself when I realized I still didn't even know his name. Not that I gave a fuck, it was just funny. I decided to get the ball rolling. I had about three days before John would be here. I figured I'd feel the guy out to see what kind of mood he was in. I wanted him to have to react to me before he wanted to. I knew I'd be able to read his reaction. From what I remembered, he was pretty stupid. I grabbed another beer and started walking downstairs toward the pool. As I was walking past the entrance of the complex Wendy walked through the front gate. She yelled out, "Hey Bronx Boy, you got a beer for me?" I turned around and walked over to her. I said, "Your boyfriend's back." She said, "What are you talking about?" I said, "The idiot I threw off the balcony, he's sitting by the pool." She looked over by the pool and said, "I can't believe it, what are you going to do? Please don't start any trouble." I said, "You got me confused with him. He starts trouble not me. I'm gonna go see what's on his mind. You just go upstairs and relax. I'll be up in a minute. He ain't gonna do shit."

I waked over to the pool. I got closer. He had his back to me and had no idea I was coming. I had to set the tone right away. A long time ago, as far back as I can remember, I learned some very important things. At first they sound simple or even obvious. One thing was, if somebody thought they could fuck with you, they would. If they thought they couldn't or shouldn't, they wouldn't. It was a mindset that once established, was flawless. That's the frame of mind I wanted to put him in.

I walked up behind him, leaned over and said, "How many balconies does it take to kill an asshole." He jumped up from the chair and dropped his beer. He turned around and said, "You scared the shit out of me man. I didn't even know you were there." I said, "What are you doing here?" He said, "Don't worry, I'm not here to cause any trouble." I said, "Do I look worried to you?" He said, "It's just a figure of speech, man You New York City guys shouldn't take everything so seriously. Do all you big city boys do that or is it just you?" I laughed and said, "You really should stop trying to figure out people like me. What you should be thinking about is what's a small town retard like you gonna do when the shit comes down. The fact is, you ain't gonna be able to do anything. But that's what you should be thinking about." I turned around and started to walk away. He said, "What's that supposed to mean? When the shit comes down? I didn't do anything to you." I looked back at him and said, "I got a couple of friends flying out from New York. I'm picking them up at the airport tomorrow. They're gonna hang out for a couple of days. I'm gonna take them around town, show them a good time. Then we're gonna make an example of you and whoever the fuck else that's stupid enough to try and help you. Then, they're gonna fly back to New York and wait for a phone call from me. If they have to fly back out here, they ain't gonna leave again until you're dead. That should be enough for you to realize what you're dealing with here. If it ain't, who gives a fuck?" I started walking back to Wendy's apartment. When I got to the staircase I heard him say, "Why are you doing this to me? I didn't do nothing." I said, "You did this to yourself." Then I walked up to the apartment.

When I walked in, Wendy was on the phone. I grabbed a beer and went out on the balcony. She hung up the phone and followed me out there. She said, "Are you ok?" I said, "Yeah I'm all right." She told me that she had been on the phone with her mother. She said, she had been telling her mother what was going on. She told me that she started talking to her about two weeks ago. She said, "I hope you don't mind, but I was so afraid that night when you threw him off the balcony. I had to talk to somebody." I felt bad for her. I said, "Of course I don't mind. She's your mother. I can't blame you for talking to her." She said, "Thanks for understanding. I told her what happened that night. She knows everything especially how you protected me and my son." I said, "She don't have to thank me for that. It was the right thing to do." Then she told me that her mother didn't' want her to live there anymore. She wanted her and her son to come and live with her. I told her I thought it was a great idea. Her and her kid could spend some time with her mother and she could get away from all the assholes hanging around her apartment building.

      This was great news. The only thing I was worried about was what this guy would do if I wasn't around. If she was going to live with her mother, I wouldn't have to worry about that. Her mother lived in Encino, about forty minutes away. I told her I thought it would be a good move for her. But there was something else. She had a real dopey look on her face. I said, "What's wrong? There's something else on your mind. What is it?" she said, "My mother said, you're welcome to come and stay at the house too." She was really excited but there was no way I was gonna do that. I said, "We'll see. Let me think about it. Let's get you and your kid out of this environment first." This was great news. Her going to live at her mother's house erased the last worry I had. I knew I'd be gone in a week or two, depending on how things went. Knowing that she wouldn't be around for this guy to fuck with after I left was a big relief. Now I could concentrate on what I had to do. I had three days to get her settled in with her mother. I wanted to get this done before John came out. I knew it was gonna suck to have to spend the next few days moving her out. It was one of those things that you knew you'd be glad you did it after it was done. But while you were doing it, you were going to hate every minute of it. It would be worth it though. Once she was out of town, it would be one less thing I had to think about. Plus, by the time I was done with the move, John would be here. Then all we had to do was deal with the asshole that was causing the problem. I couldn't wait.

Chapter 15

Three days later, I pulled into the parking lot at LAX. I drove to the airport in LA with a lot of things on my mind. The last few days were exactly as fucked up as I thought they'd be. I sat in my car outside the Delta terminal and waited for John.

I called him the day before and told him where to meet me. It was a pretty funny conversation. I called him at his mother's house. When he answered the phone I said, "Hey, yo, how you doin'?" He said, "I'm doing good, how you doin'?" I said, "Yeah, whatever, are you all set?" He said, "Yeah, I'm all set. I got my suntan lotion and a couple pairs of jeans. I'm ready to go. Are you OK?" I said, "So far, yeah." He said, "Listen, I've been thinking, why don't we fuck this guy up as soon as I get there. You know what I'm saying. Get it out of the way, so we can hang out and relax." I said, "We'll talk about that when you get here." He said, "Hey man, relax. Don't worry about nothing. This is gonna be fun." That's what I loved about him. We were two sides of the same coin, and whoever didn't like it could just get the fuck out of our way.

John was on an 8AM flight out of Kennedy airport, which is about 5AM over here. He would be landing in LA at about 10AM, which was 1PM over there, something like that. To me, all that shit was just another fucked up thing about living out here. Anyway, at about 10:30, I saw him walk through the doors of the terminal. I started to laugh as soon as I saw him. He didn't know I was there yet. He put his overnight bag on the ground and lit up a cigarette. He had on a leather jacket, jeans and a t-shirt. He had sunglasses on and a cigarette hanging out of his mouth. He was New York, standing in California. I was driving a brand new rented Lincoln Continental that I had no intention of paying for. I pulled out of the parking lot, floored the gas pedal and headed toward him. As I got closer, I jammed on the brakes and came to a very noisy stop right in front of him. I leaned across the passenger seat and said, "How the hell are you?" He looked into the window and said, "You're a sick fuck, you know that?" I said, "Yeah, yeah, yeah. And you're all fucking normal, right?" He said, "I'm more normal than you." I said, "I know. I can tell that just by looking at you." I pushed open the passenger door and said, "Get in." He got in the car and we just looked at each other for a few seconds. Then we shook hands, started laughing and hugged each other. I could tell it was a great feeling for both of us. We didn't say anything because we didn't have to. I was happy to have somebody out there that I trusted. Who the fuck knows what he was happy about. Probably the action. It was definitely a weird feeling for both of us to be together in California.

We drove out of the airport and got onto the freeway. John looked at me and said, "You got anything?" We both laughed. For us, it was a line that had been around forever and probably always will be. I took a joint out of my pocket and handed it to him. He lit it up and said, "So where can we find this fucking asshole. I'm in the mood to kick some California ass." I said, "He's from Iowa." He took another drag on the joint, passed it to me and said, "Same shit." I said, "Let's just relax and enjoy the ride. I got a couple of things planned. We'll get you settled in first. Then we'll go get a steak and talk about it. I spent the last couple of days moving Wendy into her mother's house. We got the apartment to ourselves. It's perfect. We'll stock the place with everything we need and get comfortable. A couple of days ago I got in the guy's face and planted a few seeds. All we gotta do is stay at the apartment, hang around by the pool and have a good time. He'll set himself up." John said, "OK, it you got a plan, I'll go along with it. But if we're hanging out and this guy shows up acting like an asshole, I'm gonna beat the fuck out of him." I said, "I'm sure that's a possibility. All I'm asking you is to try and go along with what I'm doing as long as you possibly can." He said, "I'll try but I'm not making any promises. We'll see how it goes."

I couldn't ask for more than that. I couldn't blame him for wanting to do what I brought him out here to do. I decided to stay with my plan as long as I could. I knew what I was doing and I was sure that what I had planned was going to work. But I was going to have to speed things up. With John around, I didn't have a choice. Whatever plans I had, no matter how well thought out, would change as soon as John got pissed off. I kept that mind as we got close to the apartment. While we were driving, John started to notice what I had already become used to. He said, "Holy shit, look at all the mountains. This is where you live? You live around mountains? What the fuck is that like?" I said, "It's no big deal, you get used to it." He said, "How the fuck do you get used to looking at mountains? I could see if you were on vacations someplace and there were mountains there, but to have mountains where you live, that's got to be really strange." I looked at him and said, "Are you done? Can we forget about the fucking mountains now? That's not why I asked you to come out here. Fuck the mountains. Maybe I should have said, Hey John, are you sure you want to do this, there's mountains out here." He said, "Calm down, man. I'm just not used to this shit." I said, "What about the palm trees? Are you afraid of them too?" He started laughing and said, "OK, you prick, you made your point. I just gotta get used to all this shit out here." I said, "Don't get too used to it. We ain't gonna be here that long."

We were only a couple of blocks away from the apartment now. I told John if he thought the landscape was strange, it was nothing compared to the idiots that lived out here. I turned onto the next block and pulled into the apartment parking lot. We got out of the car and walked upstairs. We went into the apartment and got settled in. I grabbed a couple of beers from the refrigerator and we walked out onto the balcony. I wanted to have a couple and let John get used to the surroundings. We stood on the balcony, drinking and looking down at the pool area. It was a major hangout spot. The balcony was the perfect place to keep an eye on things. It was right over the pool.

I looked at John and said, "Hey, yo, here's the deal man. In a couple of minutes we'll go get a steak. Wendy is gonna meet us at the restaurant and come back here with us. We'll hang out on the balcony and watch what's going on. We'll have a few beers and see what's what. After that, the three of us go down and hang out by the pool." John said, "Hold on a minute. I don't think she should be involved like that. If we gotta do something, you don't want her around." I said, "You see how you are, you talk when you should be listening. You didn't let me finish." He looked at me and said, "Yeah, right, OK fuck you and finish then." I said, "We'll do that tonight. I want all these assholes to see us hanging around just to light the fuse. After tonight, she won't be back. It'll be just me and you. We'll do the same thing every night. We'll go for a steak and come back to the house. Then we'll have a few beers up here and check out the scene by the pool. Then we'll go downstairs and hang out. We'll check out the broads and the first time I see this guy I'll get in his face a little bit. Then we'll have another beer and see what happens" John said, "That's it, that's your big fucking plan?" Why don't we just go find this guy and fuck him up right away?" I said, "Because I want that to be the last thing we do out here. I want us to be able to hang out for a couple of days before that happens." He said, "Why? Nobody is gonna fuck with us before or after we do what we gotta do." I said, "I guess you're right, but let's just do what I had planned for tonight." At least you'll get to meet Wendy. Who knows, this idiot might show up tonight and change everything anyway. He might screw up all my plans the first night you're here." John said, "I hope he does, then we'll get everything straightened out right away. Forget about all this planning shit. You think too much. Whatever happens, we'll deal with it. And remember this, whenever that time comes, this shit's over with fast. No matter what happens. We win, he loses. Simple as that." I said, "Yeah, I know." John started laughing and said, "I know, you know. You're just thinking too much. I ain't telling you nothing you don't already know. I know what you'll do, when you have to. When this asshole came after you on the balcony the other night, what happened? You kicked him in the balls and threw him off the fucking thing, right? I ain't worried about you. And you don't have to worry about me. These assholes gotta worry about us. And as soon as we gotta prove that we will. Now let's go get a fucking steak. I can't kick anybody's ass on an empty stomach."

    We left the apartment and drove to the restaurant. It was only a couple of blocks away. We went inside and sat down at the bar. It was about six o'clock. I had told Wendy to meet me there at six-thirty, so we had some time. It was a half-assed restaurant with pretty decent steaks. I had been there quite a few times and knew some of the bartenders. One of the guys I knew came over and said, "Hey Tony, how are you tonight?" I'll get you your first round then I'm leaving. I got the night off." I said, "No problem, thanks for coming over. This is my friend John. Wendy's gonna meet us here for dinner." He and John shook hands and said hello. I said, "Get us two bottles of Bud and a couple of shots of Dewar's." He brought the drinks over and said he'd put them on our dinner tab. I put a twenty dollar bill in his shirt pocket and said, "Can you set us up with a table before you go? It's pretty crowded in here tonight." He said, "I'm sorry Tony, but I can't. This guy behind the bar is the new bar manager. He's a real pain in the ass and I can't afford to have a problem with him. I'm off duty so you're gonna have to ask him to get you a table. Sorry man." I said, "No problem, don't worry about it. I'll see you later." I picked up my shot glass and John said, "Welcome to fucking California." He picked up his glass and we downed the shots. Then he said, "So we already got a pain in the ass behind the bar? It don't take long around here, does it?" I said, "Fuck the guy behind the bar, let's just relax and have a drink." Then the "Bar Manager" came over and said, "How are you guys doing tonight?" John looked at him and said, "Why?" The guy didn't know what so say. I said, "We're doing good. Can you get us a table any time soon? We're in a hurry. There is gonna be three of us." The guy smiled and said, "We're pretty busy right now." John said, "He didn't ask you that." Then the guy said, "Do you have a reservation?" John looked at me and said, "Do you believe this fucking guy?" I started to tell the guy, "Why would we ask you for a table if we had a reservation." John looked at me and said, "Do you believe this fucking guy?" I started to tell the guy that we didn't have a reservation when John stood up and said, "Hey, jerk off, why would we ask you for a table if we had a reservation?" The guy looked at me and said, "Sir, I'm gonna have to ask you and your friend to watch your language." John said, "And I'm gonna have to drag you over this bar and kick your fucking ass if you don't walk away right now." I was sitting there watching this whole scene when Wendy showed up. She walked up behind me and put her arms around me. She said, "Hi baby, you staying out of trouble?" I said, "I'm trying." Then she asked me, "Is this your friend John?" I said, "Yeah, that's him. Ain't he something?" John turned around to say hello. While this was going on, the bartender walked away. I introduced John to Wendy. I said, "Wendy, this I my friend John. I've known him a long time. He's a great guy." Then I said, "John this is my girlfriend, Wendy." John grabbed her and gave her a big hug. He told her he was happy to meet the girl that was taking care of his best friend. Wendy thanked him. Then she told him she was happy to meet a guy that meant that much to me. I said, "All right, that's enough of this shit. We still need a table." John said, "I'll take care of that." I said, "No you won't, she will. Wendy, do me a favor. Go over to the hostess stand and get us a table." She said, "Ok, I'll be right back." We sat at the bar and waited for her. The bartender stayed on the other side of the bar. He wanted no part of us. Wendy came back and said, "They got a table for us right now, if we're ready." I said, "That sounds good, let's go." As I picked up my keys and cigarettes off the bar, John said, "Hold on a minute. Hey, bartender." The guy walked over and said, "No problem, your tab has already been transferred to your table." John said, "Fuck the tab. The hostess just got us a table in this real busy restaurant. If there's anything about the meal or the service that I'm not happy with, I'm gonna take it out on you. After we eat, we're coming back to the bar. You better hope I'm in a good mood."

  We went to our table and sat down. I had enough on my mind, without worrying about John tearing up a bartender. Dinner came and went. The food and the service was better than usual. I wasn't surprised. It was obvious to me that the bartender had put the word out. The waitress told us that we had a round of drinks on the house. Either at the table or at the bar, it was our choice. I thanked her and said, "We'll take the check." She went for the check and John said, "I guess that asshole at the bar got the message. Let's have that drink at the bar." I said, "OK, but we'll have one drink and we're gone. We got more important things to do. John, you hear what I'm saying?" We don't need another situation. Fuck the bartender. He ain't worth it. I know how you are. Leave him alone. Do it for me." John said, "I hear you man. Just let him buy us a drink, then we'll go." We got to the bar and sat down. The bartender came over and said, "How was dinner? I hope you enjoyed everything." John said, "Yeah, everything was great. Especially the part when you knew you were going to get your ass kicked if we weren't happy. That's the part we enjoyed the best." The bartender said, "As long as you were happy with everything." John said, "You're the one that should be happy. You didn't get your ass kicked. But we could always fit that in, depending on what you say next." The bartender said, "I'm sorry if I said anything that was out of line. That was not my intention. If I did, I apologize." John said, "No problem man. Forget about it. Let me buy you a drink." I grabbed John by the arm and said, "Hey, you got a crush on this guy or what? Fuck him and let's get out of here. We got enough things to do." John said, "Relax, we'll leave in a minute." I said, "Ok, whatever. While he's at it, tell him to pour us two shots of scotch. If I gotta wait until your finished playing with this guy, I might as well have a drink."

The bartender poured three shots. He picked up his glass and said, "Good Luck". As we were picking up our glasses, Wendy stepped between me and John at the bar and said, "What about me?" The bartender said, "I'm sorry, what can I get for you? She said, "I'll have a shot of Amaretto." He poured her shot and then again said, "Good Luck". We all downed the shots and then I asked him, "What do I owe you?" The bartender looked at me and said, "You don't owe me anything. Those drinks are on the house." I said, "No they ain't." I put thirty dollars on the bar and said, "Twenty dollars should cover the drinks and the other ten is for you. You acted like and asshole when we came in here tonight. We don't accept drinks from assholes. If you see us in here again and you don't act like an asshole, we'll let you buy us a drink. If you're smart enough, you'll get the message. It ain't about money. That's not what's important. Hopefully, you won't be as stupid as everybody else we've come across out here. If you are, we'll drag you out and beat the fuck out of you. Just like we did to all the other fucking jerk offs out here that thought they could fuck with us." The guy looked at me and said, "Like I said before, I'm sorry if I gave you the wrong impression. I'm not looking for any trouble." We were all standing there. John looked at me. I looked at Wendy and she looked at the bartender. Then

John said, "I think he wants to buy us that drink right now. Just to show us he ain't an asshole anymore." I said, "Come on, let's get the fuck out of here." John said, "I'm serious, look at him. We should have another shot, just to get that stupid fucking look off his face. It's the least we could do. Look at this fucking guy." At that point, I knew as soon as I looked at him I was going to laugh. I said, "Come on John. You know I can't look at him now. What are you doing this for? You know I want to concentrate on the situation at the apartment. I don't understand you sometimes." Wendy said, "Let's just have another shot and get it over with." She looked at the bartender and said, "You're buying this round, it'll make you feel better." The guy poured the drinks; we downed them and headed for the door. Finally, we were leaving.

We walked out to the parking lot and got into the car. The three of us sat in the front seat of the Lincoln. I pushed a Clapton tape into the stereo and pulled out of the parking lot. I looked at John and said, "We can't even go get something to eat without running into some kind of trouble. Why is that?" He said, "I don't know. We ain't looking for any trouble. Maybe it's because there are a lot of assholes out here. Who gives a fuck anyway? What are we supposed to do? We can't just let people fuck with us. As long as we don't do anything wrong, it don't matter what we do." I knew he was right. I just couldn't believe I couldn't go through a single day without some kind of confrontation.

We pulled into the parking lot of my apartment building and got out of the car. We were walking toward my apartment when John said, "I hope we see this guy hanging around here tonight. I'm in the mood to punch somebody in the fucking mouth. Let me know if you see him." I said, "I thought you said you didn't want anything to happen when Wendy was around? Why don't' we just stick with my plan for one night. Let's just scope things out tonight. You can't do that?" He said, "Yeah, I can do that. But just for tonight. I'm just dying to see this guy. See what he looks like. I give you my word. Nothing happens tonight, but starting tomorrow, he gets lined up and we finish this. No more plans for any other bullshit. Deal?" I said, "Deal."

We got inside the apartment and settled in. Wendy got us all a beer and we started talking about the next couple of days. We walked out onto the balcony. It was a Thursday night and there was a lot of activity down around the pool. Wendy filled us in on the people she knew. There were a couple of people there that hung out with this guy. But he wasn't there. I said, "Wendy, what is that fucking idiot's name anyway? I don't think I ever found that out." She said, "Fletcher." John said, "What kind of stupid fucking name is that?" Wendy said, "That's his name. Not a lot of people know that. I know that because I used to go out with him." I looked at her and said, "How the fuck could you ever be stupid enough to do that?" John said, "Leave her alone. She made a mistake, that's all." Wendy said, "Thanks John. He really knows how to sweet talk a girl doesn't he? I'm sure he never made a mistake in his whole life." I said, "Not like that."

She said, "Whatever. Anyway, the point I was trying to make was nobody calls him by that name. All of his friends call him "Mad Dog." Me and John looked at each other for a second, then started to laugh. And I mean laugh. We couldn't stop. The more we tried, the worse it got. Now it was a full blown laughing fit. We both tried to say something a couple of times, but that just made it worse. We sat there laughing and trying to catch our breath. We had tears in our eyes from laughing so hard. Wendy just sat there looking at us. Then she said. "What's so funny?" This only made us laugh even harder. Then she said, "I guess this guy, Mad Dog, has really got you guys worried" We were out of control. While we were holding our stomachs and laughing, John managed to squeeze out a whole sentence. He said, "Yeah, we're scared shit." And that started us off again. It was hopeless. Then, through the laughter, I managed to say, "I know what they are going to be calling him after we leave here, too." John was out of his chair now, laughing and leaning on the wall of the balcony. He said, "So do I." I said, "Dead Dog." And John said, "That's it." Then we were out of control for another couple of minutes. Wendy sat there and watched us. Then she said, "You guys are really out of your fucking minds, aren't you?" I said, "John, they call this guy Mad Dog; what are we going to do now?" He said, "I don't know. When you asked me to come out here, you didn't tell me they call him Mad Dog? I didn't know they called him that! I better get the fuck out of here." Wendy got up and said, "That's it, I'm going inside. Call me when you're finished with all the Mad Dog one liners." We just stood there leaning on the balcony wall and laughing. As she walked inside I said, "Wendy, not so loud. He might be down there." She called me an asshole and kept walking.

We stayed out on the balcony for a while. We finished our beers and were finally done laughing. Then we started to talk about what we were going to do next. A few minutes later Wendy came back out onto the balcony. She brought us both a couple of beers and said, "I thought you might be thirsty after all that laughing." I said, "Thanks. I'm sorry about breaking your balls like that. We weren't making fun of you. It all started when you said his name was Fletcher.

Then it just got worse when you told us that everybody called him Mad Dog. It never fails. It's always the chicken shit assholes that have the scary nicknames." Wendy smiled at us and said, "I understand. You guys just take some getting used to. Nothing seems to bother you. Most people in a situation like this would be nervous, maybe even a little afraid. You're three thousand miles from home with only each other to rely on. You're on unfamiliar ground with no way of knowing what kind of people you're dealing with or how many of them. But does that bother you? Of course not. That was funny enough. But what was even more unbelievable, was the way you reacted when I told you everybody called him Mad Dog. I thought I was telling you something that might cause concerns or at least make you take the situation seriously. So when the two of you became absolutely hysterical when you heard his nickname, I realized something right then. It was obvious to me that there was no hope for this guy, Mad Dog."

I looked at John and we both started to laugh. Then John said, "What a fucking coincidence. I felt the same way then Tony called me in New York. When he explained the situation to me, I said, this guy Mad Dog is fucked." The three of us were laughing now. Then Wendy said, "Come on guys, don't start all over again now." John said, "You're right. It's time to stop breaking balls and get down to business." He looked at me and said, "What do you want to do with this asshole? I thing we should just beat the fuck out of him and whoever tries to help him, and the sooner the better." I said, "There's a good chance we'll wind up doing exactly that. But I want to fuck with him a little bit first. He's a stupid fuck. I know he'll set himself up without us doing anything." John said, "Ok, we'll spend one day doing it your way. Then I'll kick his fucking ass." I said, "Fair enough. I'm sure he'll do something stupid before one day goes by."

Wendy stood up and said, "Well, I'm glad that's settled. Let's have another beer and see if you guys can talk about something else besides beating somebody up." I said, "How about if we talk about driving you home before it gets too late?" She said, "I'm not going home tonight, I'm staying here with you." I said, "I'd feel a lot better if you were at your mother's house. It would be one less thing to worry about if something were to come up." She said, "I'll leave in the morning. Nothing is going to happen tonight. Don't make me leave now. I want to stay with you tonight." I looked at her and didn't know what to say. I knew if I said anything but ok, you can stay, there was going to be a problem. I was in no mood for this shit. I looked at John and he said, "Let her stay, man, fuck it." Right then we heard somebody call out her name really loud." Wendy, are you up there? I need to talk to you and I ain't leaving until I do."

I looked at Wendy and said, "So much for nothing happening tonight." John said, "Who the fuck is that?" I said, "It's that fucking retard." We got up and looked downstairs. He was standing by the pool with a beer I his hand. We stood on the balcony for a minute, looking down at him. John said, "Look at this fucking asshole. Let's go get him." I said, "Hold on a minute. I don't want Wendy around when we do this." John said. "I can understand that. So we won't finish him tonight, but I'm going down there. I'm gonna look into his eyes and see what kind of balls he's got." I said, "All right then, let's do it." I told Wendy to stay in the apartment. I knew she could see whatever was going to happen from the balcony. I just didn't want her to come downstairs with us.

We started walking down the stairs and John said, "Let me hit him first, then you can do whatever you want." I said, "Don't hit him. Let me talk to him first." He said, "You'll be able to talk to him after I hit him cause he's just gonna be laying there."

This whole conversation took place as we went down the two flights of stairs. At the bottom of the second staircase, I stopped and grabbed John by the arm. He looked at me and I said, "Are you gonna let me do this my way or not?" He said, "Come on, man. What do you want to do? You want to talk to this guy? That ain't gonna do shit. There's only one way to deal with an asshole like that. I know you want to talk to him first. But a drunk with a beer in his hand that's screaming at an ex-girlfriend on the second floor ain't gonna listen to reason. You know that. " I said, "I know. I just don't want to take him out with Wendy around. There's no reason to. We can wait until tomorrow when it's just you and me. He'll be here tomorrow too, acting the same exact way. Especially now that the fuse is lit. Only Wendy won't be here tomorrow. But he don't know that. I got nothing against fucking him up. I just don't want to do it tonight. Let's just piss him off and set him up. You can hit him tomorrow." John said, "I guess you're right. I really wanted to hit him tonight though. " I said, I know you did. But that feeling will be even stronger tomorrow because you had to wait one more day." He said, "Ok, we'll do it your way. Can we go now?" We started to walk out by the pool. John looked back at me and said, "Hurry up, man. Let's get out there before he leaves." I said, "Relax, he'll be there, where the fuck is he gonna go?"

We went outside and started walking toward the pool. We saw him standing by one of the picnic tables. It was obvious that the two women having a drink at the table wished he wasn't there. I had to keep a close eye on John. He was dying to hit this guy. Even though I had talked him out of doing anything tonight, I knew there was a good chance he would anyway. As we got closer and I could see how fucked up he was, I said, "John, remember what I said, Not tonight, man." John said, "Yeah, I heard you the first time." We kept walking. We were about six feet away when he recognized me. He said, "Hey man, how you doin'?" I just wanted to say hello to Wendy. That's why I was calling her before. I'm not looking for any trouble. I'm serious man."

He was such an asshole. And he was so loud. As soon as he opened his mouth he caused a scene. I figured while we were at it, we might as well do these women a favor. I walked up to him and said, "Shut the fuck up. Are you bothering these ladies?" He said, "No, I ain't bothering anybody." The table behind the two women was empty. I put my arm around his shoulder and walked him over to the table. I said, "Sit down a minute. I want to explain something to you." He said, "I don't want to sit down." Right then John smacked him across the back of the head, so hard that he fell onto the table. He looked up at me and I said, "You wanna sit or get hit? You can't be that stupid?" He sat down at the table and I sat across from him. John just stood next to the table smiling. I said, "Here's the deal. I want you to pay attention because I know you're a stupid fuck. We moved Wendy out of the apartment yesterday. She's gonna stay here with me tonight and tomorrow she'll be gone. After tonight, she don't live here anymore, we do. You'll never see her again but you will see us. Before we leave, we're gonna beat the fuck out of you. If you want to get some guys together and try and do something about that, go ahead. We'll be staying in her old apartment for the next few days. If you or anybody else tries to get into the place, we'll blow your fucking heads off." He just sat there looking at me. Then John leaned over and grabbed him by the neck. He squeezed harder and harder until the guy started choking. Then he looked into his eyes and said, "I hope you're the first one who shows up." Then he let go. The guy everybody called "Mad Dog" just sat there gasping for air. About a minute later, he was able to talk again. He said, "What the fuck is wrong with you guys? I told you I didn't want any trouble. First you throw me off a fucking balcony and now this. Why are you doing this to me?" I said, "Because you don't fuckin' listen. You act like you were just minding your own business one night and I came over and threw you off a balcony for no reason. You were acting like an asshole that night, just like tonight. Then you tried to throw a punch at me. That's how you got thrown off the balcony. Then, because you were an idiot, I went downstairs to explain to you why this all happened. That's when I told you, if you ever bothered Wendy again you'd wish you were dead. Because being thrown off a balcony would be nothing compared to what would happen after that." He looked at me and said "I don't remember you telling me all that." Then he ducked down covered his head with his hands and looked at John. John looked at me and said, "I guess that was bullshit, eh?" I said, "More than likely." Then I said, "Listen, Mad Dog, the good news is you don't have to remember what I said because I do. The bad new is there's no more good news. From now on things are just gonna get worse for you." Then John slapped him in the head again and said, "See, they're getting worse already."

The guy was petrified. He just sat there and did nothing. It was pathetic. John said, "Why don't we just get rid of this fucking guy tonight, man?" I said, "Because we don't have to. We can do that whenever we want. I want to give him one more chance before we do that. You want another chance, Mad Dog?" He said, "Yeah man. I keep telling you guys I don't want no trouble. Why won't you believe me?" John said, "Fuck this shit. if we ain't gonna finish this tonight then get this asshole out of here." I said. "He's going. Hey, Mad Dog, You're leaving right now, right?" He said, "Shit yeah, No problem man." I said, "Before you go I want to tell you something. It's something I learned growing up in the Bronx. It's always the guys with the biggest mouths and the smallest balls that have something to prove. You got something you want to prove to me tonight?" He looked at me and said, "No Tony, I told you, I don't want any trouble with you." I said, "That's what I thought. Take a walk while you still can." He said, "Thanks Tony, you won't regret this." Then he walked away.

I watched him until he left the building. From the corner of my eye, I could see John shaking his head. I lit a cigarette and heard him say. "You're unfucking believable, you know that?" I said, "What's the matter with you." He said, "What's the matter with me? What the fuck is the matter with you? Why would you want to give this fucking idiot another chance? For what? We could have fucked him up tonight. We had him set up, man." I said, "I told you why, I don't want anything to happen until Wendy is gone. How many times do I have to say that? And why the fuck can't you wait until tomorrow? It's only a couple of beers and a nights sleep away. You can't wait that long?" He said, "Alright fuck it, we can wait." I said, "Thank you, now lets go back upstairs. I am gonna have to answer a million questions from Wendy. After that, well hang out on the balcony for awhile. Just in case the asshole shows up again."

We went back upstairs. We weren't even through the door yet, when Wendy started with the questions. I guess I couldn't blame her, I knew she would want to know what happened. I was just in no fucking mood to go through the whole thing again. She said, "So, what happened?" I said "You know what happened, you watched the whole thing." She said, I know, but I couldn't hear you. What did you say to him?" I was ready to snap. My mind was jumping from dealing with this idiot, Mad Dog. Then trying to control John and what he might do. After that, I get hit with Wendy asking for a play by play of the whole scene. I said, "Come on man, give me a fucking break. I don't feel like going through all that again." Then John said "Hey, Anthony, take it easy. Don't take it out on her. She just want's to know what happened." I looked at him and said, "What's your problem? You can't hit somebody without turning into a fucking guidance counselor?" Wendy said, "Don't yell at him, he's just being sweet." John started laughing and I said, "You having a good time?" John said, "Hey, don't yell at me. You heard what she said." I said, "OK, there's no way out, right? Hey Wendy, here's what happened. I said a couple of things to him, he said a couple of things to me, then John smacked him. I said another couple of things to him, he said another couple of things to me, then John smacked him again. Then I asked him a question. After he answered me, he covered his head with his hands and looked at John. After that, I had to talk John out of killing him and throwing him in the dumpster behind the building. At least for tonight. Then we came back here. And somewhere between downstairs and up here, he became "Sweet John". That's about it man. Now you're all caught up." She looked at me and said, "You don't really want to kill him do you?" I said, "Me? No. But him, I'm not so sure." John said, "I didn't say we had to kill him. And now that I've had the chance to look him in the eye, I'm sure we won't have to. He's got no balls." Wendy said, "But what about his friends?" I said, "Hey fuck him and his friends, they got no say. We're gonna do whatever we have to do. If they get involved, they'll get what he gets. Now let's have another drink and call it a night. I'm sick of talking about this fucking jerk." Wendy brought us all a beer and I said, "No fuck that, gimme the bottle of scotch." We hung out for about another hour, then went to sleep.

When I got into bed, Wendy was all over me. I was in no mood but had mixed emotions. All I wanted to do was get some sleep. I also knew I would probably never see her again after that night. She had no way of knowing this would be our last night together. I felt guilty about that. She wanted me and I guess I felt it was the least I could do. I know that sounds like shit but I really just wanted to make her happy. We had been through a lot together. She was a good kid and if that's what she wanted, I wasn't going to disappoint her. Not on the last night I would ever see her again. So we did what we both wanted to and fell asleep in each other's arms.

The next morning, the three of us went for breakfast. We ate at a local diner and it really sucked. We paid the check and left. On the way out, the guy at the register said, "Hope you enjoyed your breakfast." John said, "I hoped I was going to enjoy it too, but it sucked." We went out the parking lot and got into the car. Then we drove Wendy to her mother's house in Encino. When we got there, the goodbyes were a little sloppy but they usually are. I told Wendy that I'd call her when things calmed down. Then we started driving back to North Hollywood.

The ride from Encino usually took about thirty minutes. But I wanted to show John some of the sights. I decided to drive to the coast. I wanted to drive down the Pacific Coast Highway then east to North Hollywood. The highway was exactly what it was called. You drove right along the coast with beautiful views of the Pacific Ocean, the entire way down. I wanted John to see it. Not that he gave a fuck, but I wanted him to see it anyway. He came all the way out here to help me out. He might as well see something. John lit up a joint and we kept driving. It was really weird for us to be hanging out in California. We were together, so that was normal and felt comfortable. But there was nothing normal about where we were. I told John to be careful with the joint because the cops out here were assholes. He said, "Fuck them and everybody else out here. I didn't come out here to get my balls broke." When he passed me the joint, I took it and threw it out the window. He said, "What did you do that for?" I said, "I got more don't worry. There's a bunch of restaurants right on the ocean, off the next exit. I want to get something to eat. I don't want to pull up to the fucking place like Cheech and Chong, with smoke pouring out of the window." He said, "OK, let's get something to eat then." Now I had to pick a place. That should have been easy but I had John with me. He really was a good guy and a great friend. But you had to anticipate certain things when he was around. If we were in New York, there would be no problem. But we were in California. I knew that wherever we went, sooner or later, somebody would piss him off. And it wasn't because he would be looking for trouble. I had been living out here for nine or ten months by this time. One of the first things I noticed about being out here was how fast people picked up on the fact that I was from New York. Especially the guys. But it wasn't just that. The funny thing was, even though most of them were punks, they were usually loud and confrontational. So I knew we wouldn't go unnoticed. I was pretty sure that sooner or later, somebody would say something stupid. And I was positive that if things went the way I thought, John would beat somebody up before we left. Because, I knew this could happen wherever we went. I pulled up to the first restaurant we passed.

We walked into the place and went over to the bar. It was about three in the afternoon, so the place was dead. The bar looked out over the ocean and there were tables outside. We decided to have something to eat at the bar and head back. When the bartender came over, I told him to bring us a couple of beers and a menu. When he came back with the beers, I asked him if we could eat at the bar. He said that would be no problem. The first beer went down real fast and we got another round. It was the first time we had a chance to sit and relax and we decided to enjoy it. I told the bartender to keep the beers coming and I'd let him know when we were ready to order. He said just let him know when we were ready. I have him a twenty dollar bill and asked him to take care of us. He said, "Thanks guys, I'll handle your afternoon."

We were both having a good time. We started talking about how we were going to finish this thing with this Mad Dog asshole. The bartender was good to us and we were good to him, enough said. I told John we'd have another beer then get something to eat. He said, "That sounds good. Then we'll go see if we can find that asshole." We were sitting there, drinking and talking, when I noticed them. They were listening to what we were saying and checking us out. They were on the other side of the bar. Two guys and one nice looking woman standing between them. She was wearing a bathing suit that didn't cover much. The guys were wearing muscle shirts. Why? I have no idea. John hadn't noticed them yet, which was fine with me. The longer it took for him to get involved the better. It had only been a couple of minutes since I spotted them. So I wasn't sure yet what their interest in us was. John was talking to me about what we were going to do later that night. I wasn't really paying attention to him. I was concentrating on the two guys across the bar. They were talking to the girl that was with them. Every once in a while they would laugh and look over at us. At this point there were two things I was sure of; it wasn't going to be long before one of them said something, and it would take even less time than that before John would notice what was going on.

There was nothing I could do. By now, I was sure they knew I was watching them. I decided to sip my beer and see what happened first. I lit a cigarette and John said, "Hey, I'm talking to you over here. Where are you at man?" I said, "I'm right here, what? Let's get something to eat." He said, "Yeah, ok, gimme the menu." As we looked at the menu we heard one of them say, "Hey we got some New York guys at the bar." Then they started laughing. John kept looking at the menu and said to me, "So that's what you've been paying attention to, eh? Why didn't you tell me? Never mind. It don't matter."

We paid no attention to them at first. Not because we were worried. Without saying a word, we knew they would dig themselves a hole they couldn't get out of. Then the bartender came over and said, "Sorry guys, they hang out here all the time. Sometimes they talk too much." John said, "Yeah, like right now. Thanks for coming over and trying to help. You're obviously a nice guy but you can't help them now." Then the other guy across the bar said, "Hey are you city boys going to order something to eat?" John looked at him and said, "No, we're just gonna memorize the fucking menu, then leave." Then I just started to laugh. I couldn't help it. It was such a funny fucking line. Then everybody else at the bar started laughing. The two idiots on the other side of the bar even laughed a little.

The only person in the place that wasn't laughing was John. The guy across the bar said, "I didn't mean anything by it. It's just that we don't get a lot of New Yorkers in here." John said, "There's your problem, right there. If you did, you would have already learned your lesson instead of having to learn it tonight." The guy standing on the other side of the girl with the bikini, who by now had the dopiest fucking look on her face said, "No hard feelings, ok?" We're not looking for any trouble. John said, "As long as you shut the fuck up, there won't be any. We'll both just go on with our lives. We're done talking. If you got something else to say, we'll take this to the next level." Everybody was waiting to see what the guy would do. Except John, he was looking at the menu.

The assholes across the bar were finished. Whether they knew it or not, didn't matter. They were done. We called the bartender over and ordered a couple of steaks. It was over. Everybody started getting back to what they were doing. The bartender brought us a couple of beers. John looked at me and said, "Ok, now we can eat." I looked across the bar at them. They were just standing there, trying to figure out what the fuck just happened. John said, "Now we can get back to figuring out what we are going to do with that other asshole at the apartment." I said, "I can't eat like this." John said, "Why not? What's the matter now?" I said, "I don't think I'm gonna be able to relax and enjoy my steak with them standing across the bar." I didn't think they were going to start any shit. They were talking to each other and drinking beer. But they were still looking over at us every couple of minutes. It was really annoying and I didn't want to eat that way. Plus I knew if it kept up, especially while we were eating it would be a problem. John said, "What do you wanna do?" I waited until one of them looked at us again and said, "Hey, why don't you take your girlfriend for a walk on the beach?" The guy said, "Why? We didn't do anything. I thought we straightened everything out?" I said, "Yeah, we did. But I don't want to be looking at you while I'm eating, take a walk." They looked at us for a minute, then I said, "You can pick up your shit and leave, or we can all go outside and see what happens." The bartender came over and put our steaks down on the bar. The two assholes downed the rest of their beers and walked out. John looked at me and said, "You really should do something about that temper of yours." I said, "That temper of mine? What about yours?" He said, "Yours, mine what's the difference? Can we fucking eat now?" I said, "Yeah, you're right, fuck it let's eat. These dumb fucks might just be stupid enough to come back in here." John said, "They do that, there's gonna be a fucking mess in here."

We had our steaks and left. Before we left, the bartender thanked us for what we did. He said he was sick of watching those guys take advantage of people. He told us it was nice to see somebody stand up to them. John said, "Thanks. Don't take this the wrong way but we didn't do it for you." John took two twenty dollar bills out of his wallet and stuck them into the bartender's shirt pocket and said, "I'm glad you enjoyed it though, and thanks for the service." We left the restaurant and got into the car.

We started driving and John said, "Ok, whose next?" I said, "What do you mean?" He said, "What do I mean? Everywhere we go out here we gotta straighten somebody out." I said, "It seems that way because it is that way. That's all we've been doing since I got here." I said, "Don't dwell on it man. Let's talk about what we're gonna do about this Mad Dog asshole." John said, "See, that's what I'm talking about." I said, "See what? What do I gotta see? He said, "We're going from this asshole in the bar, to the asshole at the apartment." I said, "So what. What does that mean? You don't want to help me out with this now?" He said, "Of course not, I don't give a fuck how many of these jerkoffs we gotta deal with. I'm just saying there's a lot of asshole out here. It's amazing. I just don't understand how you were able to stay out here this long. Me and you are pretty much the same and I don't think I could have done it." I looked at him and started to laugh. Then I said, "You know what? Here's what you do. You back me up for another couple of days, until we finish this bullshit out here. Then we'll get on a plane back to New York. On the flight back home, I'll try to do everything I can to help you figure me out." John looked at me and said, "Ok, you fucking ball breaker, you made your point. Let's go finish this."

By the time we finished our verbal chess match, we were almost at the apartment. John said, "If we see this motherfucker tonight, I'm gonna beat the fuck out of him. And don't even try to talk me out of it. I think I'm sick of this fucking place already." I said, "I think you are too. And you know what? So am I. When we get back, we'll settle in and figure out what we're gonna do. Then I'm gonna call the airport and book us a flight to New York for tomorrow night. Whatever we're gonna do, is gonna get done between now and then. Fuck this, that's it. This prick ain't even gonna know what hit him. Then we'll be gone. Whatever happens, by tomorrow night we'll be on a plane back to New York." I looked at John and he said, "Welcome back, ya fuck. I've been waiting for you to come back to life since the day I got here." I said, "Well, here I am. When we get back to the apartment, we'll plan this guy's worst nightmare." John said, "That's my boy." I said, "Fuck you too."

Before we got to the apartment, we stopped at a liquor store. We picked up a case of beer and a bottle of scotch. Then we parked the car and went upstairs. I had even less time now than I thought I did yesterday. Whatever that means. But I didn't give a fuck anymore. I'm not sure when it happened but all of a sudden, I felt different about everything. Instead of trying to figure out every little thing about what we were going to do with this guy Mad Dog, I just wanted to get it over with. I was tired of trying to plan everything so nothing would go wrong. But there was also something else now. I really wanted to hit this fucking guy. When I thought about what I had to deal with because of him and what an asshole he was, it fired me up even more. I wanted something to happen. I was ready to go. Basically, I was thinking just like John. Normally, that would worry me but not this time. I told John that whatever we did or however we wound up doing it, I was going to punch this fucking guy in the mouth.

We hung out on the balcony for a while. We had a few beers and checked out the scene down around the pool. I opened the bottle of scotch and poured us both a drink. We drank and talked about what we were going to do. I didn't know what we were going to do. I didn't know if the guy was going to show up or not, but I was hoping he would. I told John that if we wound up fucking this guy up tonight, we would drive to the airport and stay at a hotel. Then leave the next day. He said, "Hey whatever you want to do, we'll do."

    We had a couple more beers and were drinking scotch from the bottle now. I handed John the bag of pot and asked him to roll a joint. While he was doing that I noticed one of Mad Dog's friends walking into the building. He was a big fat fuck. He was with him at the party that first night, when this whole thing started. I turned and walked into the apartment. John said, "Where you going?" I said, "Don't worry about it, keep rolling." I walked into the bedroom and grabbed a baseball bat out of the closet. Then I went back out onto the balcony. John said, "Nice bat. We got a game tonight?" I said, "Oh yeah, we got a game. I'm batting third and you're batting cleanup." He said, "Fuck the line-up, what did you see down there?" I said, "You see that fat bastard down there with the radio? That's Mad Dog's right hand man. He was with him that night when I threw him off the balcony." John said, "You mean this balcony, right?" I said, "This balcony, that balcony, what's the fucking difference?" He said, "I'm just trying to get into the story man." I said, "Don't start breaking my fucking balls now, man. I got enough shit to think about." He said, "Calm down, I'm sorry. What else did you see?" I said, "That's it so far. Light up that joint.

    There is nothing like the feel of a baseball bat in your hands when you are expecting trouble. I can't explain it. You either know what I'm talking about or you don't. After we finished the joint, we drank some more scotch. By now, we had a pretty good buzz working. We were standing on the balcony, watching the activity around the pool. I had the bat on my shoulder when the fat fuck walked over to the table below our balcony. The music on the radio he was carrying really sucked. And it was very loud. There were three girls sitting at the table. He put the radio down and started talking to them. They tried to ignore him but it wasn't easy. Finally one of them said, "Could you please lower that radio and leave us alone?" I looked at John and said, "You ready?" He said, "I'm batting cleanup, ain't I?" I still had the bat on my shoulder when I leaned over and said, "Hey, fatso, shut that fucking thing off, my fish are sleeping." He looked up at me and said, "Don't you know that fish can't hear?" I said, "I guess that makes you the fattest fucking fish I've ever seen. Now we're gonna find out if you're stupid, too." He looked at us for a second, not knowing what to do Then he shut the radio off. I said, "Good, you're half way there. Now pick up your radio and leave those girls alone." He said, "Do I have a problem with you guys?" John said, "Not yet, but that could change. We're looking for some asshole called Mad Dog. When we find him, we're gonna fuck him up. And whoever tries to help him, is gonna get fucked up too." The guy looked up at us and said, "I don't know what's going on here but are you guys sure you want to mess with the Mad Dog? He's a pretty bad dude." I looked at John and said, "Did you hear what he said. You think we should still do this?" John said, "Yeah I do." I said, "You think we can handle it?" He said, "Yeah, I do." I said, "Me too." I looked down at the guy and said, "Hey radio boy, we're sure. But we're not gonna mess with the Mad Dog, we're gonna leave him for dead. You can go tell whoever gives a fuck. We'll be here all night." He picked up his radio and walked back toward the pool.

    I looked at John and said, "Fuck him." One of the girls at the table downstairs looked up and said, "Hey guys, thanks for getting rid of that jerk for us. You want some company?" I looked down from the balcony and said, "Does a shark shit in the sea?" She said, "What do you mean?" I said, "I mean yes." She said, "Do you want to come down here or should we come up there?" I said, "Why don't you come up here. We gotta keep an eye on a couple of things and it'll be easier from up here." She said, "Ok, what's the apartment number?" I said, "Just come on up, the door will be open." John looked at me and smiled. I said, "What?" He said, "I think I just found out why you've been out here this long. Is it always that easy?" I said, "Yeah, it is. So let's enjoy it for as long as it lasts. It'll be a nice distraction. But I'm not gonna let it get in the way of what I want to do. I'm gonna fuck this guy up. If we gotta take a pass on the girls, then that's what we'll have to do. John said, "Hold on a minute. Maybe we can do both. Let's not rule anything out. These girls look pretty nice. We can always fuck him up tomorrow and still catch our plane." I said, "How are we gonna find him tomorrow? I don't want to leave here without beating the shit out of this guy." John said, "Let's see what happens. This guy might not even show up tonight. If we're having a good time we can cancel the flight and stay another day. We might even have some fun around here for a change." I said, "I thought you were sick of being out here and couldn't wait to get back home?" He said, "That was before these girls, who are gonna be here any minute, got into the picture. Trust me, we're gonna fuck this guy up. It might happen before, during or after we hang out with these girls. But it's gonna happen."

I was about to answer him, when the girls walked into the apartment. All they were wearing was their bathing suits and high heels. One of them said, "I hope we're in the right place." I looked at her and said, "I hope so too." I told them there was plenty of cold beer in the refrigerator and asked them to get one for all of us. They went into the kitchen and I looked at John and said, "I guess we can wait another day if we have to." He said, "I promise you before we leave, we'll do what we gotta do."

The girls came back with the beers and we went back out on the balcony. They were better looking than I thought. One of them had jet black hair; the other one was a blonde. The dark haired girl handed us a beer and said, "Thanks again for getting that creep away from us. My name is Sandra, my friend's name is Rita." I said, "No problem. This is my friend John. My name is Tony or Anthony, whatever the fuck you want to call me." She said, "Nice to meet you. Where are you guys from? We've been trying to figure it out. You're definitely not from around here." I said, "Listen, we appreciate the company. We're both from New York and we're here to deal with a situation. We'll hang out and have a couple of beers. But if the jerk off we're looking for shows up, we'll have to cut the party short."

We had a couple of beers and hung out for a while. As we talked, we realized that besides being good looking, they were good people. John and Rita were sitting at the table in the middle of the balcony. They seemed to be hitting it off pretty good. I was still standing in the same place, looking down at the scene around the pool. Sandra, the dark haired girl walked over to me and said, "Are you ever going to put that baseball bat down?" I didn't even realize I was still holding it. I said, "Yeah sure, no problem." I leaned the bat against the wall of the balcony and she said, "This guy must have really pissed you off for you to be as mad as you are." I looked at her and said, "I don't really want to get into why we're doing what we're doing. The bottom line is, he don't listen. The first time he tried to fuck with me, he wound up in the hospital. I guess that wasn't enough. Now we're gonna take it to the next level. No big deal." She said, "Ok, let's drop it." I said, "Thanks. Why don't you get us all another beer?"

She walked into the kitchen and came out with four more beers. I looked at John and said, "Have you two set a date yet?" John said, "A date for what?" I said, "For what? For the wedding. You guys must be in love by now. John hasn't talked about hitting somebody for the last half hour." We were all laughing when I saw him come in the back entrance. I didn't say anything. I just watched him. The fat fuck with the radio walked over to him. I knew he was telling him about us. Then they both turned and looked up at us. I looked back at them. Then I picked up the baseball bat and put it over my shoulder. Sandra said, "What are you doing?" I just stood there, looking back at them and said, "Hey John, we got company." He walked over to me and said, "Where is this prick?" I said, "On the other side of the pool by the back entrance." He said, "Good, that's where the dumpster is." I said, "Ok, we keep an eye on them for a while, then set them up. How's that sound?" John said, "Sounds good to me. This is gonna be easy." I said, "That's it then. Let's get rid of the girls and get the ball rolling." He said, "Hold on a minute. Let's not throw it all away, just like that." I said, "Throw what away?" He said, "All of it." I said, "You mean the girls? Don't worry about it. We can probably find two more just like them at the airport. He said, "Would you just calm down for a minute. Why go looking for something that we already have? It makes no sense." I said, "Here we go. This is exactly what I was worried about." John said, "Relax, you ain't got nothing to worry about. Calm down!" I said, "Don't tell me what the fuck to do!" We looked at each other for a second and started to laugh. Sandra walked over to me and said, "What are you guys arguing about?" I said, " We ain't arguing. We talk to each other like this all the time." She said, "Ok then, what are you talking about? I said, "You want to know what we're talking about? We're gonna go downstairs and fuck this guy up. Whatever's left of him is gonna get thrown in the dumpster back there. If anyone of those idiots down there tries to help, they're going in the dumpster too. Then we're gonna book a flight to New York for tomorrow morning. After that, we're gonna go stay at the finest hotel airport and celebrate." The two girls just stood there looking at us. Then John said, "You wanna come?" I said, "Ah shit!" John said, "What? What's wrong with that? They can keep us company." Rita said, "Can we have dinner in a restaurant at the hotel?" We all just looked at her for a minute. It was such a stupid fucking question. John started to laugh and said, "I like this girl. We're talking about leaving people in a dumpster and she's thinking about having dinner. We should take them with us just for that." I said, "This is fucking unbelievable." Then I walked to the wall of the balcony and looked downstairs. I could see Mad Dog and the fat fuck with the radio sitting by the pool.

  I said, "Ok, here's the deal. I can't be bothered with any more bullshit. It's obvious to me that you girls are just as crazy as we are, but in a stupid kind of way. I know you want to hang out with us, but it's not gonna be easy. You have no idea what this kind of thing is like. You want to come with us, fine. But I don't want to hear any bullshit. The first time either one of you starts to whine, or cause a problem, that's it. I'm serious. Either one of you starts, you both go. Wherever we are, we stop the car and you both get out. I don't care where we are. If we're on a highway, that's where you'll get out. No discussions. So, you two talk it over and decide what you want to do. But know this, if the time comes, I will throw you out of the car."

They walked over to the couch and sat down. John walked over to me and said, "Come on Anthony, don't be so hard on them. They want to come with us, is that so bad? You sound like you're trying to talk them out of it." I said, "I ain't trying to do that. I just want to make sure they know what they're in for." John said, "Listen to me for a second. You already explained to them, what they're in for. Fuck it now. If they decide to come with us, let's think about what we're gonna be in for. We got it made, man.

We throw these guys a good beating, and then we take the girls to a hotel with us. And tomorrow, we go home. It's fucking perfect man." I said, "I don't want to lose sight of what's important here. We gotta fuck these guys up. And we will. But we gotta be smart too. Yeah, it's great to have the girls with us, but it's gonna be a distraction. Maybe it won't make a difference but it might. It gives us two more people to think about. At some point it has to affect our concentration." John said, "Yeah, you're right. But I can't stop thinking about the ass on that girl, Rita." I said, "That's exactly what I'm fucking talking about. We should be thinking about doing what we gotta do. And your mind is on this girl's ass." John said, "And where's your fucking mind? You can't tell me you ain't thinking about nailing this girl, Sandra. There ain't nothing wrong with her ass either. And I know you; so don't try to bullshit me. Besides, we can do both. I keep telling you that. What is it with you? You're telling me you never kicked somebody's ass and got laid in the same night?" I said, "I ain't saying that. Of course I have." He said, "That's good, I'm glad. Because I know you have, I was there. So how's this any different?" I said, "I don't know. I guess I just want to make sure everything works out right. I don't want to leave a mess. I want to get on the plane with a clear head. I'm so sick of being here. The last thing I want is more trouble on my way out." John said, "There ain't gonna be no trouble. Let's go set this thing in motion. I can't wait to fuck these guys up."

We walked into the living room and sat down on the couch with the girls. They were still in their bathing suits. I said, "If you're gonna come with us it's time to get ready. We're gonna pack a few things. You two go back to your apartment and do the same. Get whatever you need to spend the night and meet us back here." They left to get what they needed while me and John packed up our stuff. We didn't have much so it didn't take us too long. When we were done we went back out onto the balcony. We had another beer and kept an eye on things down by the pool.

I lit up a cigarette and I felt John tapping me on the shoulder. I turned around and he handed me the bottle of scotch. I took the bottle and he said, "You ready, man?" I drank from the bottle, handed it back to him and said, "Yeah, I'm ready. Don't worry about it. You got my back right?" He took a sip from the bottle and said, "Definitely. You got my back right?" I said, "No fuckin doubt about it." He said, "That's all. These guys are fuckin' dead already." I said, "I know they are. All we gotta do is make sure these girls have nothing to do with what we do. I've been thinking this whole thing out for the last couple of hours. You know, while you were thinking about Rita's ass. Let me tell you what I came up with. I knew our best chance of pulling this off, was to have a plan that was quick and simple. This guy Mad Dog and his friends are used to intimidating people. When that doesn't work, they have to think of something else. Most people back down from them. So they never really have to back up their words. They never have to think of something else. When they come across people like us that they can't intimidate, they have a problem. Plus, they ain't too bright to begin with and they're usually fucked up. I found this all out, the night I threw that asshole off the balcony." I looked at John and said, "You know what I'm saying or what?" He said, "Yeah, I know what you're saying. I'm just waiting for the quick and simple part." I said, "Ok, so you want to break my balls now, right?" He said, "I'm not breaking your balls. I was paying attention right up until you said you had a quick and simple plan. I got a little bored when you broke into a documentary of an asshole thing, though." I looked at him and we both started laughing. I said, "That was pretty fucking funny man. I gotta give you credit for that. Anyway, here's the fucking plan. When the girls get back, we'll pack up the car by the back entrance of the building. The girls sit in the back seat and wait for us to come back. We take the car keys with us just in case. That way we don't have to worry about them doing something stupid. If they get spooked, they can get out and run, but they can't take the car. When we're done that car has to be there. Then we'll walk into the building and tear the fucking place up. When we're done we walk back to the car and get in. We drive to the airport stopping nowhere. When we get back to the airport, we pick a hotel and park the car ourselves. We carry our own luggage to the hotel and check in. We'll pay for the room in cash and carry the bags up ourselves. I'll slip the guy at the desk some cash and tell him our girlfriends are sick or some bullshit. I'll tell him to take the money or we'll give it to someone else. Once we're in the room we can relax."

We heard the front door open and went to check it out. The girls were back with their suitcases. You would think they were going away for a week. I said, "What's all this shit?" Rita said, "This is our stuff." I said, "Get the fuck outta here. You need all that shit for one night?" John stepped in front of me and said, "Just put the bags down by the front door for now. Tony and me gotta talk about a couple of things before we go. Why don't you get us all a beer and meet us on the balcony, we'll be there in a minute."

They walked into the kitchen and John looked at me and said, "Would you calm down? Forget about them for a minute. You just walked me through the whole night all the way up to the hotel room. But we still haven't talked at all about how we are going to finish those assholes." I said, "I know. I ain't gonna know what I'm gonna do until I look at him. When he looks at me, his eyes will tell me what I'm gonna do." John said, "Oh yeah? Are his eyes gonna talk to me too, or are you gonna do that?" I said, "Listen, I know you're dying to turn this into a comedy routine, but I'm gonna take it seriously anyway. Not because you ain't funny. You are funny you know. But somebody has to be serious about this." John said, "Ok, I get the message. Tell me how you want to handle this and we'll get started."

Before we went back to the girls I wanted to have a plan in place. I didn't ever want to see them again until we knew what we were going to do. I told John that we would go with the plan I had explained to him earlier that night. Once the car was parked and the girls were in the car we'd park behind the building. John said, "Whatever we're gonna do, we're gonna do fast. We ain't going in there to talk." I said, "Exactly. There's two ways to get in or out the back of the building. You go around the other side and come in that way. I'll walk in the entrance by the car. When he sees me, he might run. If he does, he'll run right into you. If that happens, you take him out. If not, we just come at him from both sides. I'm walking in with a baseball bat. That's why I think he might run. If he stays put, I'm just gonna walk over and beat the fuck out of him. Unless somebody makes a move. Then they go first, after that, we just fuck up whoever we have to.

Then just get the fuck out of there. You got that? How's that sound?" John said, "Yeah, I got it. Sounds good to me. Let's do it."

We walked back out to the balcony. We told the girls we were ready to pack up the car. They said they were ready to go too. I told them to start bringing their stuff down to the car and we would meet them there in a few minutes. When they left, me and John went back out on the balcony. I wanted to take one last look at what was going on down there. I could see them sitting at the table. It was perfect. They were all together. As I was checking them out, John put his arm around my shoulder and handed me the bottle of scotch. I took the bottle and held it out in front of us. There was about two inches of scotch left inside. I said. "Let's down the rest of this fucking bottle and finish these jerkoffs. Looks like about and inch each." John said, "Gimme the fuckin' thing." He took the bottle and drank half of what was left. He handed me the bottle and I drank the rest. I put the bottle on the table and said, "You ready?" He said, "Let's go Motherfucker!"

We walked out of the apartment and went down to the garage. When we got to the car, I could see the girls sitting in the back seat. We opened the doors and sat in the front seats. I started the car and said, "Is everybody ready?" Then Rita said, "It's about fucking time, we've been sitting in this car for twenty minutes." I turned around and looked at her. Sandra put her hand on my shoulder and said, "Tony, we're fine. Let's go." I said, "Rita, shut the fuck up or get out." She said, "I'm sorry. All I meant was we've been waiting a long time." I said, "I don't give a fuck what you meant. Shut up or get out. Pick one." She said, "Ok, calm down and let's go." I looked at John and said, "Do you believe this fuckin' shit?" She said, "Come on, let's just go." I said, "Ok, if you can get her to shut the fuck up by the time we park behind the building, she can stay. If not, I'm throwing her out as soon as we pull over."

I drove out of the garage and headed to the back of the building. It was finally quiet in the back seat. I parked behind the dumpster and shut the car off. John got out of the car and came around to the driver's side. I took the keys out of the ignition and got out of the car. I opened the trunk and grabbed the baseball bat. Then I leaned into the car window and told the girls we'd be back in about ten minutes, give or take. Sandra looked at me and said, "Tony, I know you're doing this for a reason, just be careful. And come back safe, ok?" I said, "Don't worry about it. Just make sure your friend don't do anything stupid. I'm not sure how things are going to work out. The only thing I know for sure is when we're done we're gonna have to leave fast. If she causes any trouble, she'll get what they got inside. If you care about her at all, don't let that happen." She said, "Ok, I'll keep an eye on her. But I'm starting to get nervous. What if something goes wrong and one of you gets hurt? What do we do then? What if you can't get back to the car?" I said, "Hold on a minute, calm down. I know you're afraid and I understand, but nobody in there is gonna be able to stop me and John." She said, "Ok baby, good luck."

We walked to the back entrance of the building. We stopped at the gate and John said, "Ok, you ready?" I said, "Yeah. You walk around and come in the other entrance. I'll give you a couple of minutes before I walk in." John disappeared behind the building and I lit a cigarette. I turned and looked at the car. Sandra was waving at me from the back window. I couldn't believe it. I smiled at her and turned towards the building. I took another drag of my cigarette and threw it away. I walked up to the back entrance, pulled open the metal gate and walked in with the baseball bat in my right hand next to my leg. I walked toward them. I could see John walking along side the pool coming from the other direction. I got to the table first. Mad Dog was lying in a lounge chair with a beer in his hand. When he saw me, he sat up and said, "Hey Tony, where are you going with that baseball bat, you got a game tonight?" Everybody at the table started laughing. Then I said, "It's like a game. It's called; when the asshole don't listen. You know that game, right? We played that one before, on the balcony remember?" John was about six feet from the table now. Mad Dog got up and said, "Come on Tony, what's wrong? I didn't do nothing." I said, "You didn't do nothing? If you didn't do anything, I wouldn't be here. You think I got nothing fucking better to do than come looking for you?" I lifted the baseball bat, pointed it at him and said; "Now you gotta pay for all your bullshit." The guy with the radio stood up and said "Tony, he said he didn't do anything." I looked at him and said, "What, you wanna get hit first?" John got to the table just as Mad Dog started to back away from me. He slapped him in the back of the head and said, "Watch where the fuck you're going asshole." Mad Dog turned around and looked behind him. When he saw John he said, "Oh, shit!" Then he looked back at me for a second and tried to run. John said, "Where you goin?" The he hit him. There were only a few feet between us. The punch caught him on the bridge of his nose, shattering it completely. The force of the blow knocked him back toward me. The blood that was pouring out of his nose got all over me. The front of my shirt was covered with blood. I went nuts. The fat fuck with the radio and everybody else, took off in different directions. Mad

Dog was on his knees, screaming and holding his face in his hands. I said, "You motherfucker, you got blood all over my shirt." I swung the bat and hit him across his back. He landed, face down by the pool. I pulled the bat back to hit him again, then John stepped in front of me and said, "That's enough, you're gonna kill him man!" I said, "Look what he did to my shirt!" He said, "He didn't do anything to your shirt. All he did was get hit, bleed and fall. What happened to your shirt was an accident." I said, "An accident? That's easy for you to say, you still got a shirt." John started to laugh but forced himself to stop. He stood in front of me, put his hands on my shoulders and looked right into my eyes. Then he started laughing again. And kept on laughing. I said, "You havin' a good fucking time?" He said, "No, I'm not." Mad Dog started moaning and trying to get up. John said, "Come on gimme a break. He's moaning, you got blood all over you and I'm trying to tell you something." I said, "I'm all ears man." Then I kicked the Mad Dog in the chest, as he was trying to get up. He fell back down and started to beg. I said, "Shut the fuck up." John said, "Would you forget about him, he's finished. He's crying, his nose is inside his head someplace and who the fuck knows what you did to his back!" I said, "I'm still listening." John said, "Listen to me for a minute. We're done here. We need to get out of her now. You got blood all over you. Somebody probably called the cops. We gotta get out of here before they show up." I said, "Ok. Let's go." I walked over to Mad Dog. He was just lying there. I put my foot on his head and pressed it down on the cement. I said, "Hey, scumbag. If you do anything stupid we're coming back."

    I picked up the baseball bat and we started walking toward the back entrance of the building. We walked through the gate and I couldn't help wondering what we were in for when we got to the car. I had the keys, so I knew the car would be there. But that's all I knew. I wasn't worried about Sandra. She

Anthony and John, New Year's Eve, 1984

was pretty cool. But the other girl, Rita, was an idiot. Who knew what the fuck she was doing by now. As we got closer to the car, we could see that both girls were still in the back seat. We were about ten feet from the car when they saw us coming. Sandra said, "Oh my God! Are you guys alright?" I said, "Yeah, we're ok. But we gotta move fast." Then Rita started screaming, "You guys are fucking crazy. What did you get us involved in? Let us out of the car right now. I want to get out. Let us out!" We got to the car and I couldn't believe how fucking loud she was. John got in the passenger side of the front seat. I looked in the window and said, "I gotta change my shirt. If she doesn't shut the fuck up, punch her in the mouth." I opened the trunk, threw the bat in and opened my suitcase. I pulled out a t-shirt and closed the trunk. I walked around to the driver's side and got in. I pulled off the blood soaked shirt and put on the clean one. Then I started the car and drove toward the highway that would take us to Vegas. About four blocks away, I threw the bloody t-shirt out the window. I looked at John and said, "How you doing?" He looked back at me and said, "I'm doin good, how you doin?" I said, "You don't wanna know. You got anything rolled?" He said, "Does a shark shit in the sea?" I said, "Good, light it up then."

Chapter 16

We pulled onto the entrance of the highway. I threw a Clapton tape on the stereo and John lit up the joint. I looked in the rearview mirror at Sandra and said, "Are you ok?" She said, "Yeah, I'm alright. It's just that you were covered in blood when you came back and I was afraid." I said, "Don't worry about it. It wasn't our blood." Then Rita started screaming again. She was out of control, in a heartbeat. She started yelling, "They killed somebody back there and now we're in the car with them!" I looked back at Sandra and said, "How many times do I have to tell her to shut the fuck up? I thought you were gonna keep her under control." She said, "I'm trying but she's afraid. She thinks you killed that guy back there." I said, "Yeah, I heard." Sandra put her hand on my shoulder and said, "You didn't kill anybody did you?" I said, "No, I didn't. Not yet anyway." I looked at John, he was relighting the joint and laughing. I said, "What the fuck are you laughing at? You should be talking to your girl back there. You could at least do that, instead of laughing and smoking pot! Do I gotta do all the work?" He said, "Rita, we didn't kill anybody. Don't worry about nothing. Everything's gonna be ok." Then he passed me the joint. I said, "That's it? That's your big fucking input?" He said, "Find a place to pull over where I can take a leak." I put my arm in front of Sandra and held her back against the seat. Then I slammed on the brakes and skidded to a stop. I felt John grabbing the back of my seat to hold on. Then I heard Rita hit the back of Sandra's seat and land on the floor. She started screaming again. But at least it was worth it this time. I said, "Oh shit, I'm sorry. Rita are you all right? Let me help you up." I reached back and grabbed her by the arm. She said, "Don't touch me. You did that on purpose, you crazy bastard." I said, "Don't say that. Why would I do that? Come on, let's be friends." John helped her up and said, "Let's get out of the car. We'll all feel better after we take a piss." We all got out and took a leak. Me and John pissed by the car and lit up a cigarette. The girls walked off the road and went behind a cactus or whatever the fuck that was. It was really weird for me and John to be standing in the middle of the desert. We were New York guys, inside and out. We were used to hanging out on the west side of Manhattan. We grew up dealing with everything the streets of New York could throw at us. That experience, right or wrong, allowed us to laugh at almost everything else. To us this whole California thing and everything that was happening out here was a fucking joke. We dealt with everything from that point of view. Nothing felt real to me out here. And standing in the middle of the desert just made me homesick. And anybody that didn't understand that could just go and fuck themselves. Without saying a word, we know we both felt the same way.

  The girls started walking back to the car. Rita said, "Isn't it beautiful out here?" John and me looked at each other for a second then John said, "Let's get the fuck out of here." We were walking toward the car when we saw something run across the road, in front of the car. John said, "What the fuck was that?" I said, "I don't know. It looked like a dog." Then whatever it was, it started howling. When the howling stopped, we heard something run across the road behind us. The girls freaked out and jumped into the back seat of the car. I got in the front seat with John. I put the car in reverse and backed up about thirty feet. Rita said, "What are you doing? Let's get out of here. Those were prairie dogs, wild dogs! They're very dangerous. They're nasty unpredictable and will attack anybody." I said, "Yeah, yeah, yeah, just like a nigger on welfare." John said, "Yeah, and you know what we do to them."

  I popped the trunk and got out of the car. I grabbed the baseball bat from the trunk and walked to the front of the car. John was waiting for me there. He lit up a joint and said, "What are you gonna do?" I said, "I don't know yet." Rita looked out the window and said, "What is wrong with you guys? Why can't we just leave? Do you have to fight dogs, too?" I said, "Hey, there ain't gonna be a fight. We're gonna finish smoking this joint. If that thing comes near us, I'm gonna open its head like a melon."

  We sat on the hood of the car and finished the joint. As we were talking, we couldn't help noticing the sky. It was all around us. It was dark but there must have been a million stars up there. The land in front of us was completely flat. Everything else was sky. I looked at John and said, "Look at the sky. That's some sight, ain't it?" He said, "Yeah, it's amazing. But you're starting to sound like them now." I said, "Maybe you're right. Come on let's go." Then I heard something. We slid off the hood of the car and stood there. The howling started again. But there were more of them this time. John said, "Get ready, man, we got something going on over here." Then we saw them. There were four of them that we could see. They got within ten feet of us, and then slowed down. They were checking us out. But they looked like they were sniffing around for something. I turned my head and said, "Sandra, is there any food in the car?" Then incredibly Rita screams out, "I told you they're crazy! He's gonna get us all killed. There's wild dogs out there and he wants to eat now?" I said, "Shut your mouth, you unbelievably dumb fuck! Sandra, answer me!" Sandra yelled back, "Yeah, there's food in the back seat." The dogs were walking towards us again. I said, "John, that's it. They smell the food." He said, "Well they ain't gonna get it. Let's get in the car and run them the fuck over." Then, one of the dogs started growling and running toward us. He was showing his teeth. I picked up the bat just as the dog jumped into the air. He was coming right at me. John looked at me and yelled, "Now! Hit 'em!" I swung the bat and caught the dog flush across the side of his head. There was a cracking sound. Then his head exploded. His eyeballs flew out of his face and the rest of him landed about six feet away. The other dogs backed away a couple of feet, as its body skidded in the dirt in front of them. John said, "Nice shot man!" I said, "Yeah, I got all of that one. Let's get out here." We jumped into the car and I slapped the gearshift down into drive. When we looked in front of the car again they were taking another run at us. But there were six of them now. Sandra and Rita were both screaming when I floored the gas pedal. I headed straight for them. As we got closer the dogs started to scatter, trying to get out of the way of the car. Some of them made it. But not all of them. We saw the first one hit the front of the car. We felt the others under the car, as we drove over them. The car bounced and swerved on the road, until the last one of them shot out behind the car. The scene inside the car was unbelievable. The Clapton tape was blasting on the stereo. John and me were laughing our balls off and the girls were still screaming. I just kept driving. What else could I do?

  After a while things started to quiet down in the back seat. It had been about twenty minutes since the dog thing. Nobody had said a word since then. We were all sick of being in the car. And I was bored to death. Then we saw the lights. Way in the distance down the highway. It was Las Vegas. It was a strange sight. It was pitch black for as far as you could see, then it was real bright. It cheered us up and changed the mood inside the car. We were getting close. Rita said, "I hope that's where we're going." I said, "Yeah, that's the Emerald City, Dorothy. You got your slippers?" John and me started laughing. Then Sandra put her hand on my shoulder. I turned around and said, "I'm sorry, I was just kidding around. Let's forget about everything else and start having some fun. It looks like we'll be there in less than an hour." John said, "Yeah, come on. We'll check into the hotel and get ourselves a nice room. Then we'll go to a nice restaurant, get something to eat and relax." Sandra said, "You think we'll be able to do all that without either one of you hitting somebody? That would be really nice. When you stop and think about it, it's not a lot to ask." I said, "Yeah, no problem. We could do that." Then she said, "John? How about you? You've been known to hit a few people, here and there." He said, "Yeah, ok. I could use a relaxing night anyway. Sandra said, "Ok, great." Then we drove on.

  About a half hour later, we were just about there. It was really something. The closer we got to the city the more impressive it looked. The hotels and casinos were bigger than I had expected. And the lights got brighter and brighter. It was about 10pm when we pulled into Vegas. We drove down the strip and took it all in. It was amazing to me that this gigantic fucking place was in the middle of nowhere. We had to pick a hotel to stay at. To me it didn't matter which one. And I knew John didn't give a fuck. So I told Sandra to pick one. She said, "I don't know Tony. Any one of them would be fine with me. Rita, which one do you like?" I said, "Don't ask her, she's nuts." Rita said, "Fuck you Tony. You think I'm nuts? What about you and John? We met you guys about five hours ago. And all you've done since we met you is beat people up and run over a few wild dogs in the desert. Except that first dog. You didn't run him over. You just knocked his eyes out of his head with a baseball bat." I said, "You know what, if I didn't know you were a nut, that would have been a really good point. But the fact is I'm just a regular guy trying to go home. It ain't my fault that every guy out here is an asshole with something to prove. Can I help it if I got guys fucking with me, and dogs leaping at me? What am I supposed to do? I can't let that happen, I gotta react!" I looked at John and said, "You can jump in here whenever you want, ya know." He said, "What for? You're doing great. What are you arguing with her for anyway? Just pull into the next big hotel. At least we'll get her out of the fucking car." I just looked at him and smiled. He kept looking straight ahead, smiling. He knew I was looking at him. I hated it when he was right and he knew that too.

  Without knowing which hotel it was, I pulled into the next parking garage I came to. Once we got inside, I saw that it was the Sands Hotel. Even the garage was classy. I knew it was gonna cost us big time. But I didn't give a fuck. I wanted to enjoy my last night out here. I also knew what came with the price of staying in a place like this, and that was high-end service. I had some money to play with so I didn't care. I was gonna have some fun. There was one thing on my mind that was more important than anything else. I was going home. By this time tomorrow night, I'd be in New York. I had about three thousand dollars in my pocket. I figured I'd have two thousand left, after the airfare and the hotel room. I couldn't wait to hit the casino. I was either gonna make some money or lose it all. When I got to New York, I'd be ok. I wouldn't care if I was broke or not. I'd been broke in New York before. It wouldn't bother me. If that happened, I'd just get a job and start all over again. At least I'd be home.

Somehow all of that went through my mind before I pulled into the parking space. The next thing I heard was Rita saying, "I can't believe you picked the Sands Hotel. It's not even the nicest place. You could've asked us where we wanted to go." I shut the car off and turned around to look at her. John lit up a cigarette and said, "Oh shit, here we go." I said, "Rita, let me ask you something." Then Sandra put her hand on my shoulder again. I said, "No. No way. Not this time, Sandra. She's on her own now. Hey Rita, how does somebody get to be as annoying as you? I'm serious. I mean, I don't really give a fuck but I'm curious now. You either had a chump boyfriend, who put up with all of your shit, or you took a two week course on how to be a completely annoying motherfucker. I don't know what else it could be. What the fuck is wrong with you?" She said, "Maybe you're the one with the fucking problem, Tony. Did you ever think about that?" I said, "No, I haven't. I can't even believe I'm talking to you. Get the fuck out of the car and don't say another word. Do yourself a favor and hang out with John. At least he's got a reason to want to talk to you."

We got out of the car and took the suitcases out of the trunk. We walked through the garage and into the hotel lobby. It was beautiful. There was a sitting area by the front desk. The girls sat down on one of the couches. John and me carried the bags over to the front desk and waited to check in. There was one person in front of us. When he was done, we walked up to the desk and put our bags down. The guy said hello to us, then the phone rang. He asked us to wait and picked up the phone. While he was on the phone, he snapped his fingers and motioned for one of the clerks to come over. I was talking to John about the kind of room we wanted, when he got there. He said, "Gentlemen, are we ready then?" We just looked at him for a second. He was a black guy with an English accent. To us, there was almost nothing funnier than that. I said, "Yeah, we'd like a suite with two bedrooms. You got one of those? There's gonna be four of us." He said, "I'll check into that for you straight away. Will there be four of you then?" That accent was killing me. Then

John said, "No, there won't be four of us then, there's four of us now. There was gonna be eight of us but four of us couldn't make it. That's why there's four of us now!" I looked at John and said, "What the fuck are you talking about? He ain't gonna understand that, I don't even understand it." John said, "Who cares? I don't understand him either. Then the black English guy said, "Shall we start from the beginning then?" John said, "No, we shall start from the beginning now!"

I couldn't believe what was going on. At the same time, I guess I really wasn't surprised. Especially the way the last couple of days had gone. But I was looking forward to ending my California experience on a high note. I thought staying in a fine hotel the night before we left would be a good idea. But a black guy with an English accent was just too much. I never expected that. I mean, how the fuck could you see that coming. And there's no way it wasn't going to be funny. So that's where we were at.

We were standing at the front desk looking at this guy. He just stood there looking back at us and smiling his ass off. Right then, I knew it didn't matter what we said, or did. He was just gonna keep smiling at us. It was pathetic. And, I was in no fucking mood for this shit. I just wanted to get a room and relax. Now I had to do something fast. Because I knew as soon as he started talking again with that fucking accent we were just gonna laugh in his face. And who the fuck knew what John was gonna do after that. Right then, John looked at me and said, "How long do you think this idiot can keep smiling?" I said, "Who the fuck knows. Do me a favor. Leave the bags here with me and take the girls to the bar. I'll meet you there. I'll take care of the room and have the bags sent up. I gotta try and figure out what the fuck this guy is talking about. I don't want you around while I'm trying to do that." He said, "Why not? Maybe I can do something to help." I smiled at him and said, "I'm sure you'll do something. But there's no way it's gonna help. Don't argue with me, please. I got enough to fuckin' think about. Holy shit, am I ever gonna be able to relax tonight?" He said, "Ok man, calm down. I think he likes you better anyway."

The three of them walked over towards the bar. I went back to the front desk. This guy was still standing here. He said, "God evening again, Sir. I do hope we'll be able to square you away this time, then." I just looked at him. Obviously, he was still smiling. I said, "You're a pretty happy guy, aren't you? You think you can end a sentence without the word, then?" He looked at me and said, "I'm sorry sir. I don't think I understand what you mean." I said, "Congratulations. You did it. Now do me a favor.

Don't say you're sorry anymore. Just get me a room, ok?" He said, "Right away, sir. I'll just be a minute." He went over to a computer and started typing away. While I was waiting I thought about how everything we did was a problem. I couldn't deal with this guy anymore. I just wanted a room key. My mind was all over the place. I thought about John and the girls. I couldn't help wondering what was going on at the bar. Who the fuck knew what I'd be walking into by the time I got there. I started thinking maybe I shouldn't have sent them to the bar. As I'm thinking this, I heard the English black guy say, "Here's your keys sir. I'll have your bags sent up to your suite. Will there be anything else, then?" I looked at him and said, "So, now you're back to that "then shit" again? No problem. No, there won't be anything else." "Are we all settled then?" He said, "Very good sir." I walked away and said, "Whatever, man."

Chapter 17

It was almost midnight when I walked into the bar. There was food everywhere and the bar was huge. I walked around the other side of the bar. John and the girls were sitting at a table eating and drinking. I was relieved. I sat down with them and had something to eat. When we were done, we went up to the room. We opened the door and went inside. We just stood there for a minute and looked around. This place was unbelievable. Basically what it was, there were two complete apartments on either side. And in the middle there was a sunken living room. A horseshoe shaped couch framed the room. And in the middle of that there was a Jacuzzi and a heated swimming pool. The doors to the balcony were on the other side of the pool. And to the right of the balcony there was a full bar and stools. We looked at each other and John said, "How much does this fuckin' place cost?" I said, "Don't worry about it; I'm taking care of it. Let's all take a shower and hit the casino. Then we'll come back and enjoy this fucking place."

After my shower, I walked over to the bar and poured myself a scotch. I had started rolling a joint when John walked over. He said, "What's going on man?" I handed him the joint, then I picked up the bottle of scotch and said, "Let's go outside. I lit up the joint and for the second time that night, we stood on a balcony drinking scotch from the bottle. We stood there looking out at the Las Vegas strip. John passed me the joint and said, "That's some fucking view, ain't it?" I took a sip from the bottle and said, "What the fuck are we doing here?" John said, "I don't know how the fuck we ended up here, but I'm glad we did." I said, "You don't know how? You kept breaking my balls saying I wanna see Vegas, I wanna see Vegas. What choice did I have? We had to come here!" He started laughing and said, "You're a sick fuck, you know that?" Then the girls came out on the balcony. They were wearing high heals and not much else. Sandra said, "Hey Bronx boy, you feel lucky tonight?" I said, "I'm feeling a lot of things, let's go spend some money." Rita said, "Can I play the slot machines?" John said, "Only if I can grab your ass every time you pull the thing down." She said, "Every time?" John said, "Every time."

It was one o'clock in the morning when we walked into the casino. Before Rita opened her mouth again, I gave Sandra $50 to play the slots. told her we'd either be at the craps table or playing black jack. We walked over to the crap table. I bought $50 worth of chips and put five on a number. I tried to look the part but I had no fucking idea what I was doing. My brother, Joey, could work a crap table. But he wasn't there. He tried teaching me. Every time we were in Atlantic City, he'd take me to the crap table.

Then he'd explain everything he was doing. I just never had the patience. Tonight was no different. I tried to remember what he used to tell me but it was no use. As soon as I heard the guy next to me say, "Press the hard six," something Joey had explained to me a hundred times, I got pissed off. I said, "Fuck this, let's get out of here." I heard John laughing as I picked up my chips. Then he said, "You really know your way around a crap table, don't you?" I laughed and said, "Don't worry about what I know. Let's try something else." We walked over to the roulette table. I asked John how long it took us to wipe out the Mad Dog earlier that night. He said, "About 15 minutes, why?" I put a twenty dollar chip on fifteen black and we hit it.
The dealer gave me a hundred dollars worth of chips. John looked at me and said, "You're unfucking believable, you know that? You're a sick bastard." I split the hundred with John and said, "Let's go play some cards."

We sat down at the black jack table and played a few hands. We started out losing but had won the last couple of hands. I felt lucky and wanted to win back the hundred we had already lost. I won a hundred on the next hand. I beat the dealer's nineteen, when I held with twenty. After that, he started paying more attention to us. Then, John got hot for a couple of hands. We were up two hundred and feeling pretty good. We played for a few more hands and kept winning. I could see Sandra and Rita playing the slots. Everything seemed to be going good. We were playing our next hand when I noticed him. He was playing the slot machine next to Sandra's. And he was paying way too much attention to them. "We gotta go." John looked up at me and said, "Go where? I'm just starting to get hot over here." I said, "We're gonna be getting hot all night, let's go." He shook his head and started to pick up his chips. I said, "Let's go to the bar. I want to talk to you about something." On his way to the bar, John said, "What happened now?" I said, "Nothing yet." He said, "Ok, what's gonna happen? If you want to talk to me it's either one or the other, I know you."

When we got to the bar, I handed the bartender a hundred dollar bill and said, "We're gonna have a few drinks and you're gonna keep the change. Take care of us, ok?" He smiled at me and said, "You got it man." I said, "Dewar's on the rocks for me and my friend." John sat down next to me and said, "What's going on man?" We were behind them now, which is what I wanted. John hadn't seen them yet. I said, "The girls are at the slot machines straight ahead, you see them?" He looked at me and said, "Yeah, I see them, so what?" I said, "Check out the guy on the slot next to Sandra.

The bartender put our drinks on the bar. I picked them up and gave one to John. He took the drink and looked over at the guy again. I said, "He might have to be next man." John said, "Come on man. I thought we were supposed to relax tonight. That's why we came here." I said, "Calm down. I said he might have to be next. I didn't say he was definitely next. Let's have a drink and keep an eye on him. Then, you tell me."

We sipped our drinks and watched him for a while. To me, what he was doing was obvious. I knew it would be obvious to John too. But I wanted him to see for himself. It didn't take long. Every time the girls hit something on the slots, he tried to become part of their celebration. We were close enough to hear their conversation. But we were positioned perfectly, behind a cashier's booth. So they had no idea we were there. Rita pulled down the lever on her slot machine and got three of something. The coins started pouring out and they both started screaming. They hit for three or four hundred dollars and were really excited. The bartender came over and poured us another drink. He said, "That's on me, guys. Good Luck." We thanked him and started drinking. We looked back over at the girls. They were still celebrating and hugging each other. This guy was still standing there behind Sandra. Then, he made the move that would decide his fate. He walked over to Rita and said congratulations. Then he picked her up and kissed her on the lips. John looked at me and said, "You're right, he's next."

The guy looked like he was about forty years old. When he put Rita down she said, "Who the fuck do you think you are? Get the fuck away from me." The guy said, "Hey, no hard feelings. I'm sorry, ok? Rita said, "I'm trying to do you a favor. We came here with two guys from New York. They're at the crap table right now. We just met them today. They already beat up some guys that were bothering us. After that they killed some dogs in the desert on the way over here." Sandra said, "That's enough Rita. Don't say another word." Then the guy said, "Yeah, sure they did. I'm not afraid of a couple of punks from New York or anywhere else. But thanks for your concern." Rita said, "Hello, I'm not concerned about you. I just don't want to watch these guys beat somebody up again." He started laughing and said, "Why don't you let me worry about them?" Rita said, "If you're smart, you'll start worrying as soon as possible. I wouldn't be surprised if they already knew about this. Just leave us alone and maybe you'll get lucky." The girls started to walk away toward the crap tables. Then the guy started getting loud. He said, "I'm gonna have a drink at the bar, I'll be worrying over there, if you change you mind."

I looked at John and said, "Here he comes man. This poor bastard is gonna walk right into the belly of the beast." John said, "Good, we don't even have to go get him." I called the bartender and asked him if he knew this guy or had seen him before. He told me that he sees him around about once or twice a month. I said, "What's his story?" He looked at John and me and said, "Listen guys, I've been around a long time. I've dealt with all kinds of people around here. I can read somebody and know what they're about pretty quick." I said, "Hold on a minute." Then I turned around to see where this guy was. I didn't want to interrupt the bartender because he was about to give us all the information we needed. I just wanted to make sure he wasn't following Sandra and Rita. I saw him playing one of the slot machines. A cocktail waitress had just handed him a drink. So I knew we had some time. I turned back around and looked at the bartender. Then I said, "Sorry about that, I had to check something out. You were saying you've been around and could figure people out." He looked at me and said, "Yeah, something like that. Getting back to this guy you're interested in. When he's staying in the hotel, he's a regular at this bar. He hangs around the slot machines trying to get laid." I said, "So he's not connected to anybody we gotta worry about here, right?" He said, "Definitely not. He's nobody. But let's back up for a minute. Like I was saying, I know people. You guys are obviously New Yorkers. And you definitely ain't cops. That tells me that you are definitely gonna fuck this guy up. That aside, my instinct tells me you guys are all right. So you probably have a good reason for whatever you're gonna do. Just do me a favor and don't do it at the bar. If that happens, I'll be here all fucking night answering questions." I looked at John and said, "This guy's alright man." John said, "Yeah he is." Then John reached over to shake his hand. The bartender grabbed John's hand and looked at both of us. John said, "Don't worry about nothing. It ain't gonna happen here. We'll make sure of that. You're a good guy. You helped us out and we won't cause you any trouble.

We turned around on our stools and the bartender walked away. I looked at John and he looked back at me and said, "What?" I said, "That was really touching what you said to that guy." John laughed and said, "Don't start." I said, "No really, I'm serious. Especially that part when you said, you helped us out, now we're gonna help you. That was really something." He looked at me and said, "Why do you gotta do that shit? You gotta break my balls, right?" I said, "Hey, if you can't take a compliment that's you're problem. Let's check out what this asshole is doing. You see him?"

We were looking around by the slot machines when John said, "I hear him, but I don't see him yet." John stood up and walked to the end of the bar. I was getting us another round of drinks when I saw him walking back. As he got closer to me he started to laugh. I said, "What's going on?" He said, "Nothing. He's playing one of the slots and talking to some fat broad." I said, "So what's so funny?" John sat down next to me and picked up his drink. He downed half the glass and looked at me. I looked at him and started laughing. Then I said, "It's your turn to talk to drama boy. I'm at the edge of my seat." John just kept laughing. Then he said, "He's at the end of the first row of slot machines. He's standing behind a woman that's playing one of the slots." I said, "What's so funny about that?" He said, "Nothing's funny about that. It didn't get funny until I was close enough to hear what he was saying. He's standing behind this fat lady and talking about us. First he told her about what happened with Sandra and Rita. Then he told her what they said about us. When he picked up his drink and downed the whole thing, I started to walk away. As I was walking, I heard him tell the fat broad that he was going over to the bar. He said he wanted to see if those New York punks had the balls to show up. That's why I was laughing."

We sat at the bar, drinking and talking to the bartender. I couldn't believe we had another idiot to deal with. I was hoping he wouldn't come to the bar. But I knew he would. I also knew that the girls were looking for us. And it was only a matter of time before they would check the bar. I looked at John and said, "You know what's gonna happen. This guy is gonna come to the bar acting like a jerk. We'll be drinking and talking about how we're gonna fuck him up. While we're doing that the girls are gonna show up." Then he looked at me and we both started laughing. I said, "Why do these things keep happening to us?" John said, "I don't know, all I know is we ain't bothering anybody. People just keep fuckin' with us. What are we supposed to do?" I said, "Yeah, I know they just keep coming. But let's try something different this time. If we're right and this guy does what we expect him to do, sooner or later, something is gonna happen. Because it always does. When that time comes, this guy is gonna realize two things. There will be a split second when he'll know he's about to get his ass kicked. And he's gonna be scared. At that point, instead of kicking his ass, we'll give him a chance to punk out." John said, "Why don't we just kick his ass?" I said, "Because I'm sick of having to do that all the time. I'm trying to relax. What about you? You gotta be tired of hitting people by now, right?" He said, "No, not really, not if they deserve it." I said, "Come on man." John looked at me and started laughing. Then he said, "Ok, maybe you're right. We'll see how it goes."

    We got another round of drinks and hung out at the bar. We were talking about all the crazy shit that happened over the last couple of days. We were laughing and having a good time, for a change. For a few minutes we were actually able to relax. Then the idiot came over to the bar. We heard him before we saw him. He was real loud when he said, "Hey bartender, I got an empty glass in my hand. Where's the service? What do I have to do to get a drink around here?" The bartender looked at me for a second, then he said to the guy, "I'm sorry to keep you waiting Mr. Santiago, I'll get you a refill." John looked at me and said, "Ok, here we go." I said, "Not yet, remember my new approach." He laughed and said, "Yeah, yeah, yeah."

    I was hoping for the best and expecting the worst. I couldn't help wondering where the girls were. As I was thinking about how sick of this shit I was, Mr. Santiago sat down next to John. While he was waiting for his drink, he looked at John and said, "Que Pasa, my friend?" John kept looking straight ahead and said, "I ain't your friend." The guy said, "It's just a figure of speech." Then he leaned over the bar and said to me, "What's the matter with your friend?" I said, "Nothing, what's the matter with you?" He said, "Sorry guys, I was just trying to be friendly. I'm not looking for any trouble. I had enough of that at the slot machines. I was talking to a couple of fine looking women. But they turned out to be nasty bitches." John said, "Maybe they just didn't like you. I don't!" The guy looked at John for a second not knowing what to say. Then he said, "That's just it. If that's what it was, I could understand that. Then she started telling me she was with a couple of guys from New York. She said they liked beating people up. Can you believe that shit? Like I'm gonna believe a stupid thing like that. And even if I did, you think I'm worried about a couple of punks from New York?" John sipped his drink and elbowed me in the ribs. Then we both started laughing. He looked at us and said, "I laughed at them too. It's funny how people think they can intimidate you, ain't it?" John looked at him and said, "It's funnier than you think." We started laughing again. The guy looked at us and said, "Yeah, whatever." Then he called the bartender over.

The bartender's name was Frank. He was a good guy. He was taking care of a customer at the other end of the bar. I don't think he heard the guy calling him But I knew he didn't want to deal with this fucking asshole. So he could have been ignoring him. Then, the guy got loud again. He said, "Hey Frank, how long do I have to wait for a fucking drink?" The bar got quiet as everybody turned around and looked at him. The bartender looked at me as he started walking toward him. Even though we told him we wouldn't fuck this guy up at the bar, I knew he thought we might. I looked back at him and said, "Don't worry about anything. You got nothing to worry about." He smiled at me and I could see he was relieved. He said, "Mr. Santiago, Let me get you another drink." The guy said, "It's about time. Get me a menu, too. I'm going to eat at the bar."

I finished my drink and lit up a cigarette. I didn't give a fuck anymore. Then I heard John say to me, "I don't want this guy eating next to me." I said, "That should smooth out the rest of the night." The bartender put a menu down in front of Mr. Santiago. I didn't know what was gonna happen. But I was sure that whatever it was would happen before this guy even saw his food. He gave the bartender his order and downed the rest of his drink. I said, "Hey Frank, when you get a chance." He came over and said, "Sure Tony, another round?" I said, "Yeah, but we'll take them straight up from now on." He brought us our drinks and said, "Tony, I got this round. I know it won't be easy but try to control yourselves, please? I gotta go get this guy a set up to eat at the bar." John said, "Set him up about three stools down. That's where he's gonna eat." The bartender looked at me. I told him to do what John said and everything would be ok. He did what I said and put a setup about three stools down. While he was doing that, the guy yelled out. "Hey Frank, I'm empty again." John slammed his hand down on the bar. The guy jumped and looked at him. John looked back at him and said, "The next time you open that big fucking mouth of yours I'm gonna slap it shut."

The guy was stunned. Then he said, "I'm sorry, man. I didn't realize I was talking so loud. I'm not looking for trouble. I'm just gonna sit here and have something to eat. Hey Frank, I'm buying their next round." John said, "No you ain't. We pay for our own drinks. And you ain't gonna eat here either. We told the bartender to set you up over there. That is where you're gonna eat." He looked at both of us. Then he started talking about how he didn't have to move if he didn't want to when John interrupted him. He looked at the guy and yelled, "Move the fuck down." He got up and did what he was told.

John looked at me and I said, "You didn't have to yell at the guy like that." He said, "Fuck him, he's lucky that's all I did. He was giving me a fucking headache. Why don't we just give the bartender another hundred dollar bill and fuck this guy up right here?" I said, "Because we said we wouldn't. Let's relax and have a drink. At least he ain't right next to you anymore."

We sat at the bar drinking. Twenty minutes had gone by without anything happening. It was like a fucking vacation. The idiot finally got his food. He was eating where we told him to, three stools down. The bartender came over to us and said, "How you guys doing? Thanks for not losing your temper with that guy." John said, "Don't thank us yet." The bartender looked at me and I just smiled at him. Then he said, "Seriously though, it was a great idea to get him away from you guys." John said, "Yeah, but he's still too close. Let's move him again." The bartender started to panic. He said, "Come on, guys, don't do this. Tony, I thought we talked about this." I said, "Yeah, I know. But I've been talking to John for years. Sometimes it don't help." John started laughing. The bartender looked at him and said, "John please, I don't want to be here all fucking night." John said, "Alright, fuck it. Let's have a drink instead." The bartender brought us another round, then John said, "Give that fucking idiot a Shirley Temple and put it on our tab." The bartender said, "Come on man, don't make me have to do that." I said, "Hey, don't bring him nothing. We got our drinks. We're ok for now. Go do what you gotta do. Check us out in a little while." The bartender walked down to the other end of the bar. I looked at John and said, "What is wrong with you? Why do you want to start fucking with this guy again? We just got rid of the fuckin' idiot." He lit up a cigarette and said, "Don't worry about it." I said, "Oh, now I understand. Thanks for explaining everything." He said, "Hey, whatever it takes." I just laughed and said, "At least we got a fresh round." He said, "That's all we need." I said, "Let's drink to California." We lifted our glasses and took a sip. I put my glass down on the bar and started laughing. John said, "What's so funny?" I said, "I'm just wondering how many other things are gonna happen before we finish this drink. John said, "Who the fuck knows." Then I heard Rita's big fucking mouth. "There they are, Sandra. They're at the bar. I told you that's where we'd find them. I looked over at Mr. Santiago. He was still eating. I kind of felt sorry for him but not really. His dinner and probably the rest of his night, was about to be ruined.

John was already laughing when the girls got to the bar. I grabbed Sandra and gave her a hug. She said, "How are you doing Bronx boy?" I smiled at her and said, "I'm doing better now. I missed you." We sat them down at the bar to our left. John and me stood next to them on their right. John called the bartender over and ordered some drinks. I leaned over, kissed Sandra on the cheek and whispered in her ear, "The shit's about to hit the fan but I guess you're used to that by now. There's nothing to worry about, though. The guy is already punked out. I just wanted you to know what was going on." She looked at me and said, "Tell me you're not serious. What is it with you guys? You can't even have a drink without getting into trouble? What happened now?" I said, "Hold on a minute. First of all, we're not in any trouble. We don't get into trouble. We get out of it. You should know that by now. The guy that's eating at the bar is the same asshole that was bothering you at the slot machines a little while ago." She said, "How do you know about that?" The bartender brought over a round of drinks and said, "Tony, on your tab right?" I said, "Wait a second, Rita how'd you do on the slots?" She said, "I won!" I said, "She's buying." Rita put her arm around John's waist and said, "He's such an asshole." John laughed and said, "Not all the time though." She said, "I'm glad you ain't nothing like him." John said, "Yeah, me too."

We were laughing and hanging out at the bar. I kept an eye on Mr. Santiago. At some point, I knew he would recognize the girls. Then, sooner or later he'd put it all together and freak out. As I'm thinking this, Sandra put both of her hands on my face and turned my head to face her. I looked at her and said, "What?" She looked into my eyes and said, "How did you know what happened?" I said, "We were sitting right here and saw the whole thing. We heard everything he said. Then he came over to the bar and told us about the whole thing. We played dumb and let him talk. He told us about how he wasn't worried about any punks from New York or any place else." Sandra looked at me and said, "Oh my God. And you didn't do anything? Did John hear him too?" I said, "Yeah, we both heard him. I told John I was tired of having to hit people all the time. I talked him into letting me handle things differently this time." She said, "How did you do that?" I said, "I'm not sure but I think he'll go along with whatever I do."

John was keeping Rita busy, who knows how. The whole time I was talking to Sandra she kept looking over my shoulder. I grabbed her face with my left hand and said, "Will you stop looking at the fuckin' guy. I don't want him to know you're here yet." She said, "What are you going to do?" I said, "When he sees you two with us, he's gonna start getting nervous. Then, it will all hit him like a ton of bricks. He's gonna start thinking about things he said to us. How he didn't give a fuck about any punks from New York. Then he's gonna know he was talking to the people he was talking about. When he realizes that, he's gonna be petrified. Sandra was looking over my shoulder again. I said, "Will you stop fuckin' doing that?" She said, "I think he knows we're here. He keeps looking over at us." I said, "I'm sure he is. Anyway, we ain't gonna fuck him up. We're gonna let him punk out. Believe me, he'll be relieved. He might even thank us." She looked at me and smiled. Then Rita got up off her stool and gave Sandra a hug. I knew it was all about to happen. I said, "Rita, thanks for the drink. You didn't have to do that." John started laughing and said, "You're unfuckinbelievable, leave her alone." I said, "What? I just wanted to thank her for buying us a drink. What's wrong with that?" Rita said, "That's ok, John." Then she looked at me. Right then, I knew she would see him. She said, "You know what, Tony? Believe it or not, I'm starting to get used to you." I saw her eyes look past me for a second. That's when it happened. Everything she said was loud. She saw the guy and said, "There's that fucking guy again. The one who grabbed me at the slot machine." John looked at me and we started laughing. Everybody heard her and looked at the guy. Mr. Santiago sat there with his fork in his hand looking back at us. John said, "What fuckin' guy?" Then he turned and looked at him. He said, "Oh yeah, him. This won't take long." I grabbed John by the arm and said, "It's time for my new approach. Remember what we talked about?" He said, "Yeah, I remember. I just want to tell him something. Let's go." We walked over to the guy. He was still holding his fork. He was scared shit. He sat there, looking up at us. John said, "You're looking at John Donovich and Tony Genelli. We're the two punks from New York that you ain't worried about."

The bartender and everybody else at the bar stopped whatever they were doing. They all just stood there watching this guy, waiting to see what he was going to do. There was dead silence. We were both looking right at him. For a few seconds, the only things moving at the bar were his eyes. They were dancing in his head as he looked back and forth between John and me. Then he said, "No, no, that's not what I said. You're making a mistake. That's not what I meant. Maybe you took it the wrong way." I leaned over and grabbed him by the back of the neck. I squeezed his neck harder and harder as I said, "No, no, that is what you said. And you're the one who's been making mistakes tonight over and over. Don't tell us that's not what you said because that's bullshit. We were sitting right here about an hour ago. Our girlfriends were playing the slot machines while you were trying to move in on them, we were watching you. We saw everything you did and heard everything you said. Then, like an idiot, you came over to the bar and told us about the whole thing. So, this is the deal. It's real important for you to pay attention right now. Because this is really the only chance you got at being able to walk out of here on your own tonight. And you don't want to fuck it up. You know what I'm saying? Plus, if you do anything we didn't tell you to do, John is gonna go nuts. He hates you already. You know that right?" He looked at us for a second and I said, "John, tell him." John said, "I can't stand this fuckin' guy. I wanted to hit him an hour ago." I said, "See what I mean?"

  Mr. Santiago grabbed his glass and downed the rest of his drink. Then he looked at me and said, "Tony, I'm sorry man. I know John hates me. Just tell me what you want me to do. I didn't realize who I was dealing with, please!" I said, "Good, you're half way there. I'm gonna call the bartender over and tell him you want to pay our bar tab. You with me so far?" He said, "Sure Tony. Whatever I have to do." I said, "John stay here with this punk. If he does anything you don't like, punch him in the fuckin' mouth. John stood up in front of the guy and said, "Love to."

  I walked over to the girls and Sandra said, "Tony, what's going on over there?" I said, "Don't worry about it. You and Rita are gonna walk over there with me. Then, if John didn't him yet, that asshole is gonna apologize to you. After he does that, he's gonna pay our bar tab. Then, we'll finally go up to our room.

  I started to laugh as I walked back over with the girls. John was still staring at the guy. When we got to them, Rita said, "That's him, that's the guy." I looked at her and said, "You know, you should have been a fuckin' detective." The bartender laughed, then Mr. Santiago said, "Ladies, I'm sorry about the way I talked to you before. I was out of line." Then he looked at

John. John leaned over and whispered something in his ear. He looked back at the girls and said, "I'm an asshole." The girls laughed and Rita said, "You're damn right you are." John looked at her and said, "Shut up." Then he looked back at the guy and said, "What else?" Mr. Santiago turned toward the bar and said, "Bartender." Then John smacked him in the back of the head and said, "His name is Frank." He looked back at the bartender and said, "Frank, I would like to pay their bar tab. You can close me out too." He put his credit card on the bar and just sat there. I slapped him on the back and said, "You're doing good man!" He didn't move. The bartender came back with his credit card and the voucher. He took a pen from his shirt pocket and John said, "The bartender gets a fifty dollar tip." He totaled up his check and handed it to the bartender. Then he turned around and looked at us. He looked drained and hopeless. I looked at him and said, "Now, you can go." He stood up and started to walk away. Then John put his arm around him and whispered in his ear again. He stopped walking and turned around. For a few seconds he just stood thee looking at us. Then he said, "I'm a punk." As he turned to walk away again, everybody was laughing. The poor fuck. We were just never part of his equation.

We turned around and sat down at the bar. Everybody was looking at us but that was nothing new either. The bartender came over and handed me the hundred dollar bill I had given him earlier. I said, "What's that for?" He said, "It's your money. He paid your bar tab, we're even. Anything you guys have for the rest of the night is on the house." I said, "Hold on a minute. Don't worry about it, keep the hundred. Just do me a favor. Send somebody up to my room with a bottle of scotch and a six-pack of beer. Can you do that?" He looked at me and said, "It's done. And thanks Tony. I mean for everything. You reduced the guy down to nothing. It was one of the funniest things I've ever seen. I'm glad I won't have to be staying late, believe me. But it almost would have been worth it to see him get his ass kicked." He started laughing but I could tell he was still nervous. When I looked at John, he just started laughing. He knew what I was thinking. Then I started to laugh and said, "You know, you're right. It would be worth it. John, find out what room he's in and bring him back down here." John stood up and said, "No problem, man. I'll be right back." Sandra caught on and said, "Tony please just let's go." I said, "No way man. Frank is right. We should make an example out of him right here at the bar." John said, "He's right, I'll go get him." The bartender freaked out and said, "No. I ain't right. I said it would almost be worth it. Come on John, please. Have a drink with me. Don't bring that guy down here again." Then Rita, who was the only one that didn't know we were breaking his balls said, in that annoying voice of hers, "My God, Frank calm down. Before you go all to pieces can I have another Sea Breeze, Jesus. You can't stop them anyway. They're both confrontation junkies. It's no use, my God!" The bartender looked at me and said, "Holy shit, can we stop all this shit?" Tony, let's just forget what I said. Can we do that, before I have a fucking stroke tonight?" I looked at John and said, "Should we forget what he said?" He looked back at me and said, "I don't give a fuck." Then we both started laughing.

The bartender looked at us and realized we were fucking with him. He said, "You guys are some fucking ball breakers man." I said, "You're right about that Frank. But we had you going pretty good there for a minute. Look at it this way, though, you probably just had one of the most interesting nights you've ever had behind a bar. Everything turned out ok; you even had a few laughs. And we put a hundred and fifty dollars in your pocket for your trouble." He said, "I know and don't think I don't appreciate your generosity. You guys have been good to me. I just never knew what you were gonna do next." Then John started laughing and said, "Nobody does." Rita said, "You think this was bad? You should have seen them in the desert!" I said, "Yeah well, we don't have to get into that." Then Sandra said, "No, we don't. The bottom line is, nothing bothers these guys. It's really unbelievable. I've never met anyone like them before. I've been around guys that talked and acted tough. But it was just talk. If somebody stood up to them, they would back down. I've never seen anybody follow through like these guys. It's funny because they're different in a lot of ways. But when they're challenged, they react the same exact way. The more dangerous the situation, the more fun they seem to have!"

We were all laughing now. The bartender and everybody at the bar, who had just seen what went on, were laughing too. We downed our shots and the bartender filled our glasses again. I heard Rita say to Sandra, "When the fuck do you think we're going to be able to enjoy our hotel room?" I was really getting sick of her shit. I was really glad she wound up with John. I couldn't remember how that happened. But I was happy it did. Then John looked at Sandra and said, "Are you done now, with the fuckin' documentary?" She looked at him and said, "I don't know yet. I can't help it; you guys are just too funny." As I'm listening to this, some of the other people at the bar came over and thanked me. They said they were all sick of his big mouth and enjoyed watching us shut it. They offered to buy us drinks, whatever we wanted. I said, "Don't worry about it. There's no need for that." I thanked them and told them to just enjoy the fact that he wasn't here.

    I turned around, pulled out a bar stool and sat down. John was sitting right next to me, trying to comprehend whatever Rita was talking about. She was sitting on his lap, sipping her drink. He looked happy and it was nice to see him relaxed. But I knew he didn't give a fuck what she was talking about. Sandra walked up behind me and put her arms around me. Then she said, "Hey Bronx boy, are you finished dictating the events of the evening?" I said, "Not yet." Then I leaned over the bar and said, "Hey Frank, when you get a second." He walked over to us and I said, "Did you get a chance to take care of our room service?" He said, "It's all taken care of. Everything you asked for was sent to your suite half an hour ago. I threw in a couple of bottles of champagne, on the house. It's all packed on ice chilling. I had it set up on the balcony. I heard you guys do your best thinking out there. I looked at Rita and said, "Oh yeah, where did you hear that?" She looked at me and started whining, "All I said was you guys are always drinking on the balcony, My God! I'm sorry. I didn't know I couldn't say that. Maybe you'll be happy if I don't say anything at all!" I said, "Congratulations! You opened your mouth and nothing stupid came out. Let's just leave it at that." John looked at me and said, "Is that it now?" I said, "I hope so. Let's finish our drinks and check out our suite." John said, "If there's nothing else, I'll go upstairs with Rita and start opening the champagne. You guys finish your drinks and meet us upstairs. Don't take too long. And don't make me have to come back down here!" I lifted my glass and said, "Yes sir." He looked at me and said, "Yeah, I got you sir right here. Just hurry up." Then he grabbed Rita's arm and they walked away.

    I sat at the bar and watched them until they got to the elevator. When the elevator doors opened, John turned around and looked at me. I picked up my drink and held it towards him. He just laughed and got on the elevator. I put my drink on the bar and turned toward Sandra. She was looking right at me. I said, "What?" She shook her head and said, "Do you guys always talk to each other like that?" I said, "Like what? Yeah, why?" She said, "I don't know!" I said, "You have to understand something about me and John. It don't matter what we say to each other or how it sounds. I don't give a fuck how he talks to me. And he don't give a fuck how I talk to him. I know I could never intimidate him. And he knows the same thing about me. It's almost like we cancel each other out. So we're always on the same page. But, if somebody else talks that way to either one of us, that's a different story. Then it becomes personal. And we take that very seriously. It doesn't matter who it is. That person will pay a price. Because we will always respond. You know what I'm saying?" Sandra sat there looking back at me. Then she smiled and said, "Do I know what you're saying? Not really. But in a very strange kind of way, I think I know what you mean. And it's ok that you feel that way." I looked at her and said, "What a fuckin' relief. I don't know what I would do if you didn't understand." She started laughing and said, "Bronx Boy, you really are a piece of work." I said, "Whatever. I have to talk to the bartender again. Then we'll get the fuck out of here." I stood up and said, "Hey Frank, when you get a second." He walked over and said, "What can I do for you?" I said, "We're gonna go upstairs. I want you to do me a favor if you don't mind." He said, "No problem, what is it?" I said, "I know it ain't gonna happen but I like to cover all bases. I'm in suite 376. If that asshole comes back down here looking for us, I want you to call me." He said, "He ain't gonna do that. He's scared shit." I said, "I know he is, but you never know. Maybe he kept drinking and found some liquid balls or he called some friends, whatever. If he comes back, you call me. If that happens, make sure you leave after we hang up. Tell the manager you're sick or something. But make sure you're not here when we get down here. Because we'll just get off the elevator and tear him up. If anybody tries to help him, they'll get what he gets. It will all happen fast and we will leave a mess. Trust me, we're very good at this." He said, "I understand what you're saying. I'll keep an eye out for him." I said, "Thanks. That's all I'm asking. If none of that happens, it's been nice meeting you." He shook my hand sand said, "Same here, Tony. And again, thank you. I'll remember this night and talk about it for a long time. When I do, I'll think about you and John; two lunatics from New York. And I'll have a few laughs." I said, "You do that. Take care of yourself and don't take no shit."

    He poured us two more shots and thanked me again. Then he started walking toward the other end of the bar. I lit up a cigarette and started to get up from my stool. Sandra was standing behind me. She put her hands on my shoulders and pushed me back down. Then she turned the bar stool around until I was facing her. She looked at me and said, "That was beautiful what you said to that bartender. Really, very touching. It's a good thing we're leaving because I was almost ready to cry." I looked at her and said, "You're turning into a real fuckin' ball breaker, you know that?" She laughed and said, "And this surprises you? Look who I've been hanging out with for the last 8 hours!" I just looked at her. Then I turned around and picked up our drinks. I handed her glass to her and held mine up in front of her then I said, "Here's to drinking with strangers." We laughed and downed our shots. I picked up my room key and my cigarettes off the bar. I lit another cigarette and said, "Let's get the fuck outta here."

We started walking toward the elevator. Then Sandra said, "I've never gone to a hotel room with a stranger before." I said, "Me neither." She said, "I don't believe that. I said, "Believe whatever you want. This whole fuckin' day has been strange. I'm sure the rest of it will be too. Look at it this way. We got a beautiful suite to hang out in. We'll eat, drink and do whatever we want to do. And just so we're clear on this, you don't have to do anything you don't want to. So just relax." We got to the elevator and pushed the button. Then Sandra grabbed my hand and said, "You really are an interesting guy, you know that. Your personality changes from one second to the next depending on what's going on around you. No matter what it is. You can go from violence to what you just said to me without missing a beat. Are you sure you have to leave tomorrow? You can stay at my place for a few days and see what happens." I said, "Don't think I haven't thought about that. You're a good person, who just happens to be beautiful. But I fucking hate it out here. If I met you when I first came out here, things would be different. But I'm not the same guy I was when I got here. In my mind, I'm already back in New York. I never realized how much I loved it there. But being away from it opened my eyes. Now, I can't wait to go back. If I stayed here with you, I wouldn't be happy. No matter how much fun we'd have. I would always be thinking about leaving. It would tear me up inside. And sooner or later I'd start to blame you for it. So let's just have some fun."

I knew she didn't like what I had just told her but she smiled at me anyway. The elevator got down to the lobby and the doors opened. I was shocked and surprised at what I saw. But I had no time for that. Standing in the elevator was Mr. Santiago. I said, "What the fuck are you doing here?" He just stood there. He looked even more surprised than we were. Finally, he said, "I came down to get a pack of cigarettes." He started to get off the elevator and I said, "Fuck this." I stepped in front of him and pushed him back in. He said, "What's wrong? I didn't do anything." I said, "Don't worry about it." Sandra said, "Tony, leave him alone. He's not going to cause any trouble." I held him against the back of the elevator and told her to get in. She walked in and said, "Tony, you're making me nervous." Then, Mr. Santiago said, "Yeah, me too." I squeezed his throat with my left hand and told him to shut the fuck up. Then I told Sandra to hit the second floor button. When the doors opened we followed him off the elevator, as the doors closed behind us. He turned around and said, "I don't know how much of this shit I'm going to put up with." I looked at Sandra and smiled. Then I slapped him in the mouth and said, "I do. You want to find out?" He didn't say anything. He just stood there looking at me. I said, "You know what? You got off pretty easy, for a guy with a mouth as big as yours. I should give you the beating you should have gotten downstairs at the bar." He said, "Why can't you just leave me alone? All I wanted was a pack of cigarettes." I said, "Because I'm sick of you. I should have let John do what he was gonna do. Maybe you're gonna try and get even." He said, "I'm not stupid, I know when to back off. Just let me go, please." Then we heard the door open behind us. It was the room right next to the elevator. They must have heard me yelling at this moron. But I was in no fucking mood. When I turned around, there was a guy in a three-piece suit, standing in the doorway. He said, "What the hell is going on over there?" I looked at him and said, "Shut the fuck up and go back inside." He went back into the room and closed the door. I looked back at Mr. Santiago. I was really pissed off. And looking at him just made it worse. I really didn't know what I was gonna do next. Then Sandra said, "Tony, let's just get out of here." I said, "Yeah, you're right." Then I hit him. I leaned down and drove an uppercut into his stomach just below his rib cage. It took all the air out of him and he just collapsed. When he hit the floor he couldn't breath. Sandra said, "Oh my God. Please Tony, let's get out of here." I said, "Don't worry about it, we're leaving. Push the button for the elevator. I'll be right there." I leaned over and said, "Hey, tough guy. I got your room number from the idiot at the front desk. If I see your face again, I'll let John deal with you." I got up and saw the elevator was there. Sandra was standing inside waving at me. As I walked toward her I could hear Mr. Santiago coughing and trying to catch his breath. I got on the elevator, put my arm around Sandra and looked back at him. He was trying to say something, but he still wasn't breathing right. As the doors to the elevator started to close, he managed to stand up. Before the doors closed he was starting to say something like "No hard Feelings", or something stupid like that. We could still hear him talking after the doors had closed. I looked at Sandra and said, "What a fucking asshole. I wonder what it's like to be a punk like that." As the elevator shot up to whatever fucking floor we were on, Sandra said, "You'll never know."

Chapter 18

We got off the elevator and found our suite. I didn't feel like finding my room key and banged on the door. John opened the door and said, "How the hell are you?" I said, "You don't wanna know." He said, "Is everything ok?" I said, "It depends who you ask. I ran into Mr. Santiago on the elevator. I wasn't sure what he was up to so I took him out." John started laughing and said, "Is it over or are we going back downstairs?" I said, "No, he's done. We ain't going anywhere. Let's hang out." He said, "Are you sure? If not, it ain't a problem. You know what I'm saying? We'll just do whatever we gotta do." Then Sandra said, "Can you both just shut up now? I mean, really. What is it with you two? Can you just not hit anybody for a while? At least for the rest of this night. Is that asking too much?" I said, "Calm down. We ain't gonna hit nobody else, right John?" He said, "No, why would we do that?" Sandra said, "Wow, that really puts my mind at ease." I said, "Good, let's just settle in then."

We walked out onto the balcony. Everything was set up for us. There were sandwiches and salads. And the beer was all iced up. John handed out the beers and we started drinking. I lit up a joint and passed it to John. Then I said, "Where the fuck is Rita?" Sandra said, "Holy shit, that's right. I forgot all about her. Is she ok?" John said, "Yeah, she's ok. But that reminds me Anthony, come over here I want to show you something." I followed him back into the suite. We walked across the room toward a door next to the entrance. We stopped in front of the door. I could hear music coming from inside the room. I looked at John and said, "What the fuck is this?" He laughed and said, "Check this out man." He opened the door and we walked inside. The music was coming from a jukebox in the corner of the room. It was a huge room. The only thing in there besides the jukebox was and eight foot pool table. Rita was laying on the pool table smoking a cigarette. She was half naked. All she had on was a pair of panties. John said, "What do you think?" I said, "Nice fuckin' pool table man. Get her off there and rack em' up." John and Sandra started laughing. But I was serious. Sandra said, "He's really something isn't he?" John said, "Yeah, he's beautiful." She said, "How do you put up with him?" He said, "He makes me laugh, man. He makes everybody laugh. And if you leave him alone, that's all he'll do." Sandra said, "Simple as that?" John said, "Yeah, simple as that."

I walked back out to the balcony with John. We picked up a few beers and one of the ice buckets then went back to the poolroom. When we got there the room was empty. I racked up and John cracked open a couple of beers. We were shooting some balls when Sandra walked back into the room. I was lighting up a joint when John said, "Where's Rita?" Sandra said, "She's throwing up in the bathroom." John said, "Are you fuckin' kidding me?" I banked the nine ball into the side pocket and said, "I guess tongue kissing is out of the picture." Sandra said, "Tony that's really disgusting. Why would you put a thought like that in his head right now?" John said, "Because he's a fuckin' ball breaker, that's why!" I said, "You're right, I'm sorry. John, don't worry about it. She'll probably brush her teeth, anyway." Sandra said, "There's nothing you won't make fun of is there?" John was already laughing when he said, "Don't worry about it, Sandra. I appreciate what you're saying, but you're wasting your time with him. He ain't gonna stop, trust me." I said, "I'm sorry John really. I realize this is an emotional moment for you and I shouldn't be joking around." He looked at me and said; "Don't start your shit now. I ain't from California. Don't play with me." I said, "I'm sorry you feel that way, John. I only wanted to lend you some support. But I understand. It's natural for somebody in your situation to attack the person they're most comfortable with." I was fucking with him and he knew it. But I was doing it because I was sick of Rita's shit. And he knew that too. Who the fuck knows how we were able to read each other like that, but we could.

Sandra said she was gonna go check on Rita. I said, "We'll be here, let us know what's going on and don't take too long. It's already the middle of the fuckin' night." She said she would be right back and walked out of the room. We kept drinking and shooting pool. Then John said, "I'll tell you what, we're either gonna get laid or stay another day. One or the other." I said, "Then make sure you do what you gotta do. Because we ain't staying another night. I can't wait to get the fuck out of here." He said, "Hey, you know what I'm dealing with. She was already drunk when we were downstairs at the bar. Plus she wasn't too bright even before she was drinking. And now, she's throwing up in the bathroom. When she's done doing that she'll probably pass out in one of the bedrooms. And after all we've been through starting with that asshole at the apartment and the whole trip through the desert, that's just not good enough. I gotta at least get laid. You know what I'm saying?"

We were both laughing when we turned toward the door and saw Sandra walking into the room with Rita. They were both naked. I said, "Hey look who it is." Then I looked at John and said, "Hey and she's awake. Now you don't even have to make believe." Rita had her attitude level turned way up. In a way, I couldn't blame her. She had just finished throwing up and she was probably feeling like shit. Plus, I knew she was still drunk. So I could understand how she must have been feeling. I just didn't give a fuck. Especially when she said, "Tony, I don't feel so good. So I'm telling you right now, I'm not in the mood for any of your shit, ok?" I looked at John and Sandra then back at Rita. I said, "I don't remember asking you what you were in the fuckin' mood for. Sandra, rack 'em up. We're gonna play partners. And before I forget, Sandra you look great."

Sandra was racking up when Rita walked over to John and said, "Thank God you're here. At least there's one decent guy in this room. You know, I know I told you this once before but you are nothing like him." John said, "I know, I don't know what's wrong with him. He can be so mean sometimes." Rita said, "That's what I'm saying. I can't imagine you talking to somebody like that." John said, "Yeah, me either." Sandra finished racking up and walked over to where I was standing listening to all the bullshit. I was leaning against the wall, holding my stick in front of me. John said, "OK, let's flip to see who breaks." I just stood there looking at them. Rita said, "Look at him; he thinks he's hot shit." John said, "What are you gonna do, that's the way he is. We just won't stoop to his level. That's the only way to deal with people like him." I looked at John and said, "Get the fuck outta here. She might be buying your shit but I ain't." I walked over to the ice bucket and grabbed another beer. John said, "Calm down, man. I'm just breaking your balls, a little bit." I said, "No shit! You ain't got nothing else to do?" Sandra walked over and stood in front of me. She put her arms around me and said, "Hey Bronx Boy, I'm completely naked. Can't you think of anything else to do?" I kissed her on the lips and said, "Yeah, I can. We'll play one game of eight ball. Then we'll pull the fuckin' plug on this night."

As we walked back to the pool table Sandra said, "Just don't lose your temper Tony, ok?" I barely heard her. I was thinking about how weird everything was. Not just at that moment but everything that had gone on before it. In a few quick seconds things were flying through my mind. Here we were. Somehow we had wound up in a Las Vegas hotel room. Who knows how. And we were shooting pool with two girls that had no clothes on.

Something that under normal circumstances would be a good thing. But I was aggravated.

John lit up a joint and handed it to me. Then he said, "You ready now? Let's flip for the break." I said, "Don't worry about it. We'll spot you the break." He said, "Ok, no problem. Rita, break 'em up." She picked up a stick and walked to the other end of the table. Then she said, "You're going to lose, Tony. I always beat Sandra when we play. And I'm sure John is better than you." I said, "Yeah, whatever." She leaned over the table and started aiming at the cue ball. She was holding the stick like an idiot. When I saw that, I started laughing. She looked up and said, "What the hell are you laughing at?" I said, "Nothing. Just hit the fuckin' ball." She started aiming again and slammed the stick into the cue ball. The ball hit the side of the rack and flew off the table. It hit the wall behind us and bounced across the room. Sandra ducked behind the table, John was laughing while I just stood there and said; "What a fuckin' idiot Rita, you're supposed to hit the front of the rack." She said, "Fuck you Tony, don't you think I know that?" I said, "Oh, that's right. I'm sorry. You must know that because you always beat Sandra. Why don't you go find the cue ball, I want to talk to John." While she went to look for the ball, I walked over to John and said; "Fuck this game, man. I ain't into it." He said, "Yeah, me either." I said, "I'll tell Sandra we're gonna call it a night." John grabbed my arm and said, "Hold on a minute, before we do that let's all go out on the balcony and smoke a joint. How many times are we gonna be in a Vegas hotel room with two naked women?" I said, "I guess you're right. But that's it then. We'll have another beer and smoke a joint. Then we're going to bed." He said, "You got it man." Then Rita came back with Sandra and said, "I got the ball." John said, "Fuck the ball. The game's over." She said, "What are you talking about? We didn't even play yet." We didn't say anything. We just walked out onto the balcony and lit up a joint. It was beautiful out there. We could see the whole strip. I passed the joint back to John and said, "This is fuckin' unbelievable, look at that view." He said, "Wow man, what the fuck are we doing here?" I said, "Who the fuck knows." Then the girls came out onto the balcony and Rita said, "You guys got some fucking nerve." I handed the joint to Sandra and said, "You just figured that out? Why don't you just stop looking for daisies in the snow? It ain't gonna happen." John started laughing and Rita said, "What's that supposed to mean?" I said, "What you see is what you get. When you find a blind horse in the desert, you don't ask for directions." John was laughing harder now. He fell back into one of the lounge chairs and said, "You're a sick fuck, what are you talking about?" Then Sandra said, "No, wait a minute. I think I know what he means. He's saying, you know how we are by now, so what do you expect?" John stopped laughing and said, "What are we gonna do now? I think she figured us out!" I said, "Finally! It's about fuckin' time. I've been waiting for somebody to figure me out since the day I got here. And when does it happen? On my last night out here. I guess you just never know when something is gonna happen."

Sandra picked up the joint and walked over to me. She stood in front of me and said, "You got a light? I took the joint out of her hand and lit it up. I took a hit and gave it back to her. She looked right into my eyes and took a couple of hits. Then she turned and walked over to John. Just like that she had gotten my attention and she knew it. As I watched her naked body walk across the room, I had to smile. She knew what she was doing. And it was a classy move. She could have bitched and complained about all that had been going on. But she didn't. She had decided to take a different approach. I respected her for that. She knew I was looking at her. After she handed the joint to John, she looked over her shoulder and winked at me. I said, "Sandra, ain't you cold like that?" She said, "Hey Bronx Boy, we're in the desert. Can't you feel the heat?" I started laughing. Then Rita said, "My god, can somebody make me a Seabreeze. I mean, really." I looked at John and started to laugh. He looked back at me and said, "Come on, we'll all have one last drink. Then we'll call it a night." I said, "I know you want to get laid, but she really is an asshole." I knew she heard what I said but I just didn't give a fuck.

I went inside with John and started making our drinks. Actually, we made one drink, Rita's, then we got three beers for the rest of us. By now, we were both pretty fucked up. We didn't give a fuck about anything when we were straight. When we were fucked up, we cared even less. We brought the drinks out onto the balcony. On the way out, we lit up a joint and had a few hits. We were laughing and carrying on when we got back outside. John handed Rita her drink and I gave Sandra a beer. Then Rita said, "Seriously, who made my drink?" I said, "Just drink the fuckin' thing." Then Sandra got loud for the first time since I met her. She said, "Listen, let's all cut the shit! Since this is the last drink of the night, I think we should all make a toast, and just maybe we can have one drink without anything happening. At the very least, it would be something different." John said, "She's right, let's all make a toast." Sandra said, "Thank you, John." Then she looked at me and said, "He really can be sweet sometimes." I said, "Yeah, diabetics won't go near him.

Let's get this fuckin' toast over with." She said, "Ok, I'll go first. Then you guys toast to something. Here's to meeting somebody you never thought you'd know." Then she walked over and kissed me. Rita said, "Here's to finding out all New Yorkers aren't like Tony." She leaned against the railing of the balcony and downed half her drink. John said, "Here's to getting the fuck out of here." I walked over to Rita and stood in front of her. I lifted my drink and said, "Here's to balconies and people you throw off them." Sandra said, "Ok, that was pretty good. It wasn't exactly what I had in mind but it was nice to hear from everybody." John said, "Yeah, that was great." As we finished our drinks, we were leaning over the balcony and looking down at the Vegas strip. I know I've said this before, but it really was beautiful. Despite how completely out of the place it made me feel. I knew I didn't belong in Las Vegas or in California for that matter. John and the girls were laughing and carrying on. But I barely heard them. It was just background noise. I kept looking down at the streets. They were loud and jammed with people. I was wondering how many other weird fucking situations were going on, beside ours. I almost felt like I wasn't really there. Like I was watching a scene from some fuckin' movie or something.

Then, out of nowhere, which is where she's from anyway; Rita slammed into me and started throwing up over the balcony. I jumped back and said, "What the fuck?" John was hysterical and Sandra stood there, with this horrified look on her face. I couldn't believe it. I just stood there for a second, trying to deal with what was going on. It wasn't easy; believe me. I had never seen a naked woman look so unattractive. Sandra walked toward Rita and said, "Tony, we have to help her." I said, "Help her do what? She's throwing up. How do you help somebody do that?" I looked at John. Why, I don't know. He was laughing his as off. I said, "You're the one who should be helping her. She's your girlfriend." He said, "She ain't my girlfriend. She's just the girl that's here tonight." Sandra said, "You guys are unbelievable. I'm going to get some towels from the bathroom. Can you at least keep an eye on her and make sure she doesn't fall off the balcony?" I said, "Yeah, no problem." Then John said, "Don't worry about it, she ain't gonna fall."

We sat there, waiting for Sandra to come back with the towels. I told John that he should go over and stay with Rita, until Sandra got back. He said he didn't want to get any throw up on him. Then he told me to calm down. I looked over at Rita. She looked like she was almost finished throwing up. Believe it or not, I actually started feeling sorry for her. I never thought that would happen. I started walking toward Rita just as Sandra came back with the towels. I walked over to her with Sandra. She had stopped throwing up. But she was moaning and spitting up a little bit. Sandra put a towel around her shoulders and I asked her how she was feeling. She said, "I feel like shit, Tony. What do you give a fuck, how I feel?" She started to cry and Sandra put her arm around her. Then she started coughing. Sandra said, "Just calm down Rita. Try to relax." But it was no use. Now she was crying and coughing. Then, she farted a couple of times, really loud. It was just too much to take. I started laughing and turned around to look at John. I knew that was a big mistake but I didn't give a fuck. He was sitting there smoking a joint. He looked back at me and said, "I told you not to go over there man." I said, "Rita, I'm sorry. I know you're having a tough time." Then I went over and sat next to John. I said, "This is fuckin' unbelieveable. Is this night ever gonna end?" John handed me the joint and said, "What are you worried about, I gotta sleep with her tonight." I said, "Yeah, that's right. Don't worry about it. All you gotta do is wrap yourself in cellophane and stick a clothes pin on your nose. You should be ok."

    That was it. I tried to take a hit off the joint and spit it out, as we both got hysterical. We each tried to say something a couple of times but it got worse. Then Sandra walked over with Rita. Keep in mind they were both still naked. We were sitting on the couch trying to get a hold of ourselves. They were standing in front of the couch, looking down at us. And they just stood there. At this point, time kind of stood still. We both knew that whatever was said next, no matter who said it, was gonna set us off again. John looked at me and said, "Don't say it." I said, "Say what? Don't say what?" He said, "Whatever you're gonna say. Just don't say it." I said, "Don't worry about it." Then Rita said, "Fuck you Tony. Remember us? We're the two naked girls standing right in front of you." John said, "Oh shit, here it comes." I said, "Oh yeah, you girls must be here for the lingerie convention in the lobby tonight right?" Of course John was right. We were hysterical again. My stomach was killing me from laughing so hard. What happened next was the last thing I expected, the second time Sandra really surprised me, and the first time I saw Rita get pissed off at her. We were still laughing on the couch when Sandra went into a laughing fit of her own. She jumped onto my lap and said, "I think I love you, you crazy bastard." Then she grabbed my face with both hands and kissed me on the lips. I looked back at her and said, "Don't say that man. I ain't gonna be here long enough to fall in love." She said, "Then I'll love you until you leave. I don't care anymore, you're just funny." I started to laugh again and said, "Wow, thanks babe.

That was really nice." Then Rita said, "How could you love him at all? He's so annoying!" Sandra looked at her and said, "Shut the fuck up, Rita. I'm sick of your shit, ok? All you do is whine and complain about everything. The only time you're not doing that is when you're throwing up. You just need to shut up now!" John said, "Whoa, check that out! Hey Rita, I guess she shut you right the fuck up!" Sandra said, "You shut up too, John!" He looked at me and I said, "Don't play with her man. She's serious." Sandra looked at me and said, "That goes for you too, Tony! Can't we just fucking enjoy whatever time we have left? Is that too much to ask?"

    I looked around and said, "I'm sorry, you're right. We just get carried away sometimes." Sandra looked aback at me and said, "Excuse me. Sometimes?" I said, "Ok, we always get carried away." She said, "That's more like it." I looked at John again. Don't ask me why I kept doing that. It never helped. He just looked at me and smiled. I looked back at Sandra and said, "Whatever. I said I was sorry didn't I? What do you want from me?" Sandra said, "Nothing, I just want us all to be nice to each other." I said, "Fine, let's go back out onto the balcony and smoke another joint. We'll be nice to each other out there." We all started walking toward the balcony. It was hard to believe that these two girls had been naked through all of this shit. And we still hadn't gotten laid. Especially since John kept reminding me every fuckin' five minutes. While we were walking I could hear John laughing. I almost looked at him. Then I heard Rita whisper to him, "That's his answer to everything, 'let's smoke a joint'. He's such an asshole." John whispered back to her, "What can I say? That's the way he is. Just try to ignore him." I shook my head and looked over my shoulder at John. He looked right into my eyes and just lost it. He was hysterical as we got onto the balcony. Sandra said, "Tony, what did you say to him? You said you were going to be nice?" I said, "What the fuck! What do you mean? I'm nice. I didn't say. He's the one who. I'm not the one. Why do I have to? Hey, fuck this. I'm not gonna put up with. Can't you see that? Oh wow man. He's the one. I'm just standing here. Why do I have to? Don't start with me, man. I'm telling you now." John was laying face down across one of the tables, laughing his ass of. When Rita said, "What the fuck is he talking about?" John fell off the table into one of the chairs and said, "Leave him alone. He's gonna go fuckin' nuts." Rita said, "No, I want to know what his problem is." I said, "I think I'm gonna punch Rita right in the fuckin' mouth man. Here I go. Get out of my fuckin' way." John got up just as I started toward Rita. He stepped in front of me and got me in a bear hug. He put his arms around me and picked me up off the ground. I looked down at him and said, "What the fuck are you doing? Put me down, ya prick." He said, "I'll put you down when you calm down." I said, "How the fuck am I supposed to calm down like this? Put me down!" He tightened his grip on me and squeezed real hard. I thought to myself; look at this fuckin' shit. On top of all the other pain in the ass bullshit that's been going on for the past two days, I gotta deal with this now. Being held up in the air by a nut like John. Plus, he was squeezing all the air out of me. As if that wasn't bad enough, Rita and Sandra started laughing, as they watched this whole scene. With whatever breath I had left, I looked at John and whispered, "Put me down, motherfucker!" He said, "Are you gonna stop?" I couldn't take it anymore. John was pretty wasted and probably didn't realize how hard he was squeezing. I had no air left in me. I couldn't answer him even if I wanted to. Now, all three of them were laughing. Then Rita said, "Fuck him. Keep squeezing him John!" I couldn't breathe and had to do something fast. I slapped John on the top of his head as hard as I could. He dropped me and started screaming at me. When I hit the floor, I fell backwards and landed on my ass. John said, "That really hurt man. What did you do that for?" I was still sitting on the floor, trying to catch my breath. I said, "What did I do that for? I did it because I couldn't fuckin' breathe, man." John said, "I was just trying to calm you down." I said, "Yeah, I know what you were trying to do. But that's not what you were doing. What you were doing was choking me to death. You just didn't realize it. I didn't want to hit you but I had to. I had no choice." John said, "So it was a misunderstanding then. Ok, that makes sense." I said, "Yeah, it was a misunderstanding. Let's just not have another one. This shit's fuckin' wearing me out."

  I got up off the floor and walked over to John. He handed me a joint and said, "Here, light that up." I said, "Yeah, ok, how's your head man?" He said, "It's good, don't worry about it." I lit up the joint. Then Sandra said, "Hello! What the hell is going on here? I don't understand whatever just happened. But right before whatever it was that did happen; we had all agreed to try to be nice to each other. I mean, how many fuckin' times is this going to happen?" I looked at John and he said, "She's right man." I looked back at him and said, "She is?" He said, "Yeah, she is." I said, "Ok, she's right! So what do we do now? And don't hand me another joint. I think we smoked about ten fuckin' joints already. There must be something else we can do." John looked at me and said, "You're right man. We'll have one more drink and call it a night." I said, "That's more like it, but that is definitely the last one." He said, "Yeah, ok. Sandra, Rita, we're going out on the balcony." Then he put his arm around me and said, "Let's go buddy. We'll go out there and relax."

Sandra and Rita walked toward the balcony. We followed right behind them. I heard Rita say to Sandra, "I wonder what's going to happen out there this time." Sandra just kept walking and said, "Who knows." On the way out there, I couldn't take my eyes off both of their naked asses. I looked at John and said, "You know what?" He looked back at me and said, "No, what?" I said, "This is the fourth time we went out on the balcony to relax and it hasn't happened yet. What makes you think we can do it this time?" By the time I had finished asking the questions we were on the balcony. He looked at me and said, "Don't worry about it." He walked over to the ice bucket and pulled out four beers. He handed one to each of us and said, "We're gonna have one more beer out here and relax. Anthony doesn't think we can do that." Sandra said, "Gee, I wonder why." John said, "Exactly. So let's prove him wrong." I said, "That's it? That's your big fucking plan? Ok, I'll play along." Sandra walked over and sat on my lap. Then Rita said, "My God, Tony! You're such and asshole. Why can't you just go along with what John is trying to do? I don't know how he even puts up with you. You're so annoying. I mean, really. He's such a nice guy. He's even trying to be really nice to you right now. But do you give him a break? No, you don't. You just keep breaking his balls. You never just shut up. That's what I hate about you the most. You just keep talking and talking. Even when we're all sick of hearing you, you just keep going on and on. And you never stop. I mean, really. Do I have to draw you a fucking picture? We're all tired of listening to you. And I'll tell you something else. I'll bet that John and Sandra are wishing right now that you'd finally just shut the fuck up. And while I'm at it, I might as well tell you something else." I said, "No, what you might as well do is shut the fuck up. You know why? Because I'm sick of listening to you and nobody gives a fuck what you're talking about anyway. You know what I'm saying, you fuckin' whack job?"

Nobody said a word. We all just stood there looking at each other. It was quiet for the first time in God knows how long. Then John started laughing. He looked at me and I said, "You believe this shit?" Rita looked at Sandra and said, "See, there he goes again." I looked at her and said, "Hey dipwad! I ain't going nowhere again, especially with you. Once is enough. You need to count your blessings. You've been a pain in the ass for two days now. I'm ready to duct tape you to the service elevator and send you down to the compactor room." John put his arm around me and said, "Hey Tony, calm down this ain't City

Plaza." I said, "She don't know that." He laughed and said, "Yeah, but we do." I said, "Ok, I see what you're saying. Forget about the duct tape. But I gotta tell you something and I'm serious now. You gotta take this pain in the ass into the bedroom or wherever the fuck else you want to take her. But you gotta get her away from me. I can't fuckin' take it anymore. Let's do what we gotta do with these girls and be done with it. I can't wait to get on a plane and get the fuck out of here. My California days are over. You know what I'm saying." John just stood there looking at me, as only he can. He had a way of doing that. Nobody else could look at me like that. He put his hands on my shoulders and said, "Booby, listen to me." I said, "Booby? What the fuck does that mean? I never heard you talk like that before." He said, "It's a Jew word I borrowed for a second." I said, "Are you fuckin' kidding me? You're borrowing Jew words now? For what?" He said, "Forget about the Jew word. You said your California days are over. I was just trying to tell you that we were in Las Vegas now." I said, "I know where the fuck I am. What's the difference if we're talking about California or Las Vegas? They're both out here right next to each other. I wanna get back over there to New York. You know that. Why are you breaking my fuckin' balls?" I knew he was going to laugh but I had to make my point. So, while he was laughing I said, "Let's just get laid or go to sleep. I don't care anymore. Whichever is the fastest way to tomorrow. Because that's where I want to be. Finally! You know what I'm saying?"

    At some point, the girls must have gone to another room because they were gone. It was about six o'clock in the morning by now and I was done. John said, "Ok, I know what you're saying. I'll find the girls. Then we'll smoke one more joint and go to sleep." I said, "I ain't smoking no more fuckin' pot, man. When I smoke pot, I like to laugh and have a good time. If you bring Rita back out here, I ain't gonna be able to do that." He looked at me and said, "Yeah, You're right. Let's go inside and settle in for the night." We walked in from the balcony and looked around the room. It was empty. We walked toward the master bedroom and heard somebody crying. We didn't have to say a word. We both knew it was Rita. I looked at John and said, "Do you believe this fuckin' shit? Get her the fuck out of my bedroom and do something with her." He said, "I will just calm down." I looked at him and said, "Calm down? I've been trying to do that for two fuckin' days. How the fuck am I supposed to do that?" He looked at me and said, "All I said was, calm down. I didn't say I knew how you could do it." When I looked at him, we both laughed. I wasn't surprised anymore about how weird things were. I was at the point where I expected everything that happened would be weird and I was right. But I knew we both didn't give a fuck anymore. And somehow, that helped. We gave each other a hug then he went into the room to get Rita. Somehow we managed to get into our own bedrooms, finally.

    Sandra and I had a really nice night. We did what we had to do and really enjoyed ourselves. Who the fuck knows what John and Rita were doing. Anyway, when we got up, we got the girls a limo to take them back to L.A. John and me took a cab to the Las Vegas airport and booked a flight back to New York. We were on our way home, man. The flight back was almost as annoying as being in California. But we didn't care. In a few hours the plane would touch down at Kennedy Airport and we'd be home. We would deal with everything else from that point on.

Chapter 19

It didn't take long for me to get used to being back home. I sat down with Rocco and talked about working at City Plaza again. I had worked there before, and it was as good a place as any to get my feet back on the ground. Rocco was always there if you needed help, as long as you were willing to put in an honest day's work, and if you weren't an asshole, he'd help you. We had a lot of history between us, and it was really good of him to help me, but like I said, he was good that way.

Being back at City Plaza really brought back some memories. The first time I worked there was around 1976 or 1977 right after I left Cornell Medical Library. The place was just being built. It was between 42nd and 43rd Streets and 9th and 10th Avenues. It was two, 43 story towers; one on 9th Avenue and the other on 10th. In between, there was an Olympic size swimming pool, tennis courts and racquetball courts. It was really something. It was built primarily for housing the theater district and the elderly in the neighborhood. It was partly subsidized by the Government. It was affordable for people in need, but what the Government or anybody else didn't know was that it was going to be run by us.

This is not to say the place wasn't run correctly. Rocco was really good at what he did. This was no different. He was the building manager, and he was in charge, period. The building ran through him from the maintenance staff to all the contractors, engineering, plumbing, you name it. All union problems, scheduling problems and overtime also went to him. We were the maintenance staff.

There were so many different personalities. I was brought into be kind of an assistant to Rocco. I say kind of because I wasn't in the union yet. I really got the job only because of Rocco. The union staff really didn't take me seriously, but they had to because of Rocco. This caused a lot of problems at first, but of course, that didn't matter either. I took all the maintenance calls in the office and dispatched the work to the staff. I got to know the staff pretty well after a while and things began to run smoothly.

It was during this time that I began my friendship with John Donovich; a friendship that is ongoing to this day (33 years later). Looking back to those days and right up until now, I still didn't know who was more whacked, him or me. We pushed everything to the limit. We did odd work, and we kept our jobs alive, barely. The job at City Plaza could have given us stability, and if we took it seriously and put our time in, we could have been retired by now with full union benefits. But we didn't take anything seriously. City Plaza became our playground, and there's nothing we didn't play with.

We did all kinds of work. Besides dispatching the work from the maintenance office, I also worked with some of the guys. One of the guys contracted by the building was Nino Formaggi. He was an old time laborer with a temper. One of the building managers was a guy named Gerry Belzo. This guy was like a cartoon character with a voice to match. Nino hated him. My friend, John, could imitate Gerry Belzo's voice perfectly. That set the stage for one of the funniest situations I can remember.

I was working with Nino in the 9th avenue building. Electricians were done running some cable, and nothing could set Nino off more than a call from Gerry Belzo while he was working a job. John just finished a job in the building and was sitting in the office by the phones. Nino and I were working right outside the office. I could see John from the ladder I was working on. We could see inside the office, but we couldn't hear anything that was going on in there. The phone rang where we were working. Nino was up on the other ladder so I got down to answer the call. Nino hated to be interrupted while was working. He was great to work with because he knew so much about his trade, and you couldn't help but learn just by being around him. But he was the last person you'd want to be around when he was pissed off.

I answered the phone, and I could hear Gerry Belzo's voice yelling and screaming on the other end. He was really pissed off. Something about a job Nino was working on in the other building. "Get that Guinea bastard on the phone right now; I don't care what he's doing"! Gerry screamed "in that voice". You couldn't help but laugh whenever you heard it. I would have laughed if I wasn't the one that had to tell Nino what he said. I knew that him having to come to the phone would set him off, never mind what he had just said about him.

I had no choice but to put the phone down and tell Nino the phone was for him. "Anthony, I'm busy", he said in the Italian accent I was so used to. I thought for a second and then said, "It's Gerry Belzo, he wants to talk to you." "Fuck him", Nino replied,

"I'm busy. I'll call him back". I told him Gerry was really pissed, and he wanted to talk to him right now. Well, that did it. Nino started coming down the ladder cursing in Italian the whole way.

When he picked up the phone and said hello, I could hear Gerry screaming over the phone. "Get over here right now and finish this job you fucked up this morning you bastard." Nino's face started to turn red. He couldn't even talk. "I'll kill that asshole. Anthony come on, I'm gonna kick his ass this time." It wasn't until right at that moment that I happened to look inside the office. I freaked out. I could see John laughing his ass off with the phone in his hand. Right, then it hit me; John was imitating Gerry Belzo's voice on the phone. He made believe he was Gerry and was screaming at Nino. All I could think of was Gerry sitting in the office in the other building and having no idea that Nino was already on his way to kick his ass. Of course, I had to go with him. All the way there I kept thinking of the poor guy, Gerry, who didn't know he had called him.

We went through the garage to the 10th Avenue building's maintenance office. Nino was yelling and cursing in Italian all the way there. I could only imagine what was going to happen when we got there. We got to the maintenance office and Nino kicked the door open and said, "OK, you son of a bitch, you called me on the phone while I'm working, I'll kick your ass!" Of course, Gerry is sitting there with his mouth open not knowing what the hell is going on. "I never called you, what the hell are you talking about?" Nino freaked out even more. "Don't lie to me you bastard." Nino went right over the desk after him. Gerry was screaming, "Get off me you crazy bastard!" We had to break them apart, and somehow, I could hear John laughing his ass off in the other building. It was just another day at work at City Plaza.

The next day things had calmed down somewhat, and I was working a plumbing job with Nino. We had to replace the water pipes in all the showers in the women's locker room of the health club. Most of the women that went to the health club really needed to be there. But sometimes you got lucky and there were some nice looking women in there.

We were finishing up one of the shower stalls one morning. I was nailing up the sheet rock over the water lines when I saw this really sharp looking woman come into the locker room. She started getting undressed. I couldn't believe it because I was sure she saw me there. Either she didn't see me, or she didn't care that I was there. One thing I did know for sure was that I couldn't care less, one way or the other. She had her blouse off and started taking off her pants. She was doing all of this with her back to me so I still really didn't know if she knew I was there. Meanwhile, I kept hammering away at the sheet rock. I figured she must be able to hear me so I'll just enjoy the show. I was putting up the last piece when she turned around to face me. I guess she knew I was there. She put both her hands behind her back and unhooked her bra, then she dropped her arms to her side and looked at me as the bra hit the floor. She had beautiful tits standing straight out with big brown nipples. That was it. My arm came down with the hammer and drove the nail right through the sheet rock and into the main water supply line of the building. It was instant chaos. Water pressure began to drop throughout the building from the tenth floor down. Alarms started sounding through the health club and the rest of the building. Nino was running around screaming as water started shooting out from behind the sheet rock into my face and everywhere else. I couldn't believe what was happening. One minute I'm looking at a beautiful pair of tits and the next minute I'm in the middle of a full scale building disaster with the fire department probably already on its way because of the automatic alarm system. Anytime you have a drop in water pressure like that, the system figures it's because the sprinkler system is activated not because a maintenance guy with a hard on is hanging sheet rock. Plus, in the back of my mind, I'm already picturing Rocco running through the door wanting to know what the fuck is going on. I wasn't exactly going to be up for Employee of the Month for this one.

It was about four or five hours before things calmed down, and the building was functional again. Unfortunately, I didn't have to wait that long for Rocco's reaction. He was furious. I really couldn't blame him. I caused a huge problem for him, and it really didn't matter that it was unintentional.

Usually when you mess up like that, you wind up cleaning out vacant apartments to get them ready to be rented out again. This was no different It was a pain in the ass job. You had to clean every room, vacuum the rugs, clean the bathrooms until they were spotless and touch up the paint job as needed. In this case, Rocco would be inspecting the apartments I was working in.

By this time, Rocco had figured out John's role in the whole Nino, Gerry Belzo incident so he was also working with me cleaning out the apartments. As usual, we both felt bad about what we had done. Rocco was really a good guy, and he didn't deserve the things we put him through. We never meant to cause him problems, but ultimately, we were his responsibility.

* * * * *

John and I were cleaning out apartments for a day or two when things started to get really boring. That's the kind of work it was. And it was supposed to be. That's why Rocco was making us do it in the first place. Like I said, we felt bad about what we had done, but eventually, that didn't matter anymore. It wasn't long before we started to think of ways to have some fun.

We were working on the 26th floor of the 10th Avenue building, and we were really getting bored. We knew Rocco was at the track that day and that didn't help. We were cleaning the bathroom tiles when John went out on the terrace to have a cigarette. He said, "Hey, come out here and look at this". I went out on the terrace and looked down. In front of the building was Juan Cortez. He was one of the security supervisors of the 9th Avenue building, but he was a goody two shoes, jerk off that wormed his way into the security department. This was too much to pass up.

I don't remember whose idea it was, but we decided to dump a couple of gallons of water off the terrace and see if we could hit him with it. It wouldn't be easy because we were 26 stories up, but we figured it was worth a try.

The first couple of pails of water got caught up in the wind and came down across 10th Avenue somewhere. We figured we needed more weight. This time, we filled up a couple of buckets of water. We dumped them both over the terrace wall. There was no wind, and they headed straight down. He was going to get both buckets. We watched until he got nailed with the water. There he was in his perfectly pressed security uniform. We pulled our heads back in just as he started to look up. We laughed our asses off. We figured we better get back to work in case somebody saw us. We couldn't be sure if he saw us or not.

We didn't have to wait too long. After about five minutes, the doorbell was ringing continually. One of us went to the door while the other kept working as if nothing had happened. It was Juan Cortez. He was really pissed. He was also very wet. It was very hard to keep a straight face, but we had to. He kept saying, "I saw you guys, I saw you guys"! "What?" we asked him. "What the fuck are you talking about, we're up here busting our ass cleaning this apartment, and you come up here talking about people throwing water out the window. Are you nuts or something?" I told him, "Listen, I understand you're pissed off. You're all wet, but don't come up here accusing us, that ain't right." "Yeah", said John. "Think about it. Why would we do something so stupid? It must have been some kids or something,

We're not going to start throwing water off the terrace. We work here, and we're not going to jeopardize our jobs like that." He looked at us both for a few seconds and said, "Come on you guys, I'm not stupid you know." And right then I remember thinking, I can't believe he's starting to buy this line of shit we were handing him. We had him. He said, "Come on, really, you guys didn't do it?" "No", we said. "We wouldn't do something like that, not to you, you're our friend. Why would we do something like that?" He looked at us again and said, "I guess you're right, but I could have sworn I saw you." We looked back at him and said, "Come on, we just explained to you, we would never do something like that, come on."

It was unbelievable that this guy could look up, see us both, and we could still convince him we didn't do it. And this was a security supervisor! We finally got him to leave, and we closed the door behind him, looked at each other and started to laugh. We laughed our way out onto the terrace. We were laughing at what had just happened. But we were also laughing because without even saying a word, we knew what had to happen next. As soon as we saw him take his post in front of the building, we did it again! Juan Cortez, security supervisor, too funny!

Now we were in deep shit, and we knew it. But somehow we either knew things would work out, or we really didn't care if they didn't. It didn't help that Rocco's day at the track was ruined because his beeper was going off all day about what had happened. We knew what was coming, and we didn't have to wait long for it either. Rocco was really pissed. Things got really strict for us for a while after that. It took a long time for things to get back to normal after that. We knew our days were numbered, and this situation didn't help.

As I've said, my friendship with John Donovich is ongoing. Even though there was a time between the mid 80's and the mid 90's that we never saw each other. For some reason, we took ten years off, who knows why. Life takes you in different directions sometimes.

Anyway, right before we lost touch for a while, he helped me out with something I decided to do. John grew up in Manhattan. His family lived on 43rd Street right off of 10th Avenue. That section of the city was known as "Hell's kitchen." With good reason. If you were from there, you knew why. If you weren't, you didn't.

John and I became close friends during the time we both worked at City Plaza. But it didn't happen right away. I was given the job as Assistant Building Manager because of my friendship with Rocco. Not because I had any idea what I was doing. And everybody knew it. I would be running the maintenance department, that's where John worked. They weren't exactly thrilled to be working for somebody who was just handed the job because of who I knew. They also knew they had no say. It didn't matter what they thought, Rocco called the shots, bottom line. That didn't help either. There was a lot of tension at first, and it was hard on all of us. They were a tough bunch of guys. Their attitude towards me was, "Who the fuck is this asshole?" I understood how they felt and did my best to let them know I didn't expect any special treatment. I just wanted to fit in, but talk is cheap especially with people from the street.

So it took a couple of weeks, but they accepted me. And John became my closest friend. It was during this time we connected. We didn't know it then, but were so out of control we had different reasons for being that way, but that didn't matter. We handled things the same way. At that point, both of our lives were a mess, but we didn't give a fuck. We were both doing whatever we wanted to do and whoever didn't like it, could just go and fuck themselves.

Chapter 20

The year was 1984. John and I had been breaking all the rules for about eight years now. We had both been fired at our jobs in City Plaza. He was working in the theater district at several different box offices, and I worked at a building in lower Manhattan. I was a member of the International Union of Operating Engineers. Who the fuck knows why? I just wound up there.

I had no stability in my life. I was drifting from job to job. I had no idea that in a couple of years, I would meet Barbara and my life would begin to take shape. I was in and out of trouble at work and on the street. But as usual, I couldn't care less. I was so used to having problems that I thought it was normal, and whenever I thought it wasn't, all I had to do was call John. He was always in at least as much trouble as I was, sometimes more. I knew that no matter how fucked up things were or how much trouble I was in, he would understand, and if I needed him, he would back me up no matter what. So when I decided to drive to Syracuse, New York, in the middle of the night to find the girl who stole my car and walked out on me eight years ago, I called John.

I was working the four to midnight shift at the time. For some reason, I had been thinking about Malory and what she had done to me all those years ago. Probably because I had nothing better to do. I had never gotten over what she had done. We had been living together for four years. One day she packed her stuff into our new car and disappeared, while I was at work. I had always wanted to see her again, just once. Not because I wanted her back, I didn't, but it had taken me so long to get over her and what she had done. I didn't know what bothered me more, the fact that she left me or how she left me. I had always wanted to put her in a position to do what she had managed to avoid. I had been through so much shit because of her. The emotional aspect was bad enough, but she took my car. I had to ride the subway for a year until I could afford another one, which gave me a lot of time to think about what she did. What I wanted to force her to do was to have to look me in the eye. She had done all this without ever having to face me. I thought she owed me at least that.

But I wasn't stupid. It had been eight years, even if I was able to pull it off and surprise her by showing up at her parent's house, it probably would mean nothing and would accomplish even less. If I had anything else going on in my life, I wouldn't even be thinking about something like this, but I didn't. A friend of mine did some digging and got her parents phone number. We had a girl call them saying she was an old college roommate. She gave them some bullshit story about a college reunion and was able to find out that Malory was living with them. When they asked for her name and phone number, she told them she would be flying in from California in two weeks and would call back when she got to New York. Then she hung up before they could ask her anything else. This would buy us some time, and give me a two week window of opportunity to make a move.

I knew it was nuts. But now, the whole thing started to gain momentum. I started to plan the whole thing. I figured what the fuck. I couldn't tell anybody what I was going to do especially my family. They would only worry. I didn't expect anybody to understand because I had serious doubts of my own. It was a crazy plan that was based on feelings I had eight years ago, and there were risks involved. Who knew what would happen once I got up there? I knew it was stupid and would probably be a waste of time, but I already knew I was going to do it.

So I called John to tell him what I wanted to do. Whenever I was going to do something that nobody would understand, I always called him, we understood each other. We were different, but the same. Whatever the fuck that means. We never judged each other. We both just figured if we decided to do something, there must be a good reason.

When he picked up the phone, I said, "I need to take a ride to Syracuse, New York. I'm going to leave after work one day this week. I need somebody to come with me. I get off at midnight so we'll be driving all night. Can you help me out?" I could hear John laughing over the phone. I said, "I know it's a lot to ask." He said, "No, it ain't, are you alright?" I said, "Yeah, I just want to take care of something. I'll explain on the way." He said, "What night you wanna go?" And that was it. For us, it was as simple as that. Once I knew John was going with me, I relaxed a little bit. Not because it was relaxing to have him around, I just knew if anything happened that I couldn't handle, he would be the difference. If I was alone, anything could happen, but I didn't think there was anything that could happen in Syracuse the two of us couldn't handle.

I told John to meet me Tuesday night after work. We met in lower Manhattan when I got off work just after midnight. It was going to take about seven hours to drive up there so we knew we'd be on the road all night. The ride would be long and boring, and we had both just worked all night. Plus, we really had no idea where the fuck we were going. All we had was an address in Syracuse, New York that we would be looking for in the middle of the night. For some reason, none of this seemed to bother us. We figured we had everything we would need. We had a case of Budweiser on ice in a huge cooler on the back seat. And to help us stay awake all night driving up there, we brought about a half ounce of cocaine. We also had an ounce of pot in the trunk just in case. We were all set and ready to go. We hit the road around 12:30. We drove uptown on the Henry Hudson Parkway. We picked up the Major Deegan then the New York State Thruway, and we were on our way. We hit the Thruway around 1 o'clock in the morning. I figured we had about a seven hour ride ahead of us. My plan was to get to Malory's parents house before she left for work in the morning. Even though I had no idea when that was, but at least I had a plan. That was good enough for me so we drove on. I had convinced myself that I was doing the right thing.

Looking back on what we did that night, and now writing about it after all these years, really blows me away. How the fuck did we think we could do something like this without getting into some kind of trouble? The answer to that is a simple one. In those days, we just did things. The idea of getting into trouble never entered our minds, not because we were cocky or even confident in what we were doing. We just never considered it and that, more than anything else, explains how fucking whacked we were. Everything we were doing on the way up there and whatever we wound up doing once we got there was against the law. We were on the New York State Thruway, drinking, doing blow and smoking pot in the middle of the night, and we thought it was great! We were having a good time.

It was about four o'clock in the morning, and we figured we were about three hours from Syracuse. We had already gone through half the blow and almost all of the beer. Once the beer ran out, we just did more blow. We figured if we ran out of blow, we would just smoke pot. For some reason, that made sense to us. So we drove on.

The car I was driving at the time was a Fiat Strada, a real piece of shit. I bought it at a used car lot for about $1,300.00. I wasn't sure if we would make it up to Syracuse without the car falling apart. And making back was a real long shot. Of course, that didn't bother us either.

It was about six o'clock in the morning when we noticed the noise the car was making. We had no idea when it started. For all we knew, it could have been going on for hours. It sounded like one of the tires. We couldn't do anything about it so we kept going. As far as we could tell, we were about an hour from Syracuse. Somehow, we were ahead of schedule. We decided to stop at the next major town. Somewhere we thought we could get a cup of coffee and dump all the empty beer cans.

It was almost 6:30 when we pulled off the Thruway. I guess it was a town because it had a name. There was a gas station and a shit diner. We were both in a bad frame of mind. We were drunk, tired and in no mood for anybody. Plus, we knew the car was starting to give us trouble, but we needed gas and coffee. I wasn't sure which, but I knew that between the gas station and the diner, somebody would piss us off.

We pulled into the gas station first. We asked the attendant to fill the tank and check the oil. He was a nice enough guy, but wouldn't shut the fuck up until we told him to. He was okay after that. One of the tires looked a little fucked up, but so were we. So we paid for the gas and headed for the diner. We pulled into the diner parking lot. It was about seven o'clock in the morning. We parked the car and just looked at the place. I looked at John and said, "Man, look at this fucking place." He said, "Yeah, what about it? We're just going to get coffee. For all we know this could be the best place in the whole shit town." We laughed and I said, "You're probably right let's go."

We walked into the place and looked around. It was a typical, upstate, New York dump. There were two or three truck drivers on one end of the counter. On the other end there was a fat guy in overalls sitting with a pretty decent looking woman. We walked over and sat down between them. The waitress came over and she made the fat guy look good. And of course, she had an attitude that only a person that looked like shit could have. We could feel that everybody in the place was checking us out. Two guys in jeans and leather jackets without even saying a word didn't exactly blend in.

When she came over, she said, "You guys lost or something?" John said, "No, when we planned our trip, this was one of the places we wanted to see." If we thought everybody was checking us out before, we knew it now. We couldn't care less. We knew we were unwelcome. We just didn't give a fuck. We figured even though the people in the place were nasty and didn't want us there; they were also fat and stupid so we weren't worried.

So she's standing in front of us, ugly as shit, and says, "What can I get you?" I ordered coffee for both of us then John asked her where the men's room was. Before she could answer, the fat guy in the overalls said, "It's right next to the ladies room." A few people started laughing and making comments under their breath. We looked at each other then leaned back on our stools to look at that guy. I said, "John, did you hear something?" He said, "Yeah, it sounded like it came from that fat fuck over there." I said, "You think so, you think he could be fat and stupid?" He said, "Maybe let's find out." I had a black jack in the pocket of my leather jacket. A black jack is a ten inch piece of rubber filled with lead.

We both got up. I stood facing the guys on my right with the black jack in my hand. John walked over to the fat guy. When he saw John walking toward him, he turned and said, "You want something over here, asshole?" John said, "Yeah, I want something." Then he punched him right in the fucking forehead knocking him right off his stool. The guy hit the floor like he was shot. The girl that was sitting with the guy started screaming. John looked at her and said, "Shut the fuck up." Then he walked back to where I was standing. I was watching the guys on my right. I didn't know what was going to happen. If one of them made a move, I was going to crack him across the mouth with the blackjack. That didn't happen. When John came over, we sat back down at the counter as if nothing had happened.

We really didn't want any of this to happen. We had enough things going on already, but you can't just let people fuck with you. You just can't. We always felt that way, and after driving all night, being drunk, hung over and tired, the last thing we were going to put up with was an asshole. That's why I didn't think we would be able to go through this town without something happening.

Meanwhile, we're still trying to get a cup of fucking coffee. By now the guy had gotten back up on his stool, and the fat waitress was coming back. When she came over, she said, "You boys really know how to make yourselves right at home, don't you?" I said, "Yeah, well, none of this would have happened if people could just mind their own fucking business." She said, "I'll get you boys some coffee." I noticed that the girl that was with the idiot was on the pay phone. I looked at John and said, "This ain't over yet, buddy." He said, "Why, what happened now?" I said, "The girl with the guy you just hit is on the phone. She's probably calling the biggest jerk she knows." John said, "I can't believe it. How many people do we have to hit before we get a cup of coffee?" I said, "I guess we're going to find out."

I was really getting sick of this shit. We were minding our own business, not bothering anybody, and we were having nothing but trouble. I said, "John, this is what we're going to do. We'll have a quick cup of coffee here then get one to go. Then we'll hang out in the parking lot and see who shows up." Whoever was coming, I didn't want to make it easy for him. We weren't going to just sit there and have somebody walk in on us.

She hung up the phone and went back to the guy with the lump on his head. We waited a few minutes and finished our coffee. We ordered two coffees to go and paid the check. We went outside and moved the car to the back of the parking lot, then we had our coffee and waited. I took a baseball bat out of the trunk and put it on the front seat. From where we were, we could see the entrance to the parking lot and inside the diner. We could see the girl going to the phone booth two or three times. By going outside, we had obviously fucked up her plan. I knew she had told whoever she called that we were sitting at the counter. That's why we waited ten minutes after her first phone call before we went outside. I figured whoever she called would be on their way by then. Now we could just wait and watch. If a truck full of guys pulled into the parking lot, we could just drive away. By the time they walked into the diner and figured out what was going on, we'd be gone. But if another asshole showed up by himself, we were going to make him pay.

We were at the back of the parking lot, sipping our coffee, when the old Buick pulled into the diner. The guy never saw us and pulled up to the front door. It was obvious that this was the idiot the girl had called. But we waited to make sure. We kept an eye on the girl inside the diner. She would tip us off. When she saw the guy's car, she got up and started walking toward the front door. We were sure now and made our move. She came outside and walked up to the car. They were talking in front of the car when we pulled up along side. When we got out of the car, she said, "That's them." I looked at her and said, "Who's this fucking asshole?" They just looked at us. I said, "John, what do you think? Who could this idiot be?" John said, "I don't know, I guess they just keep coming." Then the guy said, "Are you guys looking for trouble?" I said, "What we were looking for was a cup of coffee and because of your big mouth friend in the diner, we wind up talking to you. So here's the deal, you can either drive back into your stupid fucking life or get hurt, real bad. Keep in mind that the first word out of your mouth is going to tell us what you've decided."

He was a pretty big guy, and he took his time before he answered me, but I expected him to. While I was, talking to him, John had taken the baseball bat out of the car. Nobody noticed but me. I looked at him and said, "So, what's it going to be?'" He said, "Fuck you, you guys think you can come up here and fuck with us?" As soon as he finished the sentence, John swung the bat and caught him flush across the chest. It was a brutal sound.

The force of the blow knocked him off his feet. He went straight back, bounced off the hood of his car and over the other side. Now the girl was screaming for the second time of the day. She ran back into the diner, and we knew it was time to leave. As we backed out of the parking lot, we could hear the guy moaning. We circled around the bar and got back on the Thruway. From the entrance ramp to the Thruway, we could see the guy lying on the ground.

We drove for about another 40 minutes and somehow found the exit. At least, it was the exit we thought we needed. We got off and somehow found the address we were looking for. As we pulled up to the house, I saw my car in the driveway. I couldn't believe it. The last time I saw the car, it was brand new. It had been about seven years, and the car looked old. But you know your car. Seeing the car made me realize how much time had gone by.

I was really pissed off. I said, "There it is. I can't believe it. She's still driving around in my fucking car." I told John to pull over. Then I realized I was driving. John looked at me and said, "Are you nuts? What do you mean there it is, I can't believe it? I thought you said you knew she was up here with the car." I said, "Yeah I said that, but I didn't believe it." He said, "So you brought me up here without knowing if she was even here?" I said. "If I told you I didn't know, would you have come?" He said, "No, no way." Then I said, "And if you had something to take care of and wanted me there, you wouldn't lie to me a little bit to make sure I came with you?" John thought about it for a second, then he said, "Yeah, I would, you're right." I said, "All right then" He said, "Next time you're lying to me, tell me. I won't give a fuck."

It was about eight o'clock in the morning. We parked across the street from the house. I couldn't stop looking at the car the driveway. It brought back so many memories. I couldn't believe I found her. That was weird enough. But the thought of seeing her again after all this time, was really too much. We had no idea if she would be coming out of the house or when that would be. So we did the only thing we could do, we sat and waited. We were pretty fucked up. We had been up all night driving we had also gone through a case of beer and who knows what else on the ride up. So my biggest fear was that we'd fall asleep. The whole trip would be wasted if we were sitting in the car sleeping when she came out. But by now, it was almost impossible to stay awake. We felt like shit. We were hung over and dead tired. We were both nodding off a little bit and would wake up when our heads dropped to our chest. I knew it was only a matter of time before we were both out cold.

I was asleep when I felt John slap me in the chest and say. "Is that her?" I was in a deep sleep when he hit me. I jumped up and said, "Who?" He said. "Who the fuck do you think? There's only one person we're looking for." I said, "Calm down, I was asleep. I forgot where the fuck I was." By now, she had gotten in the car and was backing out of the driveway. I was still half asleep and didn't get a good look at her. I started the car and when she pulled out, we followed her. John said. "Is that her, or what?" I said, "It must be. Unless she sold the car and we were sitting in front of the wrong house." He said, "What are you talking about?" I said, "Nothing. I'm just fucking with you. It's got to be her. Who else cold it be?" John looked at me and said. "I don't know, who else it could be. After this next intersection, pull up in front of her and cut her off. We'll make her pull over. Then we'll find out." I said, "I'm not gonna do that. With our luck there's gonna be a cop car around and we'll have to deal with that, too. He said "What else are you gonna do?" I told him I was going to follow her to wherever she was going. And when she got out of the car, I would deal with her then. He said. "Don't do that. Let's get this over with, cut her off." I said, "No, I'm gonna do this the way I want." He said. "I think you're making a mistake. Come on cut her off." I said, "I'm not cutting her off." He said, "Come on man, do it. Do it now, then we'll have a beer and go home." I said. "Would you shut the fuck up? I got enough problems without arguing, with you." He said. "'Who the fuck do you think you're talking to?" By now we were screaming at each other. I said, "I've got a lot of things on my mind. I'm trying to follow this broad and you're fucking yelling at me. You wanna give me a break over here or what. This is an emotional time for me. I'm weak. I'm fucking weak man!" That was it. We looked at each other and busted out laughing. We were hysterical and we couldn't stop. It was like the absurdity of whole situation finally hit us. We were in a fit of laughter, slapping the dashboard and trying to stop

We were on a two lane street, following her in the right lane. We had no idea where we were going. We were still laughing when the guy on our left cut us off. He pulled right in front of us. I had to jam on the breaks to avoid hitting him. Now we were really pissed off. I wanted to stay right behind her because I didn't know where she was going. I pull into the left lane so I could pass the asshole who cut us off and get behind her again. As we pulled up next to the guy, he sped up and gave us the finger. John rolled down the window and said. "Hey, scumbag, we lose the car we are following because of you, we'll chase you down and leave you for dead!" While we were along side this jerk off, trying to pass him from the left lane, the car we were following was getting onto the entrance ramp to the highway. John said, "She's getting on to the highway. Cut this mother fucker off." I told John to roll down the window all the way. I grabbed the beer can from between my legs and threw it out the window at the guy in the car. He was right next to us and his window was wide open. The beer can hit him right in the fucking head and he swerved to the right. I pulled in front of him and across to the entrance ramp. The guy hit the curb and smashed into the guard rail. John said. "Fuck him, he got what he deserved." I looked at John and said. "Is everybody up here gonna fuck with us or what?" He lit a cigarette and said, "Who cares, we're winning ain't we?" I said "I care, we're starting to leave a trail." He said, "Nah, we ain't leaving no trail." I said, "Yeah we are. We're leaving a little bit of a trail now."

  Somehow, with all that was going on, we hadn't lost her. We were on the highway now right behind her. I didn't know if she knew what was going on or not. She could have seen what had happened in her rear view mirror. We drove another couple of miles and traffic started to build up. John said. "We should have cut her off back there, when we had the chance." I said "Are you gonna start again with that. I don't need this." He said, "OK, stay behind her." I said, "I'm behind her, ain't I?"

  The traffic was getting worse. So was the noise coming from my tires. The noise we had heard the night before was getting louder and sounded worse now. She started changing lanes, moving in and out of this traffic. Because of all the traffic, I couldn't make the same moves as her. It was getting harder to stay with her. As we passed the next exit, she pulled into the right lane. There was a truck on my right, so I couldn't get over right away. By the time I was able to change lanes, traffic had really slowed down. Plus, we were behind a truck and couldn't see anything. We were hardly moving now. We figured she had the same problem but couldn't see her. I was starting to get a bad feeling. Which I knew would only get worse as soon as I looked at John.

After a few minutes I said, "This fucking sucks. How could this happen?" I looked at John and he said, "I ain't saying nothing." I said, "Good, I hope that ain't a temporary condition. We'll see how long that lasts." Then he said, "Why didn't you cut her off when I told you to?" I said, "Here we go, that didn't take long did it?" He said, "I knew it, that's why I said let's get it over with." I said, "If you knew we were gonna be behind this fucking truck, you should have told me. I would have cut her off." He said, "Don't be an asshole. You know what I mean." I said, "Come on John . I don't want to fight. You're my friend. If we don't have each other, what do we have. Come on, let's be friends. Don't close the door on our relationship now. Not when I'm so vulnerable." He looked at me and said. "You're a sick fuck, I know you're breaking my balls because you don't talk like that. That ain't you. You're my friend and all that bullshit. Just pass this truck and let's get the fuck out of here you sick bastard."

In a minute I was able to pull past the truck. Traffic was starting to loosen up a little bit. I started moving in and out of lanes but she was nowhere in sight. It was an awful feeling. The thought of losing her now, after all we had been through was a sickening feeling. We kept driving. I was still moving fast, in and out of traffic. I figured it was the only chance we had to spot her. Before the next exit, we saw a hospital sign. One of those blue signs you see on the highway. It wasn't much but it was all we had. I knew she was a nurse so there was a good chance she was working there. We weren't sure but we couldn't pass the hospital without checking it out. I knew she could be working as a nurse anywhere. It didn't have to be at a hospital. I also knew that she could have been off today and just going somewhere else. But we couldn't pass up the hospital.

We didn't want to talk about it but we both felt that we had lost her. We followed the signs for the hospital. We were pretty bummed out. We found the hospital and pulled into the parking lot. I parked the car near the entrance and leaned back in my seat, John said "Let's give it up. What are you gonna do? Even if she is here you can't get to her now." I said. "I can t just leave now, without going in there. We've come too far." He said, "I know you're pissed off. But think of it this way. We took a ride and had a good time. We kicked some ass and got away with it. If you go in there now and something goes wrong, we'll not only have to deal with that, we might get busted for everything else we did. And this ain't some diner in the middle of the night. This is a major hospital in broad daylight. Think about that. And if there's any security in there, you're the first person there gonna look at. You're all fucked up and you really don't blend in with these people." I said. "Yeah, I know what you're saying. Roll a couple of joints; I'll be back in twenty minutes.

I got out of the car and walked into the hospital. As I walked over to the information desk, I could see the security guard checking me out. I knew I was gonna have to deal with him. He was a skinny goofball whose clothes looked way too big for him. He got to me just before I got to the desk. He said, "Excuse me, can I help you?" I said, "If you could. I would have asked you something." He just looked at me. I really wanted to punch him right in his fucking mouth. I knew I couldn't but I was in no mood for a jerk like him. I said. "Yeah, maybe you can. My cousin works here. She's a nurse. I wanted to surprise her. Her name is Malory Collins, can you help me?" He said, just ask the girl at the desk if she's working today. I said, "That's your idea of helping me. Telling me to do what I was going to do before you stopped me." He said. "Don't be a wise guy."

I said. "Let me tell you something. I just drove up here from New York City. I've been on the road all night long. I'm in no mood for somebody like you. I'm not bothering anybody and I haven't done anything wrong. So why don't you just leave me alone before you get hurt." Then I turned and walked away from him.

When I got to the desk, I waited for the girl to get off the phone. She hung, up and said. "Can I help you'," I said. "I hope so. I'm from out of town and wanted to surprise my cousin. She's a nurse and works at this hospital but I'm not sure which department. Can you tell me if she's working today?" I told her what her name was and waited while she looked it up. She looked back at me and said "'I'm sorry, we don't have anyone by that name working here." I could tell she was lying but there was nothing I could do. I thanked her and started walking out of the lobby. I was walking toward the door when I saw the idiot security guard standing by the door. I decided to just walk out. We didn't need any more trouble. As I was walking through the door I heard the guy say, "'Stay out of trouble wise guy." I turned around and walked back inside. He had a smirk on his face. I walked over and got right in his face. He was taller than me, but I didn't give a fuck. I was ready to take everything out on him. We were less than an inch apart. I looked up at him and said, "Listen jerk off, you wanna say something to me, say it now. I'll tear you up, motherfucker. And when I leave, you'll just be a mess on the floor.'" His eyes told me he wasn't gonna do anything. I thought about hitting him anyway. Then John walked through the door. He said. "Is she here?" I said. "No. she ain't here." I was still staring at the guy. John said. "So let's get out of here then. Who's this fucking idiot?'" I said. "This guy's been fucking with me ever since we got here." John looked at the guy, and said, "This asshole, fuck him. He ain't gonna cause us no trouble." Right then the guy said to us, "Listen, maybe I made a mistake. I shouldn't have talked to you that way. I'm sorry." I said, "No problem but if we get pulled over by the cops when we leave, we're gonna come back for you." He said, "I ain't gonna call the cops, don't worry." John said, "You better hope nobody else does either."

We walked out of the hospital and got into the car. We sat there for a minute and said nothing. We both knew that the whole fucking trip was for nothing. John said. "Fuck it. Let's get out of here. I said I can't believe we did all this for nothing." John said. "At least we didn't take any shit while we were up here. At least we can say that." I said, "Yeah. I know." It was depressing though. We could have gone back to her mother's house and waited again. But for how long? That really would have been tough. We were almost out of money and by now, we hadn't slept in two days. So we decided to leave.

It was going to be a brutal ride and we just wanted to get it over with. We figured the sooner we started, the sooner it would be over with. But that was easier said than done. We started out really optimistic, telling each other positive things about the trip. Which wasn't easy because there weren't many. We said things like, at least we didn't get into any trouble and we're on our way home. But I knew that wouldn't last.

We got on the thruway south and lit up a joint. We turned up the volume on the stereo and drove for two hours. We wanted to get a chunk of the ride behind us before we stopped for coffee. We went into one of those places on the thruway where everybody looks like they're from outer space. We were in and out in a hurry. We drove another two hours without stopping. It was a seven hour ride, give or take a few days. It had been almost four hours now. The reality of the trip had started to set in. Not to mention the noise the tire was making. Which was much worse by now.

We had been driving for four hours and I was already starting to nod off trying to stay awake. We had at least three more hours to go. I had no idea how I was going to stay awake. John was in worse shape than I was. He had already been falling in and out of sleep. I let him sleep just in case I needed him to drive. Not that I thought he could, or if he even had a license

Somehow, another hour had passed. The tire was making a really fucked up noise and I was finding it harder and harder to stay awake. I had to do something. I reached back and flipped open the lid of the cooler that was on the back seat. I knew it was empty and the ice had melted by now. But there was cold water in there. I grabbed a small towel off the back seat. I leaned back and dropped it into the cooler. I pulled it out of the cooler and squeezed it out. It was still dripping when I tied it around my head. It was ice cold and dripping, down the back of my neck. I threw in a Clapton tape and turned the volume up. I started singing along with the song, "Blues Power". My head was fucking frozen but I was wide awake. I'm flying down the thruway with a towel around my head and ice water dripping down by back. I looked like a fucking Arab, driving a Fiat. The music was blasting and I was singing along with it when John woke up. I didn't notice and was singing, "Bet you didn't think I knew how to rock and roll", when I heard John say, "What the fuck are you out of your fucking mind?" I jumped and said, "You fucking idiot. You scared the shit out of me. What's wrong with you?" He said. "'What's wrong with me? You got any idea what the fuck you look like!" I said, "What, I'm trying to stay awake. What is your problem?" He said, "You think that explains what you look like. I open my eyes and you're singing out loud with a towel wrapped around your head. And you want to know what is wrong with me?" I said, "Don't make a big deal out of it. I don't know why you give a fuck. You were sleeping. What do you care what I look like." he said, "You got a towel on your fucking head. You think that ain't funny?" I said, "Yeah, I guess it is. You looked pretty funny for the last twenty minutes with your mouth open snoring like a seal with your head back and you didn't hear me yelling at you, did you?" He said, "I wasn't snoring like a seal." I said, "You were snoring like a fucking seal man. How the fuck do you know what you were doing, you were sleeping." He said, "Alright calm down, maybe you're right, but it would be a lot easier to believe you, if you didn't have that fucking towel on your head. You sick fuck." I said. "Hey, this fucking towel is helping me stay awake. You should try it, man. I'll get another towel from the back seat. I'll dip it in the ice water and you can put it on your head." John looked at me and said, "I ain't putting nothing on my head." I said, "Put the fucking towel on your head man." He said, "Hey, fuck you and your towel. Are you out of your fucking mind? Why don't you just drive and leave me alone" I said, "I don't want to leave you alone, you're my friend. I thought this experience would bring us closer together. That's why I asked you to come with me."

      John said, "Don't start talking like a fucking idiot. You always do this. Stop breaking my balls." I said, "Alright then roll another joint." So that's how the next hour of the ride went. We smoked some pot, tried to stay awake and listened as the noise from the tires got worse and worse. We were about an hour and a half from the city, give or take. We kept going and hoped for the best. An hour later, we were almost home. I couldn't believe it. It was about three in the afternoon. In an hour, we'd be in the neighborhood.

As we got closer, I thought the tires were going to fall off. John was living on the west side of Manhattan. I was going to have to drive right past the Bronx to get down to his apartment in the city. I looked over at John and said. "When we get to the Bronx I'll drop you off at the train station." I didn't want to drive all the way down to the city and then back, up town. The tires were failing apart already. On top of that, I would have to do this during rush hour. John looked at me and said "Get the fuck out of here. Are you out of your fucking mind? You think I'm gonna take a train home after all this? You gotta drive me home. I ain't taking no train. You've got some fucking balls." I said, "I don't think the tires are gonna make it." He said. "They'll make it. You're driving me home. You can stay at my house if you want." He had a point, and I knew he was right but I was dead tired. He looked at me and started laughing. I said, "What is so funny?" He said. "You're unfucking believable. I drop everything so I can spend two days with you. We drive seven hours to some stupid fucking town upstate. We smack a few people around; don't get to do what we went there to do. Then we drive back for another seven hours and you want me to take a fucking train home.'" I said, "Well, when you say it like that it sounds fucked up." He said. "Anyway you say it, it sounds fucked up. You know what, you're lucky you've got me for a friend. Somebody who knows how fuckin weird you really are." I said "Yeah, you're right and guess who's lucky they got me for a friend. Because I understand all the same shit." He said, "That would be me. But I'm talking about you right now." I said. "Yeah, I know, and right now I'm talking about you. So, now what do we do'" He said, "Now you shut the fuck up and drive me home. Then we'll live the rest of our lives." So that's what we did.

I drove him home and headed up to the Bronx. Somehow I made it back to my apartment before the tires blew out. I parked in front of my house and went upstairs. I woke up at about ten o'clock that night. I had the same clothes on and I didn't remember going to sleep. I was starving but at least I was back in the neighborhood. It was the best place to be when you were hungry I decided to take a ride to "Frankie & Johnnie's" to get something to eat. I went downstairs and walked over to my car. When I got to the car, I was really pissed. Three of the tires were flat and sitting on their rims. It was hopeless. There was nothing I could do. It wasn't like I had three spare tires lying around. I looked at the car and said, "Fuck this, I'm gonna go eat." I could walk to the restaurant from my apartment, so that's what I did. It was about eight blocks, no big deal. On the way, I had time to think. I was pissed off, but mostly at myself. I knew that the whole trip was a waste of time. I also knew that I would be without a car again. It was a piece of shit car that needed three tires. Probably wasn't worth what the tires would cost me; even if I did have the money for tires, which I didn't.

So, that's where I was at. I was a couple of blocks from the restaurant when I realized what I was dealing with. In a way, this was the second car I would be without because of her. Starting tomorrow, I would be taking the subway to work again. If I decided to go; or if I even had a job anymore. I would be going to work without a car, or looking for a job without a car. I really didn't give a fuck either way. At that moment all I wanted to do was eat. That's how I was back then. I lived my life about an hour at a time. I rarely looked any further ahead than that. There was no point. When things worked out, I was surprised. When they didn't, I just said fuck it. That was good enough for me. As I pulled open the door of the restaurant, I decided on the steak and lobster

Chapter 21

Construction of the West End Cafe was completed a few months earlier. It was a restaurant that was built into the complex. We really weren't supposed to frequent the place but of course, we did. We were involved with the construction of the place because we worked there. But the people who owned it didn't want us hanging out there. The two guys that owned the building were gay and they lived together in the building. This presented obvious problems because we were the furthest things from gay possible. We pushed everything to the limit, and the West End was no different.

We would meet there before Clapton concerts at the Garden. In those days, Clapton was around about once or twice a year. And we were always there. I met this girl there one night, but I don't even remember her name. She lived on 43d Street right off 10th Avenue in this weird apartment. I started fooling around with her at the West End. This wasn't a good idea because we weren't even supposed to be in the place so anything that called attention to us while we were there was bad. The owners of the building always had people in there watching what we were doing. Anyway, I was messing around with her a little bit at one of the tables by the bar, and somehow I convinced her to go into the ladies room with me for a blow job. She agreed, and it wasn't bad. We came out when we were done and decided to go back to her apartment. We got back to her apartment, and we started fooling around. One thing led to another, and of course, we had sex. But while this was all going on, I kept hearing these noises coming from the adjoining apartment. It sounded like someone or something walking. It was really weird. Anyway, after we had sex, she fell asleep. I started looking around, and I came to the door leading to the other apartment I opened the door and saw about four or five huge bird cages. They must have been at least three feet high. I couldn't believe it. I guess she had some kind of exotic birds or something like that. That must have been what I was hearing in the middle of the night. Anyway, I didn't wait around for any explanations; I just got the hell out of there before she woke up. Of course, it didn't end there. I had to duck this girl for weeks after that, which wasn't easy because she lived about a block away from City Plaza. Whatever, she got the message after a while, but not before I got my balls broken by the guys at work.

Chapter 22

So, here we go. The year was 1990, and I'm living in New Jersey (of all places). I was bartending at Cafe Sport, a bar inside the Embassy Suites Hotel in Clifton. Barbara and I were living in a house we rented on Lake Shawnee. Our son, Danny, was about three or four years old. I got to meet a lot of people tending bar, especially hotel bars. This was my third hotel. Some of the people I met became friends, for a while anyway.

Tom and Lisa were a couple I became friends with while I was at Embassy Suites. They were good people. Lisa's father owned a bar in Hillside called the Mt. Hillside Inn. They were staying at the hotel one weekend and came to the bar. That is how we first met. We became friends right away. Sometimes that happens.

The town of Hillside was just one exit before mine off of Route 80. When Tom and Lisa found out where I lived, they told me to stop by on my way home no matter what time it was. They told me that even after closing time, certain people were allowed in, and I was welcome whenever I got there. This was great news because I was always happy to know about a place that I could stop in and have a beer or pick up a six pack to take home after work. And to know the people who owned the place was always a plus.

I started to stop by there on my way home a couple of times a week, just to check the place out. Even though it was kind of a red neck type of bar, I got to know a few people. Tom and Lisa were usually there, and it wasn't long before everybody knew I was a friend of theirs.

It wasn't long before I became part of the inner circle there, especially after I got to meet Lisa's father, who owned the place. We got along, and he made sure everybody there knew I was welcome whenever I showed up.

At closing time when everybody had to leave, I was among the small group of people that were allowed to stay. Even the bartenders had to leave.

What I didn't realize was that there was one bartender there that began to resent me because of this. He was really pissed off that I could walk in and hang out while he had to leave. I had no way of knowing about this situation that was developing even though he was the only person in the place I never became friendly with. To me, he was just a big fat asshole I didn't get along with.

One night, I stopped by the Mt. Hillside Inn on my way home. It was pretty late when I got there, and as usual, I was told to hang out for a while. I was talking with Tom and Lisa when they gave last call. People started closing out their tabs and began to leave. The bartenders completed their closeouts at the register and then they left. The jerk off bartender that I mentioned before was there too. I think his name was Chuck, not that it matters. I noticed him looking at me on his way out, but didn't pay much attention.

After he and the other bartenders left, I hung out with Tom and Lisa for a while and then left. The next morning I went out to the car for something and noticed a big dent on the passenger side door. When I looked over the rest of the car, I noticed my antenna was ripped off too. I was really pissed off. I loved that car. I couldn't figure out how it could have happened. After I thought about it for a couple of minutes, I thought about that asshole bartender, and it all started to make sense.

The next night I stopped by the bar after work and talked to Tom about what had happened. He told me it sounded like something the bartender I was talking about might do. He also said this guy had done things like that before. Now I was really pissed off for two reasons. One, because now I had this stupid problem with this asshole for no reason, and two, because now I knew I had to do something about it. I knew if I did nothing, this guy would think he could do whatever he wanted, and the situation would only get worse. And whenever I stopped at the bar, I would have to worry about my car. After that, the next problem would be him fucking with me personally. That's how these assholes were. If you didn't show them you could stop them, they wouldn't leave you alone. I had to do something so I did.

I talked to a friend of mine from the neighborhood, Bobby McNeil. He was a life long friend, and I knew he would help if he could. Bobby talked to his cousin, Dennis, and told him what had happened.

Dennis was a mountain of a man. He was about six foot seven and had to be 350 pounds. I knew him from the neighborhood, and although we weren't really friends, he was Bobby's cousin, and me and Bobby were close. In the neighborhood, that's how things worked.

Dennis was into a lot of things, and one of the things he used to do was to get paid to straighten things like this out. Of course, it wouldn't cost me anything because I knew him. The only thing he wanted to know from me was if I had done anything to cause this guy to do what he did. Once I explained the situation to him, he said he would help me.

I really didn't know what he had in mind, but I knew once he got involved, that would be the end of the problem.

It wasn't long before I got the word that I was to meet Dennis at the hotel I worked at in New Jersey. From there, we would take a ride to the bar where I had the problem. Dennis told me to make sure the guy would be working the bar that night. I talked to Tom and Lisa and told them what was going to happen. I didn't want anything to happen there without them knowing about it. It was Lisa's father's bar so it was the right thing, and she understood. They knew this guy was an asshole, and he deserved whatever he had coming.

So we were all set. I was supposed to meet Dennis at the Embassy Suites Hotel in Clifton, New Jersey, on Wednesday night. I told my wife I had to work that night. There was no reason for her to know what was going to happen. She would only worry. I was worried myself, so I could only imagine how much she would worry. After all, we were going to a redneck bar in New Jersey to straighten out a bartender, anything could happen.

The night came, and I went to the hotel early to meet my brother, Joey. It would be Joey, Bobby McNeil, Dennis and myself. What I didn't know until Dennis got there was that he brought this guy Vito with him. He was the president of the Manhattan Chapter of Hell's Angels. He was a friend of Dennis' and didn't want him to do this without any backup as if Dennis needed any help. Not only was he huge, but he was nuts.

I was sitting at the bar when the phone rang at the bar. It was Bobby. He told me they were pulling up to the hotel and to meet them in the parking lot. I downed my fourth shot of Dewar's and left with my brother.

We went out to the parking lot and got into the car. Vito was driving. Bobby, my brother and I sat in the back of the Lincoln. Dennis was up front with Vito. He barely fit in the car. On the way there, Dennis told us how the whole thing would go down. After I explained the layout of the bar, he said that my brother, him and me would go in the back door. Bobby and Vito would go in the front door and meet us at the bar. He said once we all got to the bar and the bartender came over, he wanted me to ask him if he had a problem with me. After that, he would do all the talking. My heart was pounding, partly because I wanted to show this guy he couldn't fuck with me, but also because it was a pretty dangerous situation.

We pulled into the parking lot of the bar and got out of the car. My head was buzzing. I was scared, nervous and excited all at the same time. I walked in the back door of the bar with Joey and Dennis. The place was packed. Joey and I went in first with Dennis behind us. He literally had to bend down to get through the doorway. As we walked around the bar, people had to get out of the way just so Dennis could get by. As we made our way to the other side of the bar, Bobby and Vito came in the front door. Now people started to realize something was going on. Joey, Dennis and I sat at the bar. Vito and Bobby stood behind us. This was the first time I got a look at Vito. He was driving on the way there so I really couldn't see him. He was a scary looking guy. He wasn't that big, but he had a nasty looking scar down the whole left side of his face. He looked like the kind of person you would never want to be looking for you. Vito leaned over behind me and asked me, "Who's the mark?" I told him, "The bartender." He said, "Okay" and stood back behind me.

I was sitting next to Dennis and my brother. We had to put two stools together for Dennis to sit on because he was so huge. The bartender came over to where we were sitting. His face was white. He was scared shit. He said, "Hi Tony", which was really strange because in all the time I've been there, he had never said a word to me. Right then, I knew we had him. I said, "Do you have a problem with me?" He said, "What problem, Tony?" I said, "I don't know. All I know is the last time we were both here and you left there was something wrong with my car." He looked at me and said, "I don't know, did you ask Lisa about it?" That was the first time Dennis said something. He leaned across the bar and said, "He's asking you." He stepped back and looked at the five of us for a few seconds then turned around and walked into the kitchen. Now it was obvious to everybody in there that something was going on. It was pretty intense. Almost everybody in there was staring at us now. We just sipped our beers and looked back at them. A couple of minutes later, the bartender came out of the kitchen. He came over to us and said, "I don't know Tony, if I hear anything, I'll let you know." Right then, Vito leaned across the bar between Dennis and my brother. He was only a few inches from the bartender's face when he said, "No, no, no, you don't understand. If we hear anything, we'll let you know." Now he was frozen. He just stood there. Dennis broke the silence when he said, "Don't ever make me have to come back here again. I hate New Jersey." Then Dennis stood up, which was really impressive. He towered over the guy and everybody else. Now the place got real quiet. Dennis just glared at the guy for a few seconds. The bartender just stood there looking up at him. Then Dennis said, "Let's go, he understands."

Then we all stood up and followed Dennis out the back door leaving our beers still half full on the bar. People just got out of our way. The whole scene only took about 15 minutes. We got back in the car and left.

On the way back to the hotel, Dennis told me that the real test would be when I went back there alone. I knew he was right. Then he said, "I don't think you'll have a problem. If you do, you call me, and we'll tear the fucking place down."

We got back to the hotel. Joey and I got out of the car. As Vito started to pull away to leave, Dennis stuck his head out the window and said, "Don't worry about nothing." Then as they pulled away, he yelled out the window, "How the fuck could you live out here?" and they were gone.

Joey and I went back into the hotel to have a beer at the bar. I couldn't believe what we had just done. I had been thinking about this for days, and it was all over in a matter of minutes. Originally, I had told Dennis I knew the owners of the bar and maybe we could have a drink and meet them afterwards. He said one thing to me, "This is not a social call" and that was that. Of course, he was right. Anyway, we ended the night exactly the way we started it with a couple shots of Dewar's. We toasted Dennis for what he had done for me and then we left.

A couple of weeks went by before I went back to the Mt. Hillside Inn, not purposely; it just worked out that way. The whole time, I was wondering what it would be like to walk in there alone after what we had done. I was nervous about it, no doubt, but I knew it had to be done sooner or later. I thought it would be okay, but you never know. I didn't know if I should go back there alone, but that was really the only way I was going to find out if this guy got the message.

So one night after work, I stopped by there on my way home. I was nervous driving up there alone. Then I thought, fuck it and blasted some Clapton on the car stereo. When I pulled into the parking lot, I saw the asshole's car so I knew he was there. I parked the car and walked up to the front door. I didn't know what to expect or what could be waiting for me inside. I looked at the door for a second and thought about leaving. Then I pushed the door open and went inside. I was right about him being there.

The bar was pretty crowded for that time of night. I walked up to the bar and looked around. There was nobody there that I knew. I threw my keys on the bar, lit a cigarette and waited for the jerk off to come over to me.

He was on the other side of the bar talking to four or five guys when I walked in. He came over to where I was standing and said, "Hi Tony, what can I get for you?" I looked at him and said, "Bottle of Bud." He went to get the beer, and I thought if anything is going to happen, it will be now. He was hanging out with four or five guys, and I was alone. He came back with my beer and said, "This one's on me, good luck." We looked at each other for a few seconds, and I could see in his eyes he was punked out. I said, "Thanks." And it was over. I had a couple more beers and every time he came over to me, I could see he was scared shit. It couldn't have worked out any better.

The funny thing is that the next few times I was there, I found out that a lot of people were really happy about what we had done to this guy. The cook that was working the night we were all there told me that when he walked into the kitchen that night, he was petrified. He didn't even want to go back out to the bar. He almost walked out the back door. Anyway, that was that. I was really happy about the way things worked out. I called Dennis to thank him and tell him what happened when I went back there. It just reaffirmed what I had learned growing up in the neighborhood. When something happened, you either knew somebody or you didn't. It's sad, but very true. If I was anybody else or didn't know anybody to call in that situation, I would have been at this guy's mercy. It's just one of the things the neighborhood gave you to take with you wherever you went. It was pretty amazing how these things always started and ended the same way, but you never got used to them. To say the least, I was pretty scared every time one of these situations played itself out. But it was always worth it. Right before each and every one of them, I would have loved to just back out of the whole tiling. They were all very frightening, but if I did nothing, I'm sure the outcome would have been much worse than the fear itself. It was either do something now or always worry about what might happen next.

And through it all, finding myself in these situations when I did, I could always feel comfortable with the fact that I was never the cause of any of these problems. And when I think about them and really analyze what went on, one thing stands out in my mind. It's very simple, but hard to put into words without sounding like an asshole, but I'll try. It had to do with having the ability to meet potential violence with even greater violence, not for the sake of violence itself but on behalf of innocence. It was a feeling of complete satisfaction not only to get even with these assholes, but also to watch them dissolve in fear right in front of your eyes. And the outcome was always the same in these situations. Whether it was Dennis or anybody else and especially if it was Niko. Once they got involved, the problem was over. I mean really over, no matter what. No matter who the problem was with or who they thought they knew. That was it!

As I mentioned before, this is how I grew up in the neighborhood, and this kind of belief in right and wrong stays with you forever. It's a way of thinking that's so basic. And you just apply it where need be, naturally.

Chapter 23

It wasn't long after the whole bar scene at the Mt. Hillside Inn that a situation began to develop at my son's school. He was only in pre school back then, and I would take him there every morning. My wife worked in Manhattan during the day, and I took care of him and worked at night.

Every once in a while I'd have a really late night at the bar I was working at and it was really tough waking up early enough to get him up and fed and make the bus. When that happened, I would drive him to the nursery school. It was a great place right on the lake. The kids would usually be playing outside at that time of the morning so I thought it was really strange that there was nobody outside when we got there.

I parked the car and took him inside. When we got inside, one of the teachers said to me, "Thank God you're here." I said, "Why, what's wrong?" She explained to me that for the past few days there was a strange looking guy hanging around the school watching the kids. She told me that's why they were all inside when I got there. While she's talking to me, one of the kids yelled, "There he is again." We looked out one of the windows, and I saw this guy standing about ten feet from the window looking in. I walked over to the window to get a better look at him. When he saw me, he started to walk away. I started to go outside to find out what he was doing there when the woman in charge of the school stopped me. She said she had called the police, and they were on their way. I went outside anyway and saw the police car pulling up to the building.

I knew the woman in charge. Her name was Chris Murray, and her son, James, was one of my son's friends. She was a good person, and I trusted her. I stood by and listened as she explained the situation to the cop. As she was telling him what was going on, he told her he understood, but there was nothing he could do because the guy hadn't actually done anything. They knew he owned a run down house right by the school, and they would keep an eye on him. But other than that, there was nothing they could do until he actually did something wrong.

Now, I had heard enough. I walked over to the cop and said, "You mean you're not even going to confront this guy and find out why he's hanging around the kids?" He said, "Who are you?" I said, "My son comes here every day, and if you're not going to talk to this guy, I am." He told me if I did that, I would be the one that would have legal problems. Right then, I knew there was no use. I told him I understood and that I was just upset. He said, "Okay, just don't do anything stupid." I said, "Of course not, thanks." I didn't need the cops watching me at that point especially because now I knew what had to be done. There was no way I was going to drop my son off at the school every day and just hope that nothing would happen.

    I was home during the day anyway so I figured I would just check this guy out myself. The next day I dropped my son off at the school as usual. I went back home and waited a while. I knew the kids wouldn't be outside playing for at least an hour. I had some breakfast and after an hour had passed, I went down to the basement and grabbed a baseball bat and threw it in the car. Then I took a ride to the school.

    When I got there, I saw that the kids were playing outside. I sat in the car and just waited. About a half hour later, I noticed a weird looking guy walking up to the school. He was a tall, thin guy with a straggly beard. He had an old army jacket on and dirty jeans. I gave him a chance to settle in and see what he was up to. He had no idea I was there, which is what wanted. He got to where he was about 20 or 30 yards from the playground and stopped. The parking lot I was in was between him and the kids. I was a little nervous because I didn't know what he was capable of, but all I was thinking about now was my son and the other kids. I figured if it came down to it, I would just beat the fuck out of him with the baseball bat. I was locked in, and I knew it was right for me to be there.

    I waited a couple of minutes. He was just staring at the kids. I could see my son playing with the other kids, and this guy watching them. I got out of the car and picked up the bat from the back seat. I didn't look at him yet, but I could feel him watching me. I walked up to the front steps of the school, turned and sat down on the steps with the bat on my lap. I was facing him now and looking straight into his eyes. He looked at me for a few seconds then turned away. He took a few steps back and turned towards the street. As he walked away, he kept looking over his shoulder to see what I was doing. He looked uncomfortable and unsure of what to do next. It was obvious that I was something he didn't expect. He got to the street in front of the school. I gave him a minute before I got up and walked to my car. I put the bat on the front seat and started to drive toward where he was walking. I really didn't want anything to happen. I just wanted him to know I was watching him. I drove up behind him, and as I passed him, I slowed down. When I went by him, I just stared at him. He looked right back at me, but I could see that he was spooked. Then I sped up and went about a block past him. I made a U turn and headed back straight toward him. As I passed him, I did the same thing again only this time I had the baseball bat on the dashboard so he could see it. This time, he didn't look at me. He kept his head down and kept walking.

  I went back to the school and parked in front of the kid's playground. I stayed there for almost an hour. I wanted to make sure he didn't come back, at least until the kids went back inside. As I sat there, I watched them playing. I could see my son playing with the other kids. I knew I wasn't supposed to be doing what I had done, and if the police had seen me, I would have probably been in trouble myself, but I knew I was doing the right thing and from watching the kids play, I believed it even more.

  After the kids were done with playtime and were brought back inside the school, I went back home. I continued doing this for a little more than a week. Although I only saw the guy there one other time, I kept going. I figured even if I didn't see him, it was possible he was still watching. I wanted him to know I was around. I was home during the day anyway, and I just felt better to see for myself. I never told my wife or my son what I was doing because I didn't want them to worry. The woman at the school told me they always felt better when they saw me around, which was just another reason to feel good about what I was doing.

  A couple of months had passed since I had stopped going to the school during which time, I left my phone and beeper numbers with the woman in charge. They had a parent's and teacher's meeting at the school that my wife went to. While she was there, a couple of the teachers made a point of telling my wife what I had done and asked her to thank me again for doing what I did.

  Barbara was gracious as always. When she got back from the school, she asked me, "What did you do at the school last month?" Even though she already knew, I said, "Nothing, I just helped them out one day." She said, "You're really something, I know whatever you did, you did because you love your son so I can't be upset with you." I smiled at her and said, "Thanks." And that was that. I felt good. Who knows if this guy would have done anything to hurt any of the kids? But the bottom line was that the kids were okay after that. The teachers were happy that I was around, and I felt better that I was around for my son and the other kids.

Chapter 24

September 3rd, my brother's anniversary. So many things have happened this past year; it's even hard for me to believe...

In July of 1997, I was coming home from an appointment with an eye doctor. I was trying to determine the cause of the brutal headaches I had been suffering from. My son, Danny, was at my aunt's house playing with his cousins. I called my aunt and told her to send him home. She only lived a few blocks away, and so he could walk home. After I hung up, I decided to go get him because it was so hot and humid that day. It was only a couple of blocks away and the middle of the afternoon so I paid no attention to the couple of shots of scotch I just had to try and dull the pain in my head.

I found out later that right around the time I pulled out of my driveway someone placed a call to the police about somebody going door to door around the lake selling something. Of course, I was pulled over mistakenly and arrested for DWI, which, as it turns out, was to be the least of my problems.

A month earlier I had gone for a MRI because of my headaches, as a precautionary measure, just to rule out anything serious. I was working the lunch shift at the restaurant when I got a call from the doctor. He said he saw something from the results of the MRI and that he wanted to take a closer look. I went for my second MRI around the time I was waiting for my court date. It was turning into a real fun summer.

The only good thing going on was that my wife, Barbara, a real blessing in my life, was pregnant. This was great news, of course, but with all the mounting tensions and anxiety, it never got the attention it deserved.

It was August now, and I decided to go down to Long Beach Island for a day or two just to get my mind off things. A friend of mine had a house down there for a couple of weeks during the summer. While I was packing up the truck, the phone rang. It was the doctor calling with the results of the second MRI. The news wasn't good. Turns out there was something they thought was a cyst in the middle of the two lobes of my brain. Not exactly the kind of news you want to hear on your way down to the shore, or any other time for that matter. I hung up the phone and just sat there. The only way I could try to explain how I felt at that moment was that everything just looked different to me The kitchen, the living room, the truck in the driveway all packed for the shore, everything. All I remember thinking about was that there was something inside my head that shouldn't be there. And I was wondering not only if I would be okay, but how in the world were they going to go about getting this thing, whatever it was, out of my head.

So now I am thinking, okay, my wife is pregnant, I got arrested and now there's something in my head that may or may not be causing my headaches.

After seeing a couple of doctors, I got to see Dr. Davidson, who is the head of Neurology at The Hospital for Bone and Joint Surgery in New York City. The only way you get that lucky is if you know somebody. Luckily, my brother's wife's boss was a patient of his, one of those things. He reviewed my MRI and suggested I have whatever it was removed. After listening to a bunch of things explaining my problem that I didn't really understand, I asked him if it was him or his family going through this, who would he go to. He recommended Dr. Basanti of Chatham, New Jersey. He was the president of the Neurological Society of New Jersey. Then I caught a break. Dr. Davidson checked and Dr. Basanti was in my insurance plan, and I would be covered for any procedure.

Meeting Dr. Basanti was probably the first time I felt kind of at ease with the situation. Even though he was the only one of the three doctors I saw that said he didn't think what I had was a cyst. He thought it was a tumor. Even though this wasn't what I wanted to hear. I still felt a sense of calm or security just from the way he talked about how he was going to go about handling the situation. He was always so confident about whatever he said.

I decided to have the surgery right away or as soon as possible. With the baby due in December, it was really the only time I had to do it since I would be caring for her during the day while my wife was at work.

I talked to Alice, the owner of the restaurant where I was working, about the whole situation. She was more than understanding about everything. We decided that I would come back to work after the surgery, even though I had no idea what kind of shape I would be in by then. I went ahead and scheduled the surgery for October 9th while continuing to work until about a week before.

I was working on a Saturday night during the last week of September, and one of the managers told me I had a phone call.

As usual for a Saturday night, the bar was packed. I made my way through the customers to take the call. It was my wife telling me she was at the emergency room of Dover General Hospital. She said my son needed to have surgery for appendicitis. He was going to be taken to Denville to St. Claire's Hospital for the surgery, and I was to meet them there. I couldn't believe what I was hearing. All I could think about was this poor little kid. He was only nine, and he was worrying about his dad going in for brain surgery, and now here he was going in for his own surgery.

I poured myself a glass of scotch, downed it and left the restaurant. I was going to drive to St. Claire's and meet the ambulance when it got there. While I was walking to the parking lot,

I was thinking about all that was going on. When for some reason I thought about the baby, as if there weren't enough things to think about already. I remembered thinking in about a week I was going to have brain surgery. I mean, who knew, would I be around to see her? I thought I would, but really, if you think about it, who knew?

I got to the emergency room before the ambulance and waited. In about 15 minutes it got there, lights flashing. We held his hand while they wheeled him in. He's a strong minded kid, but you could see in his eyes that he was scared. It was heartbreaking, we kissed him, who knows how many times and told him not to worry, and we would be standing there when he woke up.

About three in the morning the doctor came out and said everything was fine, although his appendix had ruptured while they were removing it. We went up to see him. The room was empty in the middle of the night. We kissed him while he slept. I was rubbing his little arm when his eyes started to open. He looked at me and with his other hand, lifted up the oxygen mask and said, "Don't bother me." What a kid and what a night.

In the days that followed, Danny regained his strength. It wasn't easy, but I was able to help him because I remembered what it was like. I had my appendix removed when I was about 13. We kind of swapped stories, and I think it helped him along a little bit.

A couple of days after my son came home from the hospital, the focus soon shifted back to me. I was due for my surgery, and although we were pretty confident that things would work out okay, there was a quiet and unspoken dread about the whole situation.

* * * * *

October 9th came along just as quickly as I thought it would. I had to be at the hospital at six in the morning. We left at 5:30 am. While we were pulling out of the driveway, I asked my wife to stop the car. I went back into the house to give my son another kiss, while he was sleeping. I remember thinking the next time I see him, the surgery would be over with.

Barbara and I headed for the hospital for what I was sure would be the most surreal day I could remember since my mother's funeral. It was a pretty strange ride to say the least. We were both worried about the surgery and how I would be afterward. But by the time this day finally started, we just wanted to get it done and deal with whatever came of it.

There was so much going on besides the surgery that I think it actually helped. Barbara was more than seven months pregnant by then and that was heavy on our minds. Me being arrested, and the court date I had to postpone were nothing to us now, but it was there. And then there was our son, Danny, who was less than a week out of his own surgery. Our minds were all over the place.

We got to the hospital and began the admitting process. That took about an hour. Finally, we got up to my room where the pre surgery tests were done. The nurse explained all the positives and negatives of the procedure, and there were papers to sign in case of this and in case of that. Then we had about a half hour before I would be brought down for surgery.

Barbara and I were talking in the room about how everything was going to be fine and all the other things people say when they're scared shit. Then the door to my room opens and this guy walks in. He introduces himself and says he's a minister or something like that. So I figure, okay, he's going to reassure me now that everything's going to be fine. It did worry me a little bit that there was a priest in my room before the surgery, but I figured it couldn't hurt even though I had no idea who this guy was or who called him.

Then he looks at me and says, "So, brain surgery, boy, you must be worried." I looked at Barbara and said, "Who is this guy, get him out of here." She said to me, "Don't say that, he's a priest." I said, "He ain't a priest, he said he's a minister." I couldn't believe it. What kind of thing is that to say to me at that point? I said to Barbara, "Whatever he is, get him out of here."

Barbara was polite and said, I don't think he feels like talking, but thanks for coming.'" He finally left, and I said to Barbara, "God forgive me, but what a jerk, who called this guy to come and see me?" Turns out, it was one of Barbara's aunts who asked him to come by. Unbelievable! Just what I needed, to get aggravated before brain surgery.

The time came to be brought down and prepped for the surgery. Right before I was wheeled into the room, I said goodbye to Barbara. As they were wheeling me through the doors, I yelled to her, "Don't leave town, I'll see you later." She said, 'I'll be here."

Now, I'm lying in this bed waiting and wondering what the hell I was in for next. Then Dr. Basanti walks in. He comes over to my bed and asks me how I'm doing. Seeing him really settled me down. He was always so confident about what he was doing. It was because of his manner and personality that I was able to relax about the whole situation. It's hard to explain, but he was so matter of fact about what needed to be done. You couldn't help feeling positive. He had that kind of affect on you. The last thing I remember was him smiling at me as we went through the double doors for the surgery.

When I woke up in recovery after the surgery, I remembered thinking, okay, well at least I woke up, and I'm still here. Then I started feeling the pain. The incision was only a couple of inches long, but it felt like my head was split wide open. I was hooked up to an IV bag in my left arm, and I had a tube hooked up to my right arm for morphine. Which was for pain, and I had plenty of it. I was in the intensive care unit for head trauma. It's hard to explain how I was feeling. I was in a lot of pain, but I was also fucked up from the morphine. I was awake, but I was drifting in and out. I think there were about four or five beds in the room. Everybody else in the room looked like they were in worse shape than me, but what did I know. For all I knew, they were thinking the same thing about me. After a while, I thought I saw Dr. Basanti going over to the other patients. When he left the room, I wondered why he didn't come over to talk to me.

I must have dozed off for a few minutes because one of the nurses was waking me up to eat something. She brought over some kind of beef broth that really sucked. I had a few spoonfuls and felt like throwing up. I was starving, but the soup was so bad, I didn't care how hungry I was. I pushed the food tray to the side and tried to relax.

I was lying there when I saw my wife, Barbara, walking in with my brother, Joey. I didn't know it then, but they had just come from speaking with Dr. Basanti. He told them that he wasn't sure about what he had removed from the middle of my brain. He said he wanted to have further tests done on the tumor and wouldn't have the results for about a week. They were pretty upset, and my brother said, "What am I going to tell him when we go and see him?" The doctor told my brother that I would probably be asleep and very tired from the surgery so he wouldn't have to know what to say to me just yet.

I was really happy to see them. Barbara and Joey came over to my bed and as soon as they got close enough, I said, "What did the doctor say?" Joey looked at me and said, "You're supposed to be asleep." I said, "Well, I ain't sleeping, so what did he say?" He told me what the doctor said, and I was really pissed off. I said, "So now I went through all this shit, and I still don't know anything. That's just fucking great." I saw the look on their faces, and I felt bad for them. I was pissed off, but they were just concerned for me, and they didn't need to hear shit from me now. I looked at the both of them and for some reason, I started to laugh. I have no idea why. Barbara was standing there, and Joey was sitting on my bed, and I couldn't stop laughing. They were looking at me like I was nuts.

What I didn't know, but soon found out, was that there was a tube hooked up to my dick so if I pissed, it would go into a bag. So, I'm lying there laughing, and I started to piss, which only made me laugh even more. Joey is sitting there, looking at me, and he says, "What the fuck is wrong with you?" I said, "I don't know, I know I'm pissing right now, but I don't know where it's going." He jumped up from the bed and said, "What's wrong with you? How could you pee in the bed while I'm sitting here?" All that did was make me laugh even more. When we all realized what was happening, we all started laughing. It was a moment I'll never forget.

* * * * *

Chapter 25

The year was 1991. Clapton was playing the Garden. As usual, I talked to some ticket brokers I knew and got excellent tickets for the four of us Barbara, Joey, Tora and myself.

Barbara and Tora were working in the City so we agreed we would meet at the Garden. I drove up to Joey's in Westchester, left my car there and drove to the City with him.

We stopped in the Bronx, had a couple of beers and headed down to the City. We were driving down the F.D.R. and saw it was all back up. We decided to cut across 116th Street and go down the West Side.

As we cut across 116th Street, some asshole Puerto Ricans cut us off real bad. We caught up with them and some words were exchanged. Before we knew what was happening, they cut us off again and forced us to stop. They got out of their car and so did we, which was a big mistake because by now we were in the middle of Spanish Harlem.

As they walked toward us, I noticed somebody behind me and that's the last thing I remember. The next thing I can remember, to this day, is waking up in the front seat of Joey's car covered in blood. My hair was all matted with blood, my leather jacket had blood all over it and I couldn't breathe too well. The car was moving, and the first thing I remember hearing was Joey asking me if I was all right. I had no idea what had happened. Joey was bleeding a little from the back of his head too.

It was obvious we had gotten the shit kicked out of us, but I couldn't remember a thing about it. Slowly, things started to come back to me, not about what had happened, but that we were on our way to meet our wives. We were going to see Clapton, and I was in a fog.

As we were driving, we noticed a sign for Lennox Hill Hospital Emergency. Joey said, "Maybe we should stop in and get ourselves checked out." We did, thank God.

Joey wasn't too bad, but they told me besides the stitches on my upper lip, I had a fractured skull, and they wanted me admitted. It wasn't until then that I realized how serious the situation was. I spent the next hour trying to sort out just what had happened. It was no use, I couldn't remember a thing. The only thing I remember thinking was how thankful I was that Joey was okay. I mean, if somebody had to get the worst of it, I was glad it was me and not him. I love him so much, and I was at least happy about that.

I was lying in a bed in the emergency room when our wives showed up. I think Joey called the bar we were supposed to meet at and told them what had happened. I was lying there and Barbara walked in. As she got close to me, she started crying. I guess I looked like shit. The doctor came over to talk to us and explained what was going on. He said I had to go upstairs for a CAT scan. Then he started checking the stitches on my lip. I didn't remember it at the time, but Barbara told me that I actually asked the doctor how my mustache was. She told me I said to the doctor, "How's my mustache? I don't want to wind up looking like Stacey Keach! Don't make my lip look like that"! They both looked at me like I was nuts. I was taken upstairs for the CAT scan, and everybody else went home. Barbara had to get home to take care of our son. Danny was only about two or three years old at that time.

While I was waiting for the CAT scan they left me alone in a wheelchair in the hallway. They said it would be about a half hour before they were ready for me.

That was the toughest part. I was sitting in a wheelchair by myself in a hallway. I started to feel sick. In a couple of minutes, I started throwing up. They told me later that it was from all the blood I had swallowed. Anyway, I fell asleep like that. Alone in a hallway, in a wheelchair, and that was the last thing I remembered about that night.

I woke up the next day in my room at the hospital, I couldn't move, and I was sore all over especially my neck and head. The doctor came in and told me I was going to be okay and that I was lucky to be alive. The way I felt, I believed him. I spent the next two and half days in the hospital before I was allowed to leave. I was real happy that I was going to be okay, but I was really pissed that I missed Clapton.

There were a lot of people that were pissed off about what had happened to us. We had a couple of offers from different people to go down and find who had done this, but it would be like finding a needle in a haystack. Plus the fact that I couldn't even remember a thing about what had happened after I got out of the car. I couldn't even imagine what Joey had gone through. Obviously, after whatever happened he had to drag me off the street and put me in the car somehow. I don't know if that was while he was getting his ass kicked too, or what. One lesson I did learn, though, was that you don't get out of your car in Spanish Harlem unless you have help, we didn't.

Chapter 26

A couple of years after I came back from California, I was lucky enough to meet Barbara. I knew she was special when I met her. And now, 16 years later, she's my wife and the mother of my two beautiful children, Danny and Maria.

Life has a way of throwing you these curve balls to see if you know what to do with them. I had just moved into an apartment on Holland Avenue in the Bronx. I was having a party there, kind of a house warming, and all of my close friends were there. My cousin, Paul, came that night too. He was dating Barbara at the time. I met her that night, and although I didn't realize it right away, I was attracted to her. To me she seemed like somebody I never deserved to meet. She was very pretty and was about five years younger than I was. She was born in Germany and grew up in New Jersey and that was about as unlike me as you could get.

I went out with her and my cousin a couple of times. Sometimes I had a date, but most of the time I didn't. We had some good times. After a while, my cousin stopped seeing her. I would ask him about her, and he said he wasn't going out with her anymore. He said he would give me her phone number if I wanted to call her. I thought it might be a little awkward, but I really wanted to see her again so I took her number.

The first time I called her was a disaster. I called and told her who I was, and she hung up on me. I kept calling her until she finally agreed to see me.

I was driving a piece of shit Fiat at the time, and I drove to Fort Lee, New Jersey, to pick her up at her apartment. I was nervous so I stopped at the grocery store to buy a couple of beers. I knew nothing about New Jersey in those days even though it was right over the bridge, but it might as well have been Ohio. So naturally, I got lost. I'm driving around with no idea what I'm doing, and of course, I noticed a cop car behind me. They pulled me over and saw I had an open beer between my legs. In those days, things were different. It wasn't like now where drinking and driving was the equivalent to being a mass murderer.

Anyway, I explained to the cop that I was picking this girl up for the first time, and I was real nervous. Believe it or not, this cop was a regular guy, and he said he understood. I was shocked. He told me to get out of the car and get rid of the beer. Then he said he would show me how to get where I was trying to go. I didn't realize it; but I was only a few blocks from her house when they pulled me over so it didn't take long to get there.

For some reason, when we got to the block where she lived, the cop put on all the lights on the cop car. I think he was trying to break my balls.

Anyway, now I'm following the cop car with the lights going, and there was Barbara standing in front of her apartment. I stopped in front of her house, and the cop car pulled away. Now I had some explaining to do. I think that's what he wanted. Barbara walked over to the car and said, "What happened, are you okay?" I said, "Get in, I'll explain on the way." We drove to the Bronx and went to the Pines for dinner. I told her what happened, and she had a look on her face like she thought I was nuts.

We had a great dinner at the restaurant and a great night. I drove her back home and somehow managed not to get pulled over again. That was our first date, and to this day, Barbara tells me that right then when she saw the cops pulling up in front of her house with me following them she should have know how whacked I was.

We kept seeing each other and got along great despite the obvious differences between us. We couldn't be more different. She was born in Germany and grew up in New Jersey. I was born in New York City and grew up in the Bronx.

When I think about it now, I think because she was five years younger than me, I saw in her a way to reach back and recapture all the years I had wasted not knowing what I was doing, if that makes any sense.

I was working at the New York Plaza in lower Manhattan for the refrigeration and air conditioning engineers union. It was good money, and the benefits were good too. Although I really couldn't give a shit about the work I was doing, it paid the bills and that was that. I was driving to work on the F.D.R. Drive one day when I had an accident and totaled the Fiat. Somehow I wasn't hurt, but I was devastated because now I had no car again.

The Fiat was always giving me trouble but at least I had a car. At one point before the accident I was taking Barbara to dinner at my father's house. She had never met him yet. The gearbox was all fucked up, and the car would only go in reverse for some reason. Anyway, we drove the six or eight blocks to my father's house in reverse. We had a great time, and my father loved her. We drove back to my apartment in reverse and that was that. I got it fixed after that, but it was always something with that car. When I totaled it, it was almost a relief

Barbara worked in Manhattan and started spending the weekends at my apartment. It was tough without a car, but there was a lot to do in the neighborhood. There were restaurants everywhere, and you could walk to most of them if you had to.

After about a month, Barbara told me that she had some money in the bank, and if I wanted it to buy a new car she would give the money to me. This really shook me up. It was the first time that I realized what a giving person she was. I felt really guilty about accepting this offer. But I have to say, it was just too tempting to turn down. I took her up on her offer, and we bought a car together.

The car we bought was a 1983 Cutlass Supreme Brougham. It was absolutely beautiful. It was white with maroon crushed velvet interior and a maroon landau roof. It was power everything with vogue tires and spoke chrome mags. I'll never forget that car. We had it for a little more than 13 years. How cool is that?

Shortly after we got the car, I moved to another apartment. In those days, I moved a lot. We moved into an apartment building that my brother lived in before he bought his house. We knew the landlord and that's part of the reason I moved there.

It was in that apartment while I was taking a shower one day that I decided I would ask Barbara to marry me. I remember it to this day. She said yes, and I couldn't believe it. I never thought this kind of thing would ever come my way. We started making plans for the wedding, and it was great. We decided to get married at St. Mary's on 18th Street in the Bronx and why not? It was a beautiful church in the heart of the neighborhood. We were both very excited. We had both had relationships before that turned to shit. We were both kind of overwhelmed at taking this next big step.

All our plans went rather well considering our completely different backgrounds. I'm sure the last place her parents thought their daughter would be getting married would be in the Bronx.

We set the date and were married on October 12, 1985, Columbus Day. Our honeymoon would be a week in Puerto Rico. I have no idea why, we just picked it.

The union I was in at work was so corrupt that I not only got paid for the week of my honeymoon, but I was also paid overtime while I was in Puerto Rico. Unbelievable! Of course, I had to invite a few assholes from the union for this to happen, but I figured it was worth it. If they ever got out of hand at the reception, believe me, there was more than enough muscle just in my wedding party alone to handle it, not to mention the guests. Once they were there, they knew it too.

Barbara Genelli

The wedding went extremely well. We didn't have a band or even a DJ, and it didn't even matter. For weeks before the wedding, we made tapes of all out favorite music. We put stuff in there for literally every generation. Everybody loved it. Of course, midway through the reception, there was a heavy dose of Clapton, his really good stuff. More than a couple of people told us it was the best reception they were ever at. By the end of the night, the entire place was up dancing to the traditional Italian dances. It was great.

My brother, Joe, and his wife, Tora, drove us to the airport that night, and we were off to Puerto Rico. When we got there, we took a cab to the hotel. It was a Sunday so there was a skeleton crew at the hotel. I could tell nobody there was really in charge or had any idea what they were doing.

The guy took us to our room, gave me the keys and left. I opened the door, walked in and couldn't believe it. It was a room with separate single beds. Not only that, they were renovating the place, and our window looked out at a bunch of dumpsters filled with the kind of furniture that was in our room. I said, "Get the fuck out of here." Then the phone rang. It was the front desk asking if everything was okay. I said to the guy on the phone, "No everything ain't alright. Everything is all fucked up. Not only are there separate beds, but I'm looking out at dumpsters. This is my fucking honeymoon." The guy was apologizing left and right and asked me to please wait until the morning when his supervisor came in. I said I would, and we stayed the night in the room with the separate beds. It was late, and we were still hung over from the reception and the plane ride.

The next morning, the phone woke me up. It was the hotel manager. He said he was very sorry about the inconvenience, and he had another room for us when we were ready. I said, "We're ready."

We met him in the lobby, and he gave us the new keys and apologized again. He said, "When you get to your room, call me if you are not happy." I thought he would at least take us up there and make sure everything was okay. Barbara said, "Let's just go see it, maybe it's nice."

We went to the other side of the lobby. This side of the hotel was already renovated so I thought it might be okay. On the way up in the elevator, I noticed the number on the keys would put us on the top floor. We got out of the elevator and noticed there were only three or four rooms on the whole floor. We found our room and walked in. I was shocked. The guy had given us a penthouse suite. It was huge, with an outside terrace, half the size of the whole place, it was really sharp. We were really excited now. From then on, we really enjoyed our stay. It just goes to show you that you have to open your mouth and say something if you're not satisfied. If we didn't say anything, we would have spent our honeymoon in a room with separate beds.

Chapter 27

When my mother died, I was destroyed not physically, but mentally and emotionally. From that point in my life and even to this day, I didn't know how to act, and at times, still don't.

Even writing this now, it's extremely difficult to find a way to put into words how something of that magnitude affects you throughout your life. I am sure it did on many levels. I was sure of one thing; I would never blame anything that happened to me after that on my mother's death. I felt that would cheapen her memory. Her death wasn't about me, it was about her. Now that may or may not be true, but that's how I felt. There were still people worse off than I was. My mother was the one that died, not me, and I didn't feel I had the right to use that as an excuse for anything I did or didn't do from that point on.

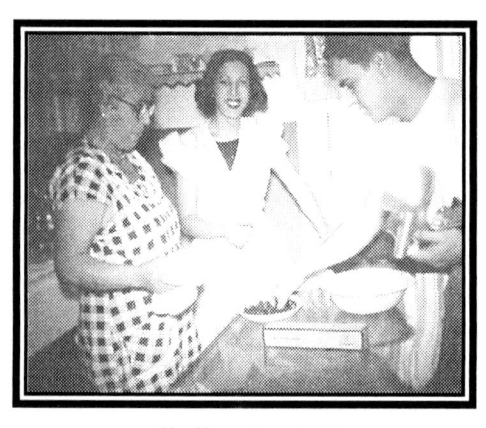

My Mom (center)

Nothing felt real to me after that. I knew that my father and brother loved me, and I loved them, but we all loved my mother too, and that didn't stop her from dying. Her funeral was just as bad as hearing the news of her death or even worse. Because I had to go see her like that, even now, 32 years later, it's very hard to talk about or think about, but I have to.

The funeral was right down the block from where she worked at Lucia Brothers on Huffman Street in the Bronx. I had walked past that same funeral parlor so many times with her when I'd meet her for lunch that was just one of the things I thought about when I walked into the place.

I blocked a lot of things out from the whole experience of her funeral. In those days, there was a wake for a couple of days before the actual funeral. I can't remember how many nights I was there, but I remember the day of the funeral, which was the worst day.

The immediate family was allowed in to view the body one last time before the ride to the cemetery. I knew this would be the last time I would ever see her. It hurt so badly to see her like that, but at least I could see her.

I stood in the back of the funeral parlor while everybody else paid his or her last respects. I was crying, partly because I was so sad and partly because I had no idea how to say goodbye to her. I had no clue what to do after that day was over. The whole experience really sucked, but in a way, I didn't want it to end because I knew I would never see her again after that.

Finally, there was no one left in the place but my father, brother and myself. I remember thinking that's all that would be left after this day. I walked up to her casket, and I can't remember if it was Joey and I or just me, but she looked like she was sleeping. I knew she wasn't. When I got to her, I put my hand on her hands. I knew I had to touch her because I wouldn't be able to ever again. Her hands were cold. I was crying now. I leaned over and said, "I love you, ma." I kissed her on her cheek. I'll never forget that feeling. Her face was cold on my lips, but I didn't care. I felt she was still there with us, and I had to kiss her. I loved her so much. I backed up, looking at her, and I was crying uncontrollably. I felt that no matter how I said goodbye, it wasn't good enough. I didn't know what else to do.

After that, at the church, it wasn't much easier. The Mass was at St Martin of Tours where I went to school, the school where she had walked me to every day. After the Mass was over, we walked behind the casket on the way out of the church.

I had no idea how to behave. I remember walking behind the casket and seeing people I knew looking at me. It felt so strange.

We drove to the cemetery, and it seemed that one thing was worse than the other. Seeing her casket closed now and prepared to be lowered into the ground was unbearable.

I had been to funerals before, but this was my mother's, and it was too much to absorb. She was only 40 years old. All I could think about was how could this happen? I couldn't understand it, let alone deal with it, and I thought if this could happen, anything could happen. Without realizing it, it shook my confidence and beliefs about everything from then on. I had no idea how to live without her.

After a few days past, I started to think about the last time I saw her alive. She was in Pelham Bay General Hospital in the Bronx. In those days, kids weren't allowed up into the hospital rooms, but that didn't matter. Somebody managed to sneak me up to her room to see her. I don't remember if it was my father or my brother.

I went into her room and walked over to her. I leaned over to kiss her, and she grabbed me and pulled me to her. I put my head on her chest and hugged her. She was holding me tight, and I could feel her starting to cry. She said, "You're getting so big." That was all she said. She held me close, and I hugged her as hard as I could. I had no way of knowing that was the last time I would ever see her alive. But she knew. I could tell by the way she held me that she knew and that's why she was crying.

Jesus Christ what she must have been going through? It's only now that I have children of my own that I can even attempt to understand. I loved her so much, and I can only hope and pray that she knew that. I hope to God that she knew how much we all loved her. She was, and is, our strength.

Life went on, so to speak, for us after the funeral but everything was strange. We were all dealing with her not being there in our own way. Who the hell really knew how to do that anyway? It was impossible for things to get back to normal because nothing was normal after that.

I'm really not sure how my brother and father were dealing with it probably the same way I was. I can only talk about myself, and even that is hard because you block so much out without even realizing it.

I do remember feeling different from everybody else after she died, especially in school. Of course, everybody knew what had happened, and they couldn't help but look at you differently.

One of my uncles was keeping an eye on my father because he started walking up and down the block where my mother used to work. I still think my father had the hardest situation to deal with. Not only did he lose the woman he loved, but he had two sons to deal with too. I'm sure he was in no condition to help anybody, even himself, let alone his two kids. Of course, he did that too. You can't help but be affected by that type of strength and courage.

Somehow, time went by. She died on July 20th, so it wasn't long before the holidays rolled around, which was the worst time of all, especially the first year. Our apartment was still the same, but she wasn't there. My father still hadn't gotten around to getting rid of all her stuff so it seemed like she was still around. It was very hard on all of us.

Then something happened that I never expected. The three of us got even closer as a family. We learned together that year, the holidays would never really be something, we looked forward to again.

Somehow we got through that first Christmas and New Years. But for us, the New Year brought with it a sense of dread because from then on, it would be, for us, a time to figure out what our lives could possibly be. We didn't know what to do now. My mother had left us with so much, and at the same time, her not being there left us with so little.

I couldn't believe that memories of her were all that we would have now, but that was it. As time went by, as good as those memories were, that was all we had. We tried as hard as anybody could be expected to, but it was no use. The void was too deep.

* * * * *

Time went by, as it always does, and we had to start living our lives without her. It was a daily struggle, but we knew without talking about it, that she would want us to go on. We did our best for her sake more than our own all the time knowing she was with us. I just thank God we had her as long as we did; she was that kind of person. Someone who could affect you for the rest of your life even without being there.

I just wish she was here now to see my kids, her grandchildren, and for them to see her and to know her. But that's my job now to make sure they know who she was and what she was like. I will do that and that will be part of their upbringing to know who she was and how much she would have loved them and how much she meant to all our lives. Even though I miss her more than I can say, it's a great comfort to know that she will live in them forever, and they will benefit, as I have, from her memory.

Many years had to pass before I could come to feel as I do now. I never thought this day would come, but somewhere along the line, I had decided to make some good come from the tragedy of losing my mother. I didn't believe that such a thing would be possible until I had my own children. My daughter is still too young, but I have already started to talk to my son about her. Even though it's very hard for both of us, it's hard for me for obvious reasons, but I've learned that it's hard for him too because he's still young, and he feels bad for me about the whole thing. So, it's hard on him too, and I have to take this into consideration when I talk to him about the whole subject.

It's okay though, because it's all about love for your mother. Although it's hard for him, it will teach him some valuable lessons about life, and it will also teach him to appreciate his own mother even more than he already does. So, it's all positive. Everything that comes naturally to me about raising my children is a direct result of my own upbringing from my mother and father, so it's very satisfying to know that what I got from my parents is what helps me give to my kids. I could never be the person I am today without the love I got from my parents. That's what I'll give to my children, and that, for me, is what will complete the cycle.

I will refer to my mother throughout this book because it is impossible not to. She is a part of every day of my life. From the time she was here with us and after she left us, I feel more in tune with her now that she's gone. Obviously, I would prefer that she was here but she's not, so I have to keep her memory alive. The sorrow and emptiness never goes away. You just find ways to deal with it. Writing about her is the best way I can think of to do her justice and to keep her alive in my heart always.

Chapter 28

What happens when you grow up somewhere and there are no boundaries for what you're allowed to do? Things can get really out of control. That's where you have to have some kind of inner strength to draw on because if you don't, you become a follower. And followers have no direction of their own they use other peoples.

There were a lot of followers in the neighborhood. Thank God I wasn't one of them. Sure, I was influenced by certain people, but when it came down to doing something I didn't want to do, I just said, "Fuck you", and if that didn't go over well with whoever, we'll that's just tough shit. That's the way I was. I never consciously tried to be that way. That's just the way I was. I made some friends because of that attitude, and I lost some friends because of it, so what. Somehow, I knew that in the long run that way of thinking would help me out. Sometimes it did, sometimes it didn't. But mostly it did. That's the thing about feeling sure of yourself. When things don't work out because of a decision you've made, you can't doubt yourself. Otherwise, you're influenced negatively about yourself. Once that happens, you're finished. Especially in this neighborhood, where weaknesses are detected and exploited all in one quick motion. Blind faith in yourself and what you believed in was the only way, even when you weren't sure; especially when you weren't sure.

We spent a lot of time hanging out in P.S. 32 schoolyard especially in the summertime. It was about a block away from the playground behind St. Martin's School. St. Martin's playground was where all the black and Puerto Rican gangs would hang out. The block that separated us became kind of a boundary between us; somewhat of a no man's land. You didn't want to be caught on that block by yourself because anything could happen.

It was during this time in the early to mid 70's that tensions were at their highest. Groups of blacks would wander around close to the neighborhood and fuck with people they came in contact with just to see how much they could get away with. They wanted to be able to come into our neighborhood.

It's important to point out that whenever there was trouble in the neighborhood, it was usually for one reason and that was when blacks came in looking for trouble. They weren't allowed in the neighborhood. Everybody knew it, and they knew it too.

It's also crucial to understand that they were kept out of the neighborhood for good reason. When I say "they or them", I'm not referring to all black people. I am talking about the kind of black people that settled into or around an area and turned it to shit.

Within a couple of short years, the areas around the neighborhood or the outskirts of the neighborhood were quickly turned into slums. This did not go unnoticed.

The simple fact was that every ethnic group had gone through this neighborhood without incident. It wasn't until now that black people were living there that the area was run down. This was not a coincidence, and it had nothing to do with prejudice. If the people who were ruining the neighborhood were pink, I would say the same thing. But they weren't; they were black. We had already been forced to give up our jobs for these people because of the city's cedar program. There was no way we were going to give up the neighborhood too!

Like I said before, this has nothing to do with hating black people. I had black people at my own wedding years later. It had to do with pride in where you lived.

Of course, you had the politicians saying that black people had every right to live wherever they wanted, but they were just full of shit assholes and nobody paid any attention to them anyway. These were the same jerk offs that attended protests and rallies for blacks and the underprivileged. They would be yelling and screaming that blacks and whites should be allowed to live together. When they were through, they'd get back in their limos and go home to their exclusive white neighborhoods in Westchester County. The bottom line was that they wanted us to live next door to the black people ruining the neighborhoods, but they would never live with them. They wanted us to live by rules and standards they themselves would never live by. They were full of shit, phony bastards. They knew it, but more importantly, we knew it.

One afternoon a couple of black guys walked down Ruthra Avenue and attempted to rob one of the shopkeepers. He was an old Italian guy who ran a modest fruit stand. He was very proud as most of them were, and unfortunately for him, he put up a fight. They stabbed and killed him right in front of his family, who worked with him. As his family started screaming at what they saw, people started chasing after them. They caught up to the two black guys right in front of where we were hanging out. There were about seven or eight guys that grabbed them. They beat the shit out of them. It was really brutal. They were kicking them in the head and beating them with baseball bats. By the time the cops got there, there was nothing left of them but a bloody heap. It was horrible. You could actually hear their bones snap as they bent their arms and legs in the opposite direction they were supposed to go.

This was justice in the neighborhood; swift and deadly. It was a very difficult thing to witness. It was the kind of thing that stayed with you. Seeing someone beaten to death right in front of you wasn't easy, but they did kill an innocent guy right in front of his family, and they paid for it with their own lives.

While I didn't always agree with the code of justice in the neighborhood; I had to admit one thing, and that was, very simply, it was a very safe place to live. That's the way things were.

* * * * *

The 70's were a wild time in the neighborhood. We had plenty to keep us busy. Most of the time, we hung out in the club in the basement of an apartment building on Beaumont Avenue.

We only went to school when it was absolutely necessary, which was hardly ever. During the day, we were in the club waiting for the girls to get out of school. They always went to school. If we got bored, we'd go down to JoJo's Candy Store. Sometimes we'd talk some of the girls into cutting out of school with us. That's when we really partied.

When we had something lined up with them, we'd usually end up at my father's apartment. Jackie and I always had something going on. Jackie was my stepbrother now instead of just my friend.

Our parents were at work during the day, and we took advantage of that just as we took advantage of everything else.

Jackie was kind of going out with Carol Bodetto. I say kind of because if she was in school that day, he would be with somebody else. We were all like that. Carol had a retarded younger brother named Milo. She would have to watch him a lot of the time because her mother, Dolly, was out doing God knows what. This really aggravated Jackie since he was always trying to get in her pants. It was really inconvenient having a retarded little brother around, to say the least.

Anyway, you never knew what you might find walking into the club or our parent's apartment. One day I came home from school, I actually went that day. As I put the key in the door of the apartment I stopped for a minute. I could hear some strange noises inside. I walked into the apartment and was shocked. I could see into the kitchen from the doorway.

There was Milo, Carol's little brother, strapped to one of the kitchen chairs mumbling. I knew right away what was going on. Jackie was probably getting laid in one of the bedrooms and had strapped the kid to a chair so they didn't have to watch him. I shouldn't have been surprised. Jackie was a good guy and a great friend, but there was nothing he wouldn't do to get laid. It was just so funny. He had used three or four belts from our pants in the closet. The kid was belted to the chair from his ankles to his chest. As I got closer to him, I could hear him. He was looking up at the ceiling saying, "Michael, Mikey, Michael."

I walked past the kid and into the bedroom. Jackie was in the bed with Carol. I walked in and said, "Jackie, what the fuck are you doing?" He looked at me and said, "What, I'm getting a little action over here." I said, "Milo's strapped to a chair in the kitchen." He said, "I know, I'm trying to get laid, gimme a break." I started laughing and walked out.

I could understand it in a way. Milo was a retarded kid, plus he was about 12 or 14 years old. He was very strong, and he was likely to do anything. Just that week, he had poured a gallon of milk into his mother's fish tank and then threw the tank out the window. The week before that he climbed into his brother's bed and shit on his head while he was sleeping. I could understand Jackie not wanting to leave him loose in his mother's apartment, but it was such a funny sight to see when I came home.

A couple of days later we were back up at the apartment only this time there were more of us. I was there with Jackie, and we had about four or five girls up there with us. I forgot who else was there, but there were about five girls and four guys including us, Debbie, Jackie's sister, was there too.

We would play spin the bottle. We'd sit around in a circle and spin a coke bottle and whoever the first two spins pointed to would pair off and then go into the bedroom for a certain amount of time, usually about ten minutes. Debbie was going out with Rocco so she usually was in charge of keeping time. Our parents were at work so we didn't expect any problems.

We went a few rounds of spin the bottle and things were going just fine. Then, while we were all paired off in the bedrooms, we heard the lock on the front door open. Well, not all of us heard it, but somebody did. Debbie started yelling for us to stop and before we knew what was going on, Jackie's mother,

Isabel, was coming through the front door. She was screaming, "What the hell is going on in here?"

We all jumped out of the beds we were in and started pulling our pants up. Here we were all running for the front door right past her. She was screaming at us, "You bastard's, what do you think this is?" The beds were all messed up, and we were all running, half naked, for the door. Once we got out the door, we started running down the flights of stairs to the streets. By this time, we were all laughing.

Jackie's grandmother lived on the first floor of the building. She was a real sweetheart of a woman. As we all ran past her and out of the building, she would be standing there with her hands covering her mouth. She started yelling at us in Italian, "What a you do? Managia, what a you do?" It was so funny.

We were in big trouble now. Isabel was really pissed. She was notorious for keeping her apartment neat and clean, and we just fucked it all up. Not to mention the smell of sex in the bedrooms, and the mess we didn't have time to clean up.

Now, we were really in trouble. It would take hours before Isabel would cool down after this one. We had been doing this in her apartment for quite awhile, but we had never gotten caught before, especially right in the middle of everything,

Anyway, we headed straight for the club, and didn't go home for a couple of days. This got us in even more trouble, but we didn't care. Trouble was trouble. And in a weird way we always figured once you were in trouble, if you just compound it with more trouble, it was tough to focus on any one thing. That's a very strange way to think. But what can I say, we thought that way, and believe it or not, it worked.

We spent a lot of time in P.S. 32 Schoolyard. It was one of our hangouts. We'd play handball, stickball, football, whatever. It was a lot of fun, and we were good at everything we played. Honestly, without trying to sound cocky, we really were. We won championships with JoJo's football teams, we were among the best teams in Little League Baseball, and we kicked everybody's ass in handball.

But there were a lot of distractions. By this time, we were partying a lot too. Nothing we would consider serious. We drank, and we smoked pot but nothing really heavy. We were in the schoolyard one day hanging out when we noticed Joe Biondi walking around the back of the schoolyard. He was the neighborhood junkie. A real pain in the ass. He was always fucked up, yelling and screaming all the time. Basically, he was always being a jerk. He would always be bothering the girls and anybody else he could intimidate. He would do this all the time and then he would just fall asleep wherever he was. He would never fuck with us because he knew better.

It was a real hot day, and we were all a little bored. Somebody came and told us that he was sleeping on the grass in the back of the schoolyard.

We decided to have a little fun. And fun for us could mean just about anything. We were already a little pissed that he was bothering the girls. This was nothing new. But the combination of it being hot and us being bored, and we couldn't stand him in the first place, gave us ideas.

I don't remember who but somebody thought it would be really funny if we lit him on fire. You know, while he was sleeping.

We talked about this while we were finishing our game of handball. One of the girls was still crying about what he had done to her. She was cursing him and saying, "Yeah, go ahead, he deserves it". The girls loved to egg us on. They were famous for putting ideas in our heads and then complaining that we were crazy for doing it. They were really annoying that way.

We took a walk to the back of the school yard, and there he was sleeping on the grass. A big, fat fuck just lying there. We sent one of the guys to the candy store around the corner for some newspapers and lighter fluid. We crumpled up the newspaper into balls and put them in a circle around him. We doused them all with lighter fluid. We didn't have to worry about him waking up since he was out cold.

Somebody lit a match and threw it on the pile of newspapers. We stood there and watched as it all caught fire. Finally, something woke him up. It was either the heat, the smoke or both. He went crazy. He tried to get up, but he was so stoned that he kept falling down. He finally got up and ran through the flames screaming. We were all laughing our asses off. He never bothered the girls again. As a matter of fact, he never even came in the schoolyard again. He was never in any real danger, but he didn't know that. We got our point across. It was too funny. Just another day in the neighborhood. That is the way things worked there. There were plenty of people that would fuck with you for whatever reason. As long as you had the ways and means to turn things around on them, you were all right. But you bad to be able to do that, and those that weren't able to, get fucked, over and over.

Chapter 29

Jean Marie Banfi was one of the neighborhood girls. She was also one of the best looking girls. I was fortunate to know her and know her well. Together, we had one of the longest on again, off again relationships in the neighborhood. It's not easy to put into words what she meant to me, and the rest of us who knew her, but I will try. I picked this night, or I should say this night picked me to talk about her because I found out today that she passed away. Those of us who knew her well, all died a little today too. At least a piece of us was chipped away and went with her.

She had been suffering from cancer for the past few years, and I guess it finally took its ugly toll on her. She was living out in California, near her sister, Carol, another sweetheart, when she died. She also had two children, a son 10 years old, and a daughter about 4 or 5. The last time I talked to her was about two weeks ago. I could hear the pain in her voice when she said she couldn't talk. She was waiting for the doctor to get there. She suffered so much at the end that if it weren't for the sake of her kids; you had to be happy for her that she was at peace now.

About a year and a half ago when I was going in for my brain surgery, she was the one trying to cheer me up when I talked to her, with everything she was going through. That's the kind of person she was. We will remember her and miss her at the same time.

Anyway, it would be unfair and a complete waste to only talk about the end of her life. She was a lot of fun, and a great friend to all of us. She was my girlfriend for a long time, and even during the times we had split up, I would still see her. No matter who I was going out with at the time, if we got caught, we got caught. Neither of us cared. She was a tough kid, and she would kick the shit out of anybody, guy or girl, that pissed her off. It made for a stormy relationship for both of us, but we loved it.

I remember a friend of mine, Anthony Astorino, knocked on the door of my apartment one day. I opened the door, and he had this huge black eye, I said, "What the fuck happened to you?" He said, "You know, you better talk to that girlfriend of yours, I'm serious." I couldn't believe it. I said, "Jean Marie? She did that to you?" He said, "Yeah, I didn't do nothing because she's your girl, but you better straighten her out." It was the funniest thing. He told me he said something about me that she didn't like, and she belted him. I was laughing my ass off. He was really pissed. He said, "You know, she's lucky she's your girl." This was really funny because if he would have tried to do anything about it, she probably would have really kicked his ass, and he would have worse than a black eye. She was really something, a real ball of fire.

We had great times, with so much fun and laughs. In the summertime, we would go to Orchard Beach and then hang out at the feast in the neighborhood at night. She would basically kick any girl's ass that showed an interest in me. Part of the reason we really clicked, I think, was because we had both lost our mothers. Of course, we never mentioned that. We were far too tough to admit that, but it was there, and we both knew it.

It's impossible to try to explain what she meant to me in a few paragraphs. When somebody is a big part of your life, especially your early life as a teenager, there are so many memories, and the memories from that time have an innocent quality because you were young. When you know somebody from that part of your life, I mean really know them, it stays with you forever no matter how much time goes by. You could talk to them after five or ten years have gone by, and it's still the same. It all just comes right back. That's the thing about friends from that time. It's all about friendship because there was nothing else. There was no responsibility. Not like later on in your life when there are car payments, house payments, jobs, wives, kids, etc. Not that those are bad things, in any way, but it was just a different time in your life that will only happen once and never again. That's okay because there are things that happen in your life later on, like your wife and your kids, that could never have happened then. Just different times.

I will refer to this part of my life over and over again because it is impossible not to. I will dedicate this small chapter to Jean Marie's memory so that in some small way, I can pay tribute to her and maybe she can live on through this book.

It was July 1999 when we all finally gathered for Jean Marie's memorial service at St. Raymond's Cemetery in the Bronx. It was a day we all looked forward to with mixed emotions. Although she had died on February 27 in California and was cremated there, now she was coming home. It was a sad day, no question, but we were all happy that we had the chance to pay tribute to her together. Obviously, she was the main focus of the day, and it was because of her we were all there. But there was no way to escape the anticipation of the day.

I was driving in from New Jersey to meet with five girls from the neighborhood that I hadn't seen for about 25 years. Not to mention Jean Marie's sister, Carol, who I hadn't seen for even longer than that. Carol always had a special place in my heart. I'm not even sure why, but she did.

As if that wasn't enough, I was also going to see Jean Marie's children for the first time. I knew her son's name was Frankie, but I didn't know her daughter's name.

Anyway, I got to where I was supposed to meet the girls on Williams Bridge Road in the Bronx. Although it had been about 25 years since we'd seen each other, we were together almost every day for years back then. So I didn't think it would take too long to get comfortable with them. There would be Laura, Anna, Diana, Joy and Phyllis. And it took even less time than I thought.

It was almost like no time had passed at all. I know that sounds like an exaggeration, but it's the truth.

I pulled up in front of Casa Mia Restaurant. Anna and Laura were there, and no one else. It was a real hot day about 95 degrees. I told them I'd be back in a few minutes. I wanted to stop at Jackie's office on Williams Bridge Road. Anna looked at me and said, "Hurry up, don't leave me roasting over here." I drove away laughing at what she said.

When I went back a few minutes later, Diana, Joy and Phyllis were there. It was unbelievable to see them all again. We said a quick hello and left for the cemetery. Diana and Joy came with me in my car. Laura, Anna and Phyllis went in Laura's car.

There was a little confusion finding the gravesite at the cemetery, but we finally found it. On the way there, Joy, Diana and I talked and caught up a little bit, or as much as you can catch up after 25 years. I really enjoyed talking to them. If was obvious we were real comfortable with each other immediately.

After the service for Jean Marie, we were talking about where we should go for lunch. That's when I heard something that froze me for a second. One of the girls suggested a place to eat, a new restaurant that was owned by Frankie Grecco. She said, "You remember his father Niko from the neighborhood?" I couldn't believe my ears. I had been writing about what I had been through with Niko for almost a year. I hear somebody mention his name, stunned me for a second. I started asking questions that day and haven't stopped since. It was the first time I'd heard his name in 25 years. But we were there for Jean Marie's funeral, so out of respect, I dropped the subject.

We wound up going to a different place to eat on Williams Bridge Road. We all ate and talked about the old days. It was great to see everybody, but it was a sad day. Jean Marie's kids were at the restaurant with us, and it was heart breaking to watch them having dinner on the day of their mother's funeral. I couldn't help thinking about my own mother's funeral, and how I felt that day. I felt so bad for her kids. As I watched them, I thought about what they were going to have to deal with. Going through the rest of their lives without their mother and how that would always make them feel different than everybody else. Not to mention the worst part of all, how much they would miss her from that day on. When you lose your mother at a young age, the only memories you have are from that day and before that day. The problem is that you have to go forward. And there will be no more memories. You have to go the rest of your life with only what you can remember. And it's never enough. Even if you're lucky enough to get through the rest of your childhood, get married and have children of your own, nothing will ever fill that hole. And it never ends. It just eats at you in so many different ways.

Although I was nervous about it, I was dying to see Niko. When things didn't work out the first couple of time we tried to meet, I decided to wait. My wife was pregnant with our third child and due to deliver, in about three weeks. Barbara knew how important it was to me, to be able to see Niko after all this time. She understood and was very supportive about what I was writing about. But she needed me now. And as excited as I was about my writing, Barbara and the baby had to come first.

The baby would be delivered by C Section and the date was set for April 18, 2000. It was an exciting time for all of us. Even thought the date was getting close, it was still hard to believe, the thought of having three kids scared the shit out of me. It wasn't because we didn't know how we would do it. It was because we did know how we would do it! Anybody who worked while they raised their kids knows what I mean. We had two children already, so we had experience. And that

Me & Maria

would help. On the other hand, knowing what it's like to have one child doesn't mean you know what it's like to have two. And the same thing goes for having three. And so on. But hey, no complaints here. What you get out of having kids, easily out weighs what you go through to raise them. You just don't always feel that way while you're raising them.

April 18th came as fast as any other day we were worried about. We drove to St. Clares Hospital, the same place we had the other two kids. When we got there, it all seemed so familiar.

It was only 2 years ago that our daughter Maria was born. We went through the admitting process and everything else as though we were in a fog or something. We were so shocked by this pregnancy that the whole thing was kind of unbelievable. We spent the last couple of months convincing ourselves that we could handle having three kids. In fact, we were so wrapped up in how we were going to do it, we forgot all about what it would be like to experience childbirth again.

That all I changed the minute Barbara began being prepped for surgery. Once we were in the operating room, it was like nothing else mattered. Everything else in your life seemed to stand still.

During the delivery, my mind was all over the place. I though about the twenty three hours of labor my wife went through, when my son was born natural childbirth. I'm proud to say that I was with her for every minute of it. For the first seven hours, all we could see was the top of his head. Because his arm was wrapped around his head, it was another sixteen hours before we had him. By the time he came out, I was a lunatic. Because of the position of the baby

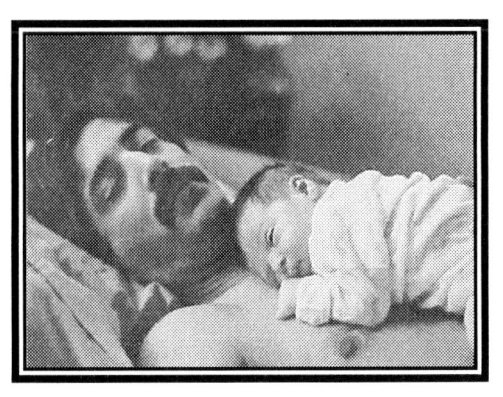

My brother Joe and my son Danny

and the pressure of the delivery, my son's head looked really weird. It freaked me out. It was almost in the shape of a football. The doctor said, "Mr. Genelli, would you like to cut the umbilical cord?" I said, "'Are you nuts? I don't want to cut nothing. What's wrong with his head?" My wife said, "Anthony calm down, it's ok." The doctor said, "Don't worry; it'll straighten out in a couple of days." I said, "Straighten out, we ain't talking about a fender over here, we're talking about his head. He's going to need that forever." Barbara convinced me to leave the room for a while, so I could calm down. I wasn't happy with the doctor's explanation of the baby's head, or how he explained it. I guess I could have been over reacting but after twenty three hours, I really didn't give a fuck. All I cared about was Barbara and the baby. When I went back into the room, the nurse put my son into my arms. He was pretty banged up from the delivery but he looked better already. He still had blood all over his face and in his hair but his head looked well. He had big brown eyes and as I held him in my arms, I could see my reflection in his eyes. It would be a waste of time to try to explain what that felt like.

When my daughter was born, she was delivered by C Section, which is a whole different ball game. I was there for that too, but didn't watch the surgery, Thank God. I want to be there for my wife but I had no desire to see what was happening. The first time I saw my daughter, she looked perfect. That was because of the C Section. I couldn't believe how good she looked.

Meanwhile, the surgery for our third child was going extremely well. We were starting to get excited because we knew we would be able to see the baby soon. I was still thinking how happy I was about not having to watch the delivery, when I heard the doctor say "Here she come, she looks great, Mr. Genelli, do you want to see your daughter being born?" I felt like a chump, not to watch. So I got up and looked over the sheet that was there. If you didn't want to see anything, that was a big mistake. When I saw what was happening, I was overwhelmed. One of the doctors was pulling the baby out of the opening in my wife's stomach, which wasn't the worst of it. The thing that really got to me was what the other doctor was doing. With one of his hands, he was pulling back the opening of my wife's stomach. His other hand was moving, God knows what, out of the way so the baby could get out. There was blood everywhere. I tried not to look at anything but the baby. No matter how hard I tried, I could still see what was going on.

As I watched my second daughter come into the world, I started to cry. It was just too much. Even though she was my third child or maybe because of that, I was overcome with the miracle of birth. I felt blessed, lucky and scared, all at the same time. I felt blessed for a lot of reasons. But mostly because of being able to survive the brain surgery I had, while my wife was pregnant with our second child. I felt lucky because I have spent almost two decades after my mother died, acting like an irresponsible asshole. And I never thought anything would work out right, after that. After all these years to wind up with a beautiful wife and three kinds, if that ain't lucky, I don't know what is. And I was scared because I knew, from first hand experience, what it took to raise a child, especially the third time around.

Chapter 30

It was the middle of May and a brand new century. The year two thousand, who could believe it? There was so much going on, but that was nothing new either. Barbara and I had our third child in April of that year. Our daughter Natalie was born on the 18th. We were both still overwhelmed by the thought of having three kids. She was so unexpected but of course, we were already in love with her. I was still trying to deal with the thought of having one daughter, now we had two. It was unbelievable. For 9½ years it was Barbara, Danny, and me. Now what seemed like all of a sudden, it was me, Barbara, Danny, Maria and Natalie. Even so, I knew we were blessed. It was just so much, all at once. As if that wasn't enough, and believe me, it was, I was going to meet Niko in the neighborhood, the following week.

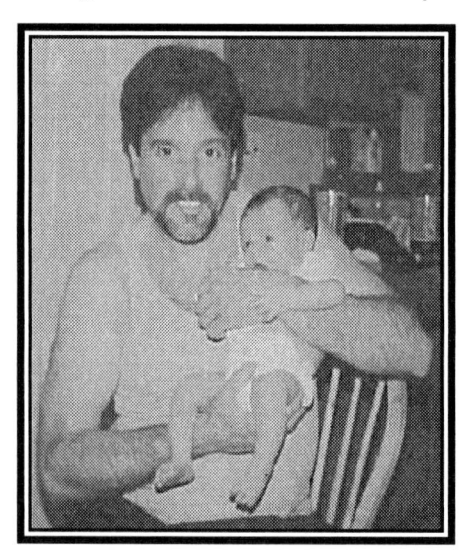

Me and Natalie

Even though I had been planning to see him for months, it was still weird. There was so much going on. Obviously, the baby being born was the most important thing. On top of all of this, a month before the baby was born; I got fired from my job. I had been working there for four years. For them to fire me a month before the baby was due, tells you all you need to know about those assholes. But that's another story. Fuck them. I wound up collecting $420 a week from unemployment that they had to pay me. Plus, I was able to be home with my wife, when the baby was born. I didn't care about the job because I could always get another one. I had been tending bar for 14 years in all kinds of places. I could find a job whenever I wanted. So I decided to let them pay me to be home with my family.

Anyway, you get the idea. Even though it was going to be unbelievable to see Niko after almost 25 years had gone by, it wasn't the only thing on my mind, which probably helped. I still couldn't believe I had found a way to get in touch with him, let alone see him. But because of everything else that was going on, I didn't have time to dwell on what it would be like. If seeing Niko were all I had to think about, it would have driven me nuts.

On May 18, a month after my daughter was born, I drove to the Bronx to meet Niko. After 25 years, I didn't know what to expect. But I couldn't wait. I was really excited to finally be able to see him. I knew I'd be nervous but I tried to block that out. I had to look past that because if I didn't I'd never be able to see him.

I got to the neighborhood a little early. I was supposed to meet him at the coffee shop, at 12:00 in the afternoon. I drove around for a couple of minutes and tried to calm down. I had been living in NJ for the past 12 years and had made this trip to the neighborhood hundreds of time. It was home to me. I grew up there, in more ways than one. It was the only place I was really comfortable at. But this was different. I loved being there and every street had a different memory. But this was unbelievable. There were two things going on here, in my mind. One was, to be seeing somebody after all these years. The other thing was who I would be seeing.

It was 12:00, when I turned onto Crosby Avenue. I figured, fuck it, let's do it. The coffee shop was in the middle of the block and as I got closer, I saw him. There were three or four guys hanging out in front of the place. And standing in the doorway, watching everything that was going on was Niko. I had spent the last year and a half trying to find him. But once I saw him, I froze and drove right by the place. I drove around the block and pulled over. It was a weird feeling. I knew it was going to be strange to see him. And it would be difficult to just walk over and say hello after all this time. But I couldn't believe how nervous I was. For whatever reason, I never anticipated that. I also never considered the fact that there would be other people around, which was pretty stupid, once you thought about it. What did I expect? It's not like he was going to be standing there by himself, waiting for me to show up. I felt like an idiot, which didn't exactly fill me with confidence. It was bad enough that I was nervous about seeing Niko. Now I had to do that with all these guys standing around. I had no choice. So that's what I did.

I drove down Crosby Avenue and looked for a place to park. I found a spot on the comer and pulled into it. The coffee shop was in the middle of the block. As I got out of my car, I could see Niko standing in the middle of the block. I tried to relax but it was impossible. I kept my eye on Niko and kept walking. Any second now, either Niko or somebody else, would see me coming. I knew that. In this neighborhood you can't walk up to a place like this without being spotted. As I got closer, it felt like everything was happening in slow motion. I kept walking. Now there was about fifty feet and twenty five years between me and Niko. Then he turned and saw me coming. First him, then the rest of them. This was the hardest part. I walked the rest of the way to the coffee shop, with all of them checking me out. It was nuts. But I kept walking. I was a few feet away when I said, "Hey Niko." I was smiling at him, I have no idea why. I was happy to see him, but I didn't know what to expect. I was also scared shit. He looked at me and said "Anthony?" I said "Yeah." We were face to face now. I said, "How the hell are you?" He said, "Good, good, you look the same. I knew it was you right away." He looked the same but different. We shook hands, and I was thinking, what the fuck do I do now? This all happened with the other guys standing there, wondering who the hell I was. But I really didn't give a fuck about them. Seeing Niko was all I cared about. I was a little uncomfortable and wasn't sure what to do next. He could see I was nervous and said, "Let's go inside."

We went inside and sat at the coffee bar. He walked behind the bar and said, "Cappuccino or espresso?" I said "Whatever you're having is fine with me." He started making espresso for both of us as I sat there watching him. I didn't know what to do with myself. I had so much on my mind, so many things to tell him and so many questions to ask. As I stood there, I thought about what I had been through with him. It was something I had done many times before, and had been writing about. I had spent years trying to put what I had experienced with him into words, but this was completely different. Now I was thinking back to those times while I was standing in the same room with him! Something I never thought would happen.

We both sat at the bar, sipping our espressos. We talked a little bit, the usual bullshit. Things like, how the fuck are you? Where have you been, it's been a long time. Stuff like that. I told him how good it was to see him, which sounded stupid to me because it didn't even come close to explaining how I really felt. I took my time as I talked to him. I was trying to pick my spots and see what I could talk to him about. It wasn't easy. I was excited, but nervous. It didn't help that the whole time I was with him, we were constantly interrupted. Every couple of minutes, somebody would walk into the coffee shop to see if he needed anything. They'd come in to say hello to him, then it would be like "Niko, you alright?" "You need anything?" "You hungry?" "Can I get you anything?" It was really something. He sent one of them to the deli around the block. He told the guy to get sandwiches for everybody. He said "Anthony, you hungry?" I said, "Go ahead and eat. I'm going to do some shopping in the neighborhood. I gotta get some bread, cold cuts and pastries to bring home with me. I'll be back in a little while." He said, "Sounds good, I'll be here."

I left the coffee shop and walked up the block to 18th Street. I did have to do some shopping but I really wanted to get out of there for a few minutes. Seeing Niko and spending some time with him, one on one, brought back a flood of emotions for me. Between that and the sense of accomplishment I felt for being able to find him, was too much for me. I wish I could explain what was going through my mind. I already knew, I couldn't, I didn't have the words. I knew any description would come up short.

I walked back to my car, opened the door and got in. I leaned back in the seat and thought about what was going on. I picked up my cell phone and called my wife. I knew she was nervous about what I was doing and wanted to let her know I was ok, but I really just wanted to hear her voice. There are a lot of things I love about Barbara and our kids, but what I love most is that we are a family. A true family in every sense of the word.

Barbara and I are very different people, but we share the same idea of what a family should be. We both felt that there was nothing as important as that. Ever since my mother died, having a complete family of my own was something I'd always hoped for. Now that I had one, especially after all the shit we had been through, it was a source of strength for me.

When Barbara answered the phone, I said "Hey Babe, it's me", she said, "Are you ok?" I said, "Yeah, I'm fine. I just needed to hear your voice." I could hear the kids in the background and that settled me down. She said, "I'm not going to ask any questions, I know how important this is to you. Just do what you have to do and come home." I said, "Thanks, That's exactly what I'm going to do. I'll be leaving in about an hour." She said, "OK" and I hung up the phone.

I got out of the car and walked around the block. My mind was all over the place. I had to go back to the coffee shop. I was dying to talk to Niko but it was impossible. There were a lot of people around and it didn't seem like I'd be able to talk to him alone. I wasn't surprised. He always was the center of attention and obviously still was. Plus I was nervous about talking to him, even without bringing up the book I was working on. That's the way it was with him. It all came back to me, just by spending a couple of minutes with him. Even though he made people nervous and sometimes uncomfortable, you still wanted to be around him. I was no different.

I started walking back to the coffee shop. I didn't know if I'd be able to talk to Niko about the book but I couldn't leave without trying. When I turned the corner I could see him standing in front of the place.

I started walking down the block. I wanted to talk to him again before I left for the day. As I got closer to him I started to freeze up a little bit. It was a familiar feeling for me. It was how I felt twenty five years ago and it was how I felt earlier in the day, before I saw him again after all that time. So when I felt nervous again, as I waked toward him for the second time that day, I just said, fuck it. He had that kind of affect on people. If you wanted to see him or talk to him, you just had to get past that.

When I got to him, he put his arm around me and told me to hang out for a while. He was talking to a couple of guys, which wasn't unusual. It sounded like they needed his help with something. Nothing new there, either. I sat down at one of the small tables, outside the club. One of the guys brought me an espresso. I sat there and took in the whole scene. Being in the neighborhood was something I always loved. Connecting with Niko after all these years, just added to the feeling of being there.

It was a beautiful day. The sun was shining and the sound of the church bells filled the neighborhood. Those church bells filled by mind with memories. I heard them as I walked these streets with my mother. That was before she died, when I was just a kid. They never sounded the same after that. But they were always there. I grew up with that sound. It meant different things to me over the next eighteen years. Depending on what was going on in my life. Then, in 1985 I heard them in a way I never thought I would. On October 12th of that year, Columbus Day, Barbara and I were married at St. Mary's. As we walked out onto the street after the ceremony, the church bells were never louder.

All of these memories were shooting through my mind as I sat there watching Niko. It was almost too much to absorb. At the time, my life and where I was living it, were worlds apart from the neighborhood. It was weird. Even though it couldn't be more different, I was completely comfortable. I sat there and took it all in. As I thought about what I was writing about, I had a tremendous feeling of accomplishment. I know that there are going to be times when I repeat myself as I try to put this story into words I just don't give a fuck at this point. I wasn't only writing about things as I remembered them, I was reliving them. So I will talk about them and explain these feelings, from that point of view.

I was sitting there, sipping my espresso when I saw three black guys turn the corner and walk toward the coffee shop. One of them was carrying a huge radio on his shoulder. I thought to myself, holy shit, this ain't good. I remember thinking; at least it ain't that loud. As I was thinking this, the three of them stopped and put the radio on the hood of a parked car. They put a tape in, blasted the volume and slapped each other five. Then they picked up the radio and walked toward the coffee shop. I just watched as they got closer.

I looked over at Niko, just in time to see his reaction. When he turned and saw them he said, "What the fuck is this?" A couple of guys came out of the coffee shop to see what was going on. One of them said, "Where's that nigger music coming from?" One of the other guys said, "It's corning from these three lowlifes walking toward us. These eggplants must be lost."

I felt bad for them. I knew nobody would make a move until Niko decided what should happen. The neighborhood had a reputation for not allowing this type of behavior. Ever since I was a kid, it was something I was always proud of. It was why the neighborhood was a safe place. Nobody could fuck with you there. Even though I understood all of this and knew the end result was a safe neighborhood, I never got used to witnessing the physical aspect of the situation. It was always brutal because it had to be.

When they got to the coffee shop, they stopped and looked at us. The music from their radio was really loud, and it sucked so bad, Niko said. "Shut that fucking thing off." One of them said, "It's a free country, we can listen to whatever we want." Niko said, "You're right, it is a free country. But when you're walking through this neighborhood, it's a little different. Things happen faster around here, you know what I'm sayin'? Shut it off."

As I sat there hoping the guy would just shut the fucking thing off, I was really getting nervous. This was all happening about ten feet from where I was sitting. The three black guys were pretty big and didn't look like they would back down. But there was something else. From where I was sitting, I could see inside the coffee shop. The guys inside were passing out pool cues and baseball bats. They were just waiting for something to happen. If Niko wasn't there, the situation would have already exploded. Because he was there, I felt there were two things that could set this whole thing off. One of them would be a signal from Niko, the other would be if these guys were stupid enough to make the first move. Somehow, every thing I had seen and thought about took place after Niko told them to shut the radio off and before anything had happened. I don't know how, but it did.

Now, Niko and the guy with the radio were standing face to face. They were looking into each other's eyes when Niko said, "Time's up." A few more seconds went by before the guy reached up to the radio on his shoulder and shut it off. Then he said, "You happy now?" Niko said, "Yeah, I am and you should be too. This works out real good for both of us. I get a new radio and you get to walk away." The three black guys started to laugh and so did Niko. The guy said, "I ain't giving you my radio, man." Niko said, "You can either leave the radio or the last thing you'll remember will be saying you won't." Niko looked toward the coffee shop and a few guys walked out carrying baseball bats. The guy with the radio put it down and said, "No problem, it's yours man." Then they started to walk away. They kept looking over their shoulders to see if anybody was following them. As they were walking, Niko said, "Don't worry about it, you just walked down the wrong block. As long as it doesn't happen again, you got nothing to worry about."

I was still sitting at the table with my espresso and I just started laughing. Niko walked over and sat down next to me. He said, "What's so funny?" I said, "I don't know. I guess all of it is." He said, "You're right. For the most part, everybody knows their place around here. But every once in a while, you're gonna get some asshole that has to be straightened out. And it has to be done." I sat there and listened to him talk about the neighborhood I had grown up in. I paid close attention to what he was saying. Just like I did the last time I saw him all those years ago. I knew then as I knew now, that Niko was somebody you should pay attention to. Not just because you had to or because you were better off if you did. These were both good reasons, but not the most important one. If you could get past all that, which wasn't easy, you realized he was almost always right. About everything.

I sat at the table with him and listened as one of the guys brought us espresso and sambuca. He talked about what had just happened and explained it in its simplest form.

He explained how these situations had to be handled. He said they should be dealt with the same exact way every time. Whether it seemed like a serious threat or not, it was the only way, whoever was causing the problem. It had nothing to do with prejudice, one way or the other. Niko looked at me and said, "People will always think it's race related. Because they've been conditioned to think that way. For whatever reason, you can't control what people think. It doesn't matter what they think anyway. So fuck them and what they think. The fact is we've had problems with white people too. And they were handled the same way. But nobody talks about that. Assholes are assholes, it doesn't matter what color their skin is. The bottom line is, you can't be an asshole around here, without paying the price. What happened here today was simple but will go a long way. These guys are gonna go back to wherever the fuck they came from and tell whoever they know, what happened here. That's what I want. Because now, they work for me. They just don't know it. They walk into the neighborhood like tough guys and they leave as messengers." I was looking at him and waiting to see if he was finished making his point. He looked back at me and said, "What are you looking at? You know how this shit goes, you grew up here. What happened, New Jersey make you stupid?" I laughed and said, "Of course not. I understand completely. I'm just happy to see nothing has changed around here after all this time." He said, "A lot of things have changed. Everything changes. This ain't the same place we remember from the seventies. That time is gone and we'll never see it again. There's people living in this neighborhood now that wouldn't even be allowed to walk through here years ago. The atmosphere has changed but the food, culture and core of the neighborhood are still the same. Yeah, things have changed. They always will. But the most important things are still the same.

    The people who made the rules around here twenty years ago, still do. We just don't live here anymore. By the end of the seventies we knew some things would be different It was a crazy time and there were bound to be some uncertainties. Other than that, there were three things about to happen we were absolutely sure of. The first was there were going to be black and Puerto Rican people living in the neighborhood. The second thing about to happen was there would be people moving out of the neighborhood. Nobody, including us, wanted to live with these people. They were animals and would bring down the quality of life around here, no question. The third and most important thing everyone could be sure of was that we could control this neighborhood no matter who was living here. We would put up with them being here but nothing more. They could walk around and shop in the stores, like everybody else. But they would be watched closely. Any sign of trouble or arrogance, would be dealt with swiftly. That's the way it was going to be. We knew it and more importantly, they knew it."

I just sat there and listened to him talk. By now I had just about gotten over the shock of seeing him again. I was relaxed and felt comfortable with him. It was amazing. I had just sat through an unbelievable scene. It was dangerous and could have gotten ugly. I was happy that everything turned out ok. But, honestly, I was more nervous about seeing Niko earlier that day than I ever was during that whole scene. I know that is hard to believe. And there is really no way to explain what I mean, unless you knew Niko. Driving into the neighborhood to see him after twenty five years made me nervous. I wasn't sure what to expect. But I knew exactly what to expect whenever he handled confrontations. These guys would either back down or I was going to have to watch them get hurt.

Chapter 31

You can't talk about the neighborhood without talking about Gino Valenti. To us kids growing up there, he was somebody you heard about but never really saw, and you heard about him a lot.

He was literally and figuratively bigger than life. Obviously, he was a big man, but his influence in the neighborhood was even bigger.

The neighborhood, in those days, was something you could only understand if you lived there. To an outsider, it might seem like a violent place. But to us, the only time there was violence was when somebody from the neighborhood or the neighborhood itself was being threatened.

The politicians in those days, whether it was John Lindsay or Abe Beam, were hell bent on giving every opportunity to black and Hispanic people. No doubt, because of their liberal views.

As I have mentioned before, a lot of us had already lost our jobs because of pressure to hire black people, and I mean, literally. One day you go to work and find out your job is gone because it was given to so called "underprivileged youths" moving in around the neighborhood. "What balls!" That was actually the reason they gave us! We had to deal with that, somehow, I mean, nobody gave us any alternatives after that. Nobody ever talks about this, which is why I am. There was no outcry for what we had lost. No "movement" for our situation; it was pathetic.

It was around this time that the Italian American organization was formed in the neighborhood. It was too late to help us or save our jobs, but maybe it would help people like us after that. In the meantime, resentment and tensions were building. It was clear that the neighborhood and the people in it would have to stand on its own without legal or political support. So that's what happened, and the stage was set.

It didn't help that the blacks that were being bussed into our schools in the neighborhood were arrogant and defiant. Busses that were loaded with blacks coming from Bartlet High School traveled right down 18th Street, which was the heart of the neighborhood. They would hang out of the windows of the busses cursing and yelling at people as they went by.

If you knew anything about the neighborhood, which they didn't, this could only end badly for them. After a couple of days of this, meetings were held at Ruthra Avenue Playground. During these meetings, there were hundreds of people that filled the playground, and the surrounding streets. All of them anxious to show their support for the streets they called their own.

Right in the middle of everything was Gino Valenti. He would organize these meetings, and he was the one everybody looked to for leadership.

My memory of this, as a kid standing there with all these people, was vivid. Gino was standing in the middle of the crowd on the base of the flagpole in the playground so everybody could see him. His message was simple and very clear.

When he started talking, the crown quieted down to listen. He said, "If you see black people walking through the neighborhood on their way to or from work, bothering no one, you leave them alone. But if you see black people bopping through the neighborhood looking for trouble, you make sure they find it. And you make sure they know where they found it." A roar went up from the crowd, and then he said, "You all know what I'm talking about. This doesn't mean its open season on all black people. If you bother innocent black people, you'll answer to me. If you have a problem with troublemakers, and you've done nothing wrong, I'll answer for you."

Now the noise level was unbelievable. Everybody there seemed to draw strength from what he was saying. The crowd was very loud, but under control. Everybody understood what he meant and nobody was going to go against what he said. It was really something to see. He had complete control over hundreds of people, which is exactly what he wanted.

No one could expect or predict what would happen in the next few days following the rallies, but the neighborhood was hot. You just knew that with the busses of black guys going through the streets that it was only a matter of time before something big was going to happen. And as usual, it didn't take long.

Two days after the rallies on Ruthra Avenue, a big statement was made. As the busses made their way down 18th Street loaded with blacks from Bartlet High School, neighborhood guys, who simply had enough, blocked the streets.

As usual, blacks were hanging out the windows of the busses cursing people and just being assholes until they got up to the block of St. Mary's. There were about 50 or 60 guys with baseball bats blocking the streets. Two busses came to a stop and they were surrounded on both sides. The drivers from both busses ran out, leaving everyone inside.

The guys started smashing windows with bats, glass was flying everywhere, and then everybody started rocking the busses side to side until they were literally turned on their sides. The busses were turned over, and it was complete panic. Black guys in the busses that two minutes ago were taunting everyone were scared shit. They tried jumping from the windows of the busses that were now lying on their sides. People were beating the shit out of them with bats and their fists.

By now, cop cars were pulling up to the scene, but it was far too late. There was nothing they could do. It was an ugly scene. There were people being beaten everywhere. The blacks that weren't being beaten were running through the neighborhood with crowds chasing them. It was complete chaos. There were bodies all over the streets, bleeding. It took the police hours before they could get control of the situation. By then, it didn't matter. A huge statement had been made that day. That was, nobody was going to come through that neighborhood threatening people and acting like assholes. No matter how much political backing or how many organizations you had behind you, you still had to come through the neighborhood.

After that day, the city changed the bus routes for the No. 12 bus. No busses were to come through the neighborhood again. To this day, that is still in effect.

When it was all over, nobody could forget the sight of overturned busses and ambulances all over the streets. Although there were still some politicians trying to get the bus routes changed back, nobody really wanted to find out how that would work out. Especially the black people that would be on the busses.

These memories stay with you for a lifetime. In one way, it made you proud, but it was not something you enjoyed seeing. This was the balance you lived with in those days. It was just another example of how the neighborhood stood on its own against whatever odds there were.

It was impossible to feel bad about the things that were going on in those days. None of these things would have happened on their own. We weren't going into other people's neighborhoods looking for trouble or forcing ourselves on them. We were just living our lives and bothering no one. It wasn't easy to witness these beatings, but you couldn't argue with the results they brought. Your sister, mother or grandmother could walk the streets day or night without worrying about anything, because in this neighborhood, if something happened, something was going to happen.

As I've mentioned over and over in this story. It was never about prejudice; it was always about pride in where you lived.

* * * * *

The Genelli Family

Not surprisingly, food was a very big part of growing up in the neighborhood. It was a way of life there, and with good reason. You couldn't go 30 feet without passing a great place to eat.

On the other side of the Bronx Zoo, on Bronxdale Avenue was a place called Frankie & Johnny's Pine Tavern. The food was great, and the portions were unbelievable. In those days, it was just a bar with a back room where you could eat. Today, it's half a block long, but the food is still the same. The restaurant has been there since 1912 or 1918, something ridiculous like that, and that's where we'd usually eat.

About eight blocks away, on Morris Park Avenue, there was the M.P.I., The Morris Park Inn. The food was good there too, but that's where you went to drink and hang out.

Contrary to what everybody thinks of the Bronx, this was a place where you could be just as comfortable hanging out with the guys or sitting at the bar with your wife or girlfriend. This is what everybody did, and God forbid if somebody fucked with you there.

Everybody was comfortable there, and along with the great jukebox, there was my buddy, Ralphie Saco, the bartender. He was one of the reasons I kept going back there.

The neighborhood was something you always went back to. It was a sense of belonging. I can't explain it. If you were from there, you understood it. If you weren't you didn't.

One night, we were hanging out at the M.P.I. My brother, Joey, and I were at the bar when this guy came in. He seemed strange, but nobody paid any attention at first.

After a few minutes, he started acting weird. I had already noticed that he was drinking green Cream De Menthe, straight up. I've been bartending long enough to know that was the first red flag.

A couple of minutes later, he took his jacket off and was staring at himself in the mirror. Then, he put his sunglasses on, even though it was about midnight, and he put his jacket back on and folded his arms in front of him. Now, he's got his jacket and sunglasses on, starring into the mirror, and he starts talking to himself. This didn't go unnoticed for too long.

Ralphie was behind the bar talking to Joey and me, but I had already noticed that Ralphie was keeping an eye on him. We had another beer and were kidding around with each other as usual when I noticed one of the guys from the back room come out and stood on one side of this guy, who was still talking to himself in the mirror.

When you've been around the neighborhood long enough, you could sense when something was going to happen. That's the feeling I was getting when I saw Ralphie walk out from behind the bar and stand on the other side of this guy.

He was still talking into the mirror when Ralphie leaned over to him and said, "Your cab is here." The guy looked at him and said, "What cab?" Ralphie said, "Yours." The guy looked back at him and said, "I didn't call any fucking cab." Before he finished the sentence, Ralphie slammed his head down on the bar and pulled it back up in one quick motion. Blood was pouring down his face as they walked him out the door. Nobody even really noticed what had happened. And he was gone.

Ralphie came in the back door and was back behind the bar serving people as if nothing had happened. He brought Joey and I another beer without saying a word about what had gone on outside. We didn't ask, and the night just went on.

That's how things go in the neighborhood. You hang out, eat, drink and have a good time. If you make trouble or look like you might bother the clientele, you get removed quickly and quietly. There's no way you're going to do anything about it. That was the reputation the neighborhood had. Every once in a while that reputation would be tested either blatantly by some loudmouth asshole. Or inadvertently by some weirdo. But it always ended the same way.

The M.P.I. became home base for me during the late 80's and early 90's and for good reason. I was tight with Ralphie, and I became friends with the other bartenders.

Chapter 32

I was bartending at a place called "The Far Turn" in Randolph, New Jersey. It was a nice restaurant with a cozy little bar. It wasn't a real busy bar, but I was being paid pretty well to run it. It was real easy for me compared to the other places I had worked, I was working there for almost a year, and I had made some friends with the staff. And I had gotten to know some of the customers pretty well too.

I was working the bar one Thursday night when a guy came in that I never saw before. He seemed okay at first. He had a couple of drinks, and I made some meaningless conversation with him.

After a while, he started acting weird. He asked me if he could use the phone. There was no pay phone so I let him use the house phone. He made one call then another. He started to dial a third call when Gus, the owner, came out of the kitchen and asked me what he was doing on the phone. I told him that the guy asked to use the phone, but now he was making call after call. Gus told me to get the guy off the phone and went back into the kitchen.

I walked over to the guy and said, "You gotta get off the phone." He said, "Okay, in a minute." I said, "Now, hang up!" He told whoever he was talking to he had to go and went back to the bar. I went back behind the bar and took care of a couple of guys sitting in the comer. I had a feeling it wasn't over yet with the guy that was just on the phone. I went back over to where he was sitting. I had to make some drinks for one of the waitresses. As I'm doing this, I hear the guy say, "You know, I didn't like the way you talked to me when I was on the phone." I thought, here we go. I looked at Cara, the waitress, then I turned to him and said, "You asked to make a phone call, not three phone calls. Besides, the owner wanted you off the phone." Then he says, "You always do everything the owner tells you to do?" I said, "You know what, finish your drink and leave." He says, "This is my first drink, I'm going to have one more then leave." I said. "Guess what, now you're not even going to finish that one. You're leaving now." Cara was watching this whole thing and went into the kitchen to call the owner. The guy picked up his money like he was leaving and said, "You're a real asshole. I think I'll punch you in the mouth." I stopped what I was doing and walked out from behind the bar. I said, "Go ahead, do what you gotta do." As he's walking towards me, I slapped him across the mouth with the back of my left hand just to stop him. I figured if he kept coming, I'd punch him in the mouth with my right. As soon as I slapped him, he screamed and lunged backward. He crashed into one of the customers having dinner at a table then fell to the floor.

Now, I knew the guy was nuts. I only smacked him hard enough to shock him and stop him from coming at me. There's no way I hit him hard enough to even knock him down, let alone send him flying into a table full of people. When he hit the floor, he just laid there like he was dead. He didn't move. I couldn't believe it. He was lying flat on his back when Gus and Cara ran out from the kitchen. Gus looked at me then looked at the guy lying on the floor in the middle of his dining room. Then he looked back at me and said, "Tony, what did you do?" "Nothing" I said. "I just tapped him. He's full of shit, he's faking it."

Now this guy laid there on his back for the entire night. People had to finish their dinner with this guy lying on the floor. Gus had to do everything by the book for the sake of his business. First, we had to call an ambulance. Then we had to notify the police because that's what the paramedics in the ambulance had to do when they got there. And it just looked better if we did it before they got there.

I couldn't believe what was going on. Nobody wanted to touch the guy until the ambulance got there. I was watching him closely, and I could see that he was breathing. I also noticed something really strange. It looked like he had some kind of wires attached to his chest. The two guys at the end of the bar yelled out, "Kick him, he'll move. He's full of shit."

Right then the ambulance showed up. Now we had paramedics trying to examine this guy with people still at their tables having dinner. It was unbelievable. Not surprisingly, people started rushing through their dinner and leaving. Who could blame them? There was one table left when the police showed up. Before the cops got there, the guys at the bar and the people at the last table told me they would back my story if I needed witnesses.

By this time, the paramedics and the police had determined there was nothing wrong with the guy. They started going through his pockets to find out who he was and to see if there was anyone to contact that would come and get him. They ran his license and plate number and got a phone number. Then they called the number, they got his wife on the phone. She told the cops that he was a patient at the local mental institution, and she had no idea why he wasn't there. The cop asked her to come down to the restaurant to I.D. the guy. After the cop hung up, he started to fill out his paperwork. The guy lying on the floor must have heard the copy talking to his wife on the phone. As soon as he heard that his wife was coming, he suddenly got up and ran for the front door. One of the other cops tackled him by the entrance to the restaurant and handcuffed him.

I'm standing there with Gus and Cara watching this whole unbelievable situation come to an end. At first we were worried that this asshole might try and sue me for hitting him or sue the whole place. Now that we knew we didn't have to worry about that anymore, we were finally able to relax a little bit.

We all had to give statements to the police before we were able to close the place for the night. It took forever. After all the bullshit was over, I finally started to clean up and close the bar. All the time I'm thinking so this wacko escapes from a mental hospital and has to come to the bar I'm working at. How fucked up is that?

This guy lay on the floor of the dining room from about 8:30 p.m. until closing time. It was probably the most bizarre situation I have ever worked through. It's one thing to write about something like this; it's another thing completely to have to work the rest of the night with some guy lying on the floor in the middle of the restaurant.

The rest of the customers were pretty gracious about the whole thing. But imagine having to finish your dinner with some guy lying on the floor by your table. If it was me, I don't know if I would have been that understanding. As it was, I felt like walking by where he was and kicking him in the fucking head because I knew he was faking it. And I also knew if I did something like that, he would have to react. But Gus asked me no to do any thing else to the guy, just to be on the safe side so I didn't.

We finally got everybody out of the place about 1 a.m. We had a couple of drinks at the bar before we left just to unwind. We knew that it would be a couple of days, at least, before we would know if the whole thing was really over.

We all went about our business at The Far Turn for the next couple of days. Everything seemed to be okay, and we never heard anything about this guy again, which was fine. You know, no news is good news and all that, but what a pain in the ass. Anyway, that was the end of that.

Chapter 33

It was January and a brand New Year. The year two thousand and one. Everybody was still having a hard time not writing the words nineteen hundred before dating something. We all knew it was the beginning of a new century. And we all thought we were ready for it. But having to write it down was still weird for everybody. My father was going to be eighty years old on August sixth of the upcoming summer. My brother Joey's mother-in-law, Nancy, who I love, was also turning eighty that year. Anyway, my brother's wife, Tora, who I also love, started planning a celebration for both birthdays. What she planned and eventually pulled off was really unbelievable. Between the two families, there would be a total of thirty-five people. Tora's plan was for all of us to take a one week cruise to the Bahamas. And believe it or not, that's what we did.

On the cruise

We were all very excited about the trip. But when you have three kids, you're only allowed to be excited a couple of minutes at a time. At the time our kids were thirteen, three, and one and a half years old. My son Danny was thirteen years old and wouldn't be a problem. But we knew if we really wanted to enjoy the trip, we should leave our daughters with someone at home. But the only people we felt comfortable leaving them with were also going on the trip. And if we left them with anybody else, which we never did, would prevent us from being able to relax and enjoy the trip. Especially because we would be gone for seven days. We had never even left them with family for that long. So leaving them with anybody else was out of the question. So even though we knew what it would be like with three kids in a cabin on a cruise ship for seven days, we decided to take them with us. We knew we would be passing up the chance to relax and enjoy the cruise. And if you have young children, you know what I mean. If you don't, you don't know what I mean. Whatever. The bottom line is kids come first, always. We both felt that way.

Nobody could believe that this trip was actually going to happen. Especially with all the people involved. But it was. Most of us had never been on a cruise, which made it even more unbelievable. The ship would be leaving from the docks on the city's west side. So, thirty-five of our family members would meet there. Each of us coming from different places, up and down the east coast. I'm sure it was just as strange for everybody else as it was for us. Except that we would be bringing three kids with us. Nobody else was doing that. We left on a Saturday in June. I worked the night before we left and that just added to the chaos. I got home at one o'clock in the morning. We had to pack the car and leave by nine o'clock that same morning. Naturally, it rained that whole night. And I mean it poured. I figured, what the fuck, by this time tomorrow we'd be on a cruise ship.

Joe Genelli

The next morning came as fast as we thought it would. It had stopped raining and was pretty nice out. We finished packing the car with suitcases and then we packed it with kids. We were finally on our way. We headed down route 80 toward the city. We were all very excited as we drove on. The kids were fine but

Barbara and I were both on edge. We didn't talk about it because we didn't have to. We both knew it wouldn't be easy to have three kids with us on a cruise ship. But we tried to cancel that out by thinking that we'd be on a cruise ship. Something neither one of us had done before. But in the back of our minds we both knew there was no way it was going to be a relaxing vacation. Somehow, we just blacked it out. We were used to doing that. Anybody with three kids knows what I mean. From that point on and through the entire cruise, our mood and mindset alternated between excitement and dread. We didn't have to wait long for the next mood swing. We drove through the Lincoln Tunnel and up the west side. It was the first time we saw the cruise ship. It was really beautiful. We couldn't believe we would be on it for a whole week. I pulled over on 45th street and waited for my brother Joey. We kept staring at the ship until he got there. Joey pulled up alongside of us and rolled down his window. I looked at him and he said, "Do you still want to do this or what?" That was him, man. To the tee. I looked at him and said, "Yeah, I got the truck all packed up, man." He said, "Fuck it man. I guess that's it then. Follow me and make sure you keep up with me." I said, "So, now we're gonna have a race to the ship? Why don't you calm down, man?" He waved his hand at me and pulled away. I pulled out and tried to stay with him. Barbara said, "What's the matter with him?" I said, "Who knows, man." I followed him to the cruise line parking area. Then up the two or three ramps and found a spot to park.

  We started unpacking the car. We were right alongside the ship. It was huge and being that close to it got us all pretty excited. But it was total chaos. Trying to unpack the car, figure out what we had to do and where we had to go and keeping an eye on our three kids was unbelievable. As I said, we were all excited. But it was our first taste to how crazy this entire trip would be. We found a wagon to put all our luggage on and headed toward the ship. Finding the customs line was easy. It was the longest one. Excitement and dread were alternating again. We pushed on. Danny was arguing with my daughter, Maria. My other daughter, Natalie, was crying. Who knows why. Joey and Tora were behind us on line. They helped us out with our luggage and the kids but couldn't help laughing at us. Barbara and I both knew it was funny but neither one of us were laughing. We both had the same feeling. This was just the beginning. Finally, we got to the customs agent and started filling out the paperwork. Actually Barbara handled that whole thing. She was better at that kind of thing than I was. Besides, by now I was starting to get fucking aggravated. I was giving

Barbara my driver's license and whatever other shit she needed when Maria came over and told me that Danny had taken her blanket away from her. I was looking for Danny to find out why he took Maria's blanket when Barbara told me she needed my signature on some documents. While I'm signing my name, Barbara asked me why Maria was crying. I told her she was crying because Danny was being an asshole. She said, "Where is he, anyway? I told him to stay right her with us." I gave Barbara the paperwork I had just signed and said, "I'll be right back. I'm gonna go see where he is." She said, "Don't be too hard on him." I said, "I won't be, keep an eye on Maria." I started to walk away when Natalie threw up in her stroller. While we were dealing with that, I heard Danny say, "Here Dad, use this." It was Maria's blanket. I just looked at him. He looked back at me and said, "What?" Then Barbara said, "That's it, let's go. We're done."

      Finally, we were boarding the ship. We had never been on a cruise ship before, so everything was amazing. Once we were on the ship we had to find our cabin. We had plenty of help with that. There were stewards everywhere that were more than willing to help. They were all black guys and all of them had English accents. They were very nice and extremely polite. In other words, they were good guys. But there was something about black people with English accents that always made me laugh. I guess it reminded me of when I was with John in the hotel in Las Vegas, all those years ago. Anyway, I was going to have to deal with them for a whole week. So I tried to block that out. We gave one of them our boarding passes and followed him to cabin. We were excited again thinking about getting settled in. We forgot for a second that excitement and dread walked hand and hand on this cruise. We got to our cabin and put our luggage down. The steward unlocked the door and pushed it open. We looked inside. There were two bunk beds and a sink. To the left of the front door, there was a bathroom that made the sink look big. I stood there looking into the room and said, "Ten pounds of baloney in a five pound bag." The black English steward looked at me and said, "I'm sorry sir?" I kept looking straight ahead and said, "Yeah, me too." Then he said, "I'm not sure I know what you mean, sir?" I said, "Don't worry about it." I handed him a twenty dollar bill and said, "Thanks, we're ok for now. I'll let you know if we need anything." Then he said, "I'm sorry if we got off on the wrong foot sir. I just want to make sure you're happy with the accommodations." I said, "Hey, I'm happy ok? I just need a little space. You know what I'm saying?" He said, "Very well, sir. I'll leave you to it then." Then he walked away. I watched him walk away and said, "Holy shit, man. How can this be happening again?" I turned around to go into the cabin and Danny was standing by the front door. He said, "How can what be happening again, Dad?" I looked at him and said, "Don't worry about it. It was before you were born." Then we went inside the cabin.

We spent the day getting familiar with our new surroundings. We took time out to be on deck as we left New York Harbor. The ship headed out into the ocean as we stood there watching Manhattan pass us by. We started out from 44th St. and headed south. Before long we had passed by lower Manhattan and were leaving the city behind. We were all standing at the back end of the ship looking at the skyline. The World Trade Center was a massive presence and the focal point of our gaze. I'm sure it was a sight that had different meaning for everybody. But I can only speak for myself. Besides having never been on a cruise ship, I had never left the city from that direction. I was standing next to my father, who was holding Maria in his arms. It was not lost on me that he had seen this sight before. That time as an eight-year old boy being taken from his mother all those years ago. I just watched him not saying anything. My respect for him growing even more, if that was even possible. As the Trade Towers and the city itself started to fade in the distance my father turned around and looked at me. Then he said, "How are you doing?" I said, "I'm your son, I'm doing fine." He just smiled at me and kissed my daughter. As I looked at him, I thought about my mother and how much she deserved to be there. Even though I was used to her not being around for these special kinds of moments by now, she was always the person I thought of whenever they happened. This was no different. And it was always a good feeling.

We all went down to our cabins and got ready for dinner in the dining room that first night. It was what would become a daily ritual for the next seven days. It was chaotic and difficult because it was the first night. We were all still excited about being on the ship, so we didn't see it coming. But being in a small cabin with three kids, would soon take its toll. It's hard to complain about being on a cruise to the Bahamas but believe me; by the second day we knew what we were in for. The daily ritual of getting three kids ready for three meals a day wasn't easy. But after all the daily activities and the trips off the ship to the beaches, we soon found out that getting us all ready for dinner would be what drained us completely. By the time we all got showered, changed and dressed in our tiny cabin, we were exhausted. When I say we, I mean Barbara and me. The kids just argued and cried through the whole process. When we finally got the five of us up to the dining room and seated for dinner, we were completely drained.

Then somehow, we had to make it through dinner. Which was the same as being in the cabin getting dressed, only in a different room. Excitement and dread were hanging around together again. There is no reasonable way to put into words, what this kind of situation is like. Unless you have actually done it yourself. So I will not try. I will only try to explain each day as it was.

Dinner came and went, as it did for the next six days. The stress and strain, mounting with each passing day. The headaches I had been suffering from for the past five years were worse than ever. During the last five years, I had been going for allergy shots, twice a week. This allergy doctor had somehow convinced me that I was allergic to grass, trees and dust mites. Who the fuck knows how. But it was becoming obvious to me that this was all bullshit, and that I had been wasting my time and money for years going for these allergy shots. Because now I was in the middle of the fucking ocean and the pain was worse than ever. There was no grass or trees within a hundred miles. And I'm sure there were no dust mites around either. Whatever the fuck they were. Anyway, the headaches came every night. Usually during dinner, sometimes later. But they always came. When they did, I would just get up and leave. No matter what I was doing. I had no choice. Barbara always knew why. I didn't really care who understood anyway. The pain was too intense. I would go back to our cabin or to a dark end of the ship, where nothing was going on that night. On the way, I'd get a cup of black coffee and find a place to sit down. Then I'd take a few pills and drink the coffee down as hot as I could stand it. I had all kinds of pills for the pain. This time I decided on Tylenol with codeine. I knew that drinking something hot would break open and dissolve the pills faster. Then I'd just sit back and stare out at the ocean trying to wait out the pain. Sometimes the pills would work and I could feel the pain subside. Sometimes they wouldn't work at all. Then I would just sit there as the pain got worse and worse, wondering what the fuck was wrong with me. Whenever the pills didn't work, I knew I was fucked. The pain would usually last for about an hour, sometimes longer. Anyway, that's what I was dealing with on a nightly basis.

One night after dinner, I hadn't gotten a headache yet and went to one of the bars on the ship. I sat at the bar with Joey and my cousin, Rob. The bartender was a real jerk, but I expected him to be. I was just happy about not having a headache, so I left him alone. We had a couple of beers and hung out for a while. Then it came. I always knew. Before the actual pain, I would always get a kind of sensation. A feeling above my left eye. Within a minute or two, the pain was with me. I didn't say anything. I just got up and left. I did my usual thing and found a spot at the back of the ship. I sat there for about forty-five minutes. Then I felt the pain start to subside. I was happy it didn't last longer and that it was still early. I knew that Barbara was probably back at the cabin with the kids by now. So, I lit up a cigarette and went to look for my brother.

I walked past a couple of bars and looked inside but I didn't see him. I thought he might be up at the bar by the pool and started to walk to the other end of the ship. As I'm walking past one of the entrances back into the casino area, I noticed someone standing there. I kept walking and a minute later I knew someone was walking behind me. I could just feel it. I figured, fuck it. He was either some kind of authority figure on the ship or a faggot. Whoever he was, I would deal with him when I had to. I was in some fucking mood already. And I didn't give a fuck who he was. He was going to have to pay a price for fucking with me no matter who he was. I got to the other end of the ship and walked into the first bar I saw. My brother was sitting at the bar and I walked over to him. He looked at me and said, "Where the fuck have you been? I turned around and you were gone." I said, "Don't worry about where I've been. I had a fucking headache and had to get rid of it." Then I

Anthony Genelli

turned around and looked at the doorway to see if this guy had followed me into the bar. I didn't see him. Then my brother said,

"What are you looking at?" I said, "Nothing, man. I thought somebody was following me." He said, "Who the fuck would want to follow you?" I said, "If I was a different type of guy, that would bother me, but I ain't." He said, "Ok, so what do you feel like doing?" I said, "I just got rid of a headache so we might as well smoke something. You got anything rolled?" He said, "Yeah. Let's take a walk."

    We walked upstairs and out onto the deck. We walked to the front of the ship and sat down at one of the tables. The ship was docked and looked out over the town we were at. I would tell you what town it was, if I knew but I didn't. I didn't give a fuck what town it was. All I cared about was that I didn't a have a headache. We sat there and lit up a joint. With three kids on a cruise, there wasn't much time to relax. But this was the one of those times. So I was going to enjoy it no matter what. We brought our drinks with us so we were all set. We smoked about half the joint and were sipping our drinks. We had a pretty good buzz already because the weed was excellent. But it was really windy and the joint kept going out. We kept trying to light it up but the wind was out of control. I grabbed the joint and lit an entire book of matches. I finally got the joint lit and gave Joey a shotgun. Then he gave me one, before it went out again. There was a cloud of smoke over the table as we started choking and coughing. When we finally got control of ourselves we started laughing and couldn't stop. That's when I saw him. Out of the corner of my eye, I noticed somebody standing there. It was the same idiot that was following me when I was looking for my brother. He was standing in the doorway of one of the bars, near where we were sitting. He was wearing some kind of uniform so I knew would have to deal with him. Joey was still laughing when I tapped him on the shoulder and said, "We've got company, man." He was a skinny oriental guy and his uniform just made him look stupid. When Joey looked at him, he started laughing again and said, "Who the fuck is that, man?" Then, I started laughing and we were both out of control. We tried to get a hold of ourselves as he walked toward our table. We had managed to stop laughing by the time he got to us but I knew it wouldn't last. I still had the joint in my hand when he said, "Are you two gentlemen enjoying yourselves tonight?" We started laughing again, and then I said, "What do you think?" Then he said, "There's a strict drug policy aboard this ship. What have you guys been doing?" I looked at him and said, "Who the fuck are you?" He said, "I am the chief of security aboard this ship." I stood up and flicked the joint over the side and into the water. Then I looked at him and said, "You're the chief of security?" He said, "Yes I am, sir." Then I said,

"So, now what are we gonna do?" He said, "That depends on what you're going to do next." I said, "I'm not gonna do anything. I'm just gonna stand here looking at you." Then Joey said, "Well somebody better do something. That's all I can say." Then the security guy said, "Well as long as we understand each other I guess everything is OK." I just stood there looking at him. Then I said, "We don't understand each other. You don't understand me. And I don't give a fuck about you. There's just nothing else to say, so let's just leave it at that. You can go back to your fucking life and we'll go back to ours." He said, "Ok, just stay out of trouble." Then he walked away. Joey looked at me and said, "I'm glad that's over. You two weren't getting along at all." I just laughed. That was my brother in a nutshell. He had a real off the wall way of distancing himself from what was going on. Whatever it was. Not many people really understood him but I always did. We finished our drinks and walked back to our cabins. But that wasn't the end of it. Nothing ever seemed to end when Joey and me hung out. Not in a normal way anyway. We walked down to the level of the ship where our cabins were. We had to make a left after the elevator bank to get to them. We were walking and breaking each other's balls as usual. We heard footsteps right before we turned to walk down the corridor. He slammed right into the both of us and fell back against the wall. It was him. The idiot Chinese security guard. I said, "What the fuck are you doing here?" He got up and said, I told you before, I'm the chief of security on this ship." Me and Joey looked at each other and then I said, "I didn't ask you who you were. Get the fuck out of our way. What the fuck is wrong with you anyway? Why were you running down the hallway?" Then Joey said, "Maybe he had to run, leave him alone." I started laughing and said, "Yeah, whatever. I can't believe this shit." Then I looked at the guy and said, "Are we free to go?" Then his walkie-talkie came on. It was real loud. Somebody was asking him if he was in position or not. Then Joey pushed me and said, "You should have let him run, man. Now he's out of position." I said, "I don't give a fuck, what are you on his side now?" Then the security guy said, "I have to go check out the other side of the ship." I said, "So, go ahead. Who gives a fuck?" He started walking down the hall when his walkie--talkie went off again. Something about him being in position or not. We watched him as he started to run again. We watched him until he disappeared around the corner. Then I looked at Joey and said, "Do you believe this fucking idiot?" Then Joey said, "At least he's running away from us now. Leave him alone." I said, "Yeah, you're right. Let's get some sleep before something else happens."

We said goodnight and walked to our cabins. This was always the toughest part of the night for me. Because I had to get into the cabin, get undressed and get into bed. To get into bed, I had to climb up to the top of the bunk bed. With three kids in the room, it was like waking through a minefield. As I walked toward the door, I felt the pain above my left eye. I couldn't believe it. I had one of my headaches again that night.

Usually, I only got them once a day. Now, I could feel another one coming on. I knew I was fucked. If I was lucky, the pain would go away in less than an hour. And it wasn't easy to pass an hour with that kind of pain. And although I was used to it this was really fucked up. Because now I would be doing it while I was trying to creep into bed without waking up the kids. As I put the key card into the door, the pain was with me. I opened the door and closed it behind me. I stood there in complete darkness. I thought to myself, "How the fuck am I gonna do this?" Everybody was sleeping. It was so quiet; I could hear my kids breathing in their sleep. Before I took my first step, the pain above my left eye was intense. I squeezed into the tiny bathroom and started getting undressed. My head was pounding. I sat on the toilet bowl with my head in my hands. I had no idea how I was gonna get to the top of that bunk bed. Not just without waking anybody up but now the pain was so bad, I didn't know if I could make it up the ladder. I figured what the fuck. I'm either gonna try it or sit on the toilet bowl all fucking night. I took three codeine pills out of my pocket and swallowed them. Then I got up and opened the door. I had to shut the light before I opened the door, so I was already disoriented. My head was killing me. I walked toward the bunk bed. I felt for the ladder in the darkness. I had both hands out in front of me. I took another couple of steps and tripped over my son's sneakers. I fell forward and landed face down onto the ladder. My foot was stuck between one of the rungs and my head was pulsating with pain. I laid there for a couple of seconds, hoping nobody would wake up. It was still quiet in the room, so I pulled my foot out of the ladder and started climbing up to the bed. When I got to the top of the ladder I heard Barbara say, "Anthony, is that you?" I said, "If it wasn't me, I wouldn't be here." I knew what I had just said didn't make much sense. But I didn't give a fuck. By now, I was in so much pain; I was just hoping she wouldn't even answer me. I got off the ladder and rolled onto the bed. I was lying on my back when Barbara said, "Are you Ok?" I said, "No, I ain't ok. My head is fucking killing me and I think I sprained my ankle. I just hope the codeine pills will kick in and I'll be able to fall asleep." I was lying there pressing my hand against the pain above my eye when she said, "Did you lock the door?" I couldn't believe what I just heard. I took my hand off my head and said, "Hey, fuck the door. If somebody comes in this room, I'll jump on top of him and kill the fuck, whoever he is." She said, "Ok, goodnight. I can't talk anymore; I'm trying to fall asleep." I said, "And what the fuck am I trying to do. I'm not talking to you, am I? You're the one asking stupid fucking questions, not me. Right or wrong?"

The room was quiet. And I realized she was already asleep. Then I said, "Oh, that's good. Now, I'm fucking talking to myself for no reason." I was alone with the pain again. But I was used to it. I lay there and tried to fall asleep. The pain in my head intensified, as I knew it would. Everybody else was in a deep sleep by now. Maria and Danny were snoring really loud, as usual. The noise didn't bother me or keep me awake. But it did add to a feeling of loneliness that I always felt at times like this. I was alone with my pain. But I didn't care. I was used to it by now. And in some strange kind of way, I was glad when the pain started. Because then I could concentrate on getting rid of it. It became a challenge to me. But it would always get real bad before the pain

Barbara Genelli

would go away. Most of the time, I would have to bite into a towel or whatever was handy, just to keep from screaming out loud. It sounds strange but in a weird kind of way, I enjoyed the fight. I guess it was just my nature. Whenever something threatened me, my first reaction was always confrontational. Who knows why? But to try to explain it would suggest that I understood it. And I didn't. Anyway, as I laid there with the pain in my head and all these weird fucking thoughts flying around, I fell asleep. I woke up the next morning the same way I always did, in a fog. The pain always took a lot out of me. The drinking with the pain pills, added another dimension.

The chaos in the room was unbelievable, but at least I didn't have a headache. Not yet, anyway. They usually came at night. The anticipation of pain always hung over me. And no matter how hard I tried, it always cast a shadow over whatever I was doing.

It was our fourth day on the ship. And it was the last day we would be going ashore. We left the ship and spent the day at one of the many beautiful beaches on the island. My wife and kids were there. So were my father and brother and their wives. My cousin Donna and her husband Rob were also there with their daughter, Randi. Most of us were looking forward to heading back home the next day. We all had different reasons for feeling that way. But for the most part, they all had to do with how many kids you had or didn't have with you for the past week. But that's another story. With that aside nothing could take away from how beautiful the beach was.

After all, it was the Bahama Islands. It was a small beach surrounded by rock formations and caves. And right before the water's edge there was a bar. Sometimes things just work out right. It turned out to be a great day. It was the first time we had a chance to relax since we left New York. We were way overdue for a day like this. But something else happened that day to make it even more perfect. I got to swim in the ocean or whatever the fuck it was, with my father and my brother. Something we hadn't done together since I was a little kid. It was when my mother was still alive. And we'd all go to Orchard Beach in the Bronx. When it was still white and before it was destroyed by people who didn't give a fuck about where they lived. But that's another story. Anyway, it all came rushing back to me. The three of us were swimming out to the deep part of the inlet. My father was eighty years old. He was still diving underwater and coming up ten or twenty feet away. When he did he would be spitting out water and pushing his hair back, just like he did all those years ago. Seeing him that way again at his age filled me with pride and respect. Especially after all he'd been through in his life. I just stood there looking at him, with all of this going through my mind. Then he looked at me and said, "What did you think, that I was an old man and couldn't do this anymore?" I just laughed and said, "Nah, I stopped doubting what you could do years ago. Right now, I'm just enjoying being your son." He started swimming away and said, "Hey, Joey, did you hear what your brother just said?" My brother started swimming alongside my father. Then I heard him say, "Hey Dad, you know I don't listen to him. It ain't worth the aggravation." I just looked at them and started to laugh. Then I swam after them. There were a handful of big moments on this vacation and that was one of them. We didn't know it at the time but the biggest moment was just around the corner.

We spent the rest of the day at the beach and then we headed back to the ship. The trip back was a pain in the ass. But by now we were used to it, I guess. When we got back, we went through our usual chaos getting ready for dinner that night. Then we all met in the dining room like we always did. But it was different this time. I mean for me it was anyway, because now we were heading back home. I don't know how anybody else felt about it, but for me it was always a special feeling to be going back home. When I say home, I mean New York City and the Bronx. I felt that way no matter where I went. Ever since the time I moved out to California and realized what the city meant to me. The streets of Manhattan where I was born and worked for most of my life, and the neighborhood in the Bronx that shaped me and made me who I was, would always draw me back there. It was where I belonged. And I never felt right until I got back there. Even though I was living In New Jersey now and made a life for my wife and kids on a beautiful lake there. The Bronx would always be home to me. My wife knew that and that's all that mattered to me. More importantly, she knew why. I didn't give a fuck if anybody else understood or not.

Anyway, we were having dinner that night and things were going pretty well, for a while anyway. It was about eight-thirty and we were all still sitting around the dinner table. Barbara looked at me and said, "Are you ok?" As I looked at her, I knew what she meant. I realized I hadn't gotten a headache yet. I said, "Yeah, I'm ok." It was such a relief. We all hung out for about another hour and enjoyed ourselves. It was the first night I didn't have a headache since we boarded the ship. It didn't mean I wouldn't get one later but I didn't have one now. And that was good enough for me. I decided to enjoy myself. By now I was used to living my life about an hour at a time. It was really fucked up. Because the fact of the matter was whenever I didn't have a headache, I got one, sooner or later. So I could never really enjoy not having one. So I did what I always did. I just said, "Fuck it."

My Father knew what I had been going through and wanted to help me out. He said, "I'll keep the girls with me tonight, you guys go out and enjoy yourselves." I looked at Maria and Natalie and said, "Do you want to stay with grandpa tonight?" They started jumping up and down saying, "Please Daddy, can we?" So, that was that. We left the girls with my father and went to a bar on the top deck of the ship. It was right by the pool and there was a band playing some stupid fucking dance music. We sat down at the bar. There were six of us. It was Joey and me with our wives, Barbara and Tora, and my cousin Donna with her husband Rob. We ordered a round of drinks and hung out for a while. Then I saw him. It was the idiot security guard from the night before. He was sitting at the bar having a drink. He was right next to Rob. He kept looking over at Joey and me. We were all having a good time and I was really happy about not having a headache. But I kept an eye on him. He was paying way too much attention to us. And I was starting to get aggravated. I said, "Hey Joe, there's that asshole from last night." Joey looked over at him and started laughing. Barbara said, "What happened last night? Can't we just have a drink in peace?" I said, "Nothing happened, don't worry about it." Joey finally stopped laughing, and then Tora said, "I guess whatever happened, must have been funny." Barbara said, "Yeah? Funny to who? If it was funny to them, I'm sure it wasn't really funny." Tora took a sip from her drink and said, "Come on Joe, was it funny or not?" Joey looked at her and said, "What are you asking me for?" Barbara said, "Oh my God!" Then Tora said, "Because you're the one who's laughing. That's why." He said, "Ok, was it funny? I guess that was the first question. Then Barbara said something about funny to who." Then Joey said, "I don't know, man. It seems like a lot of questions when you think about it, man. Doesn't it? Why do I have to answer all of them? Let somebody else do some of the talking for a change! All right, ok, fuck it! Which question do you want me to answer first?" Then my cousin Donna put her arm around my brother's shoulder and said, "Hell! I wouldn't answer any of them. Let them figure it out." Joey said, "That sounds good to me, man. I don't have to answer any fucking question." Then he looked at Tora and said, "What else do you want to know?" Now, everybody was laughing.

Everybody but me, that is. I was watching the Chinese security guard. While all this was going on he was talking to Rob and pointing in our direction. I told Barbara I would be right back. She said, "Where are you going?" Then Tora said, "Just leave them alone, they have to go through their motions." I walked over to Rob and stood between him and the security guard. I put my arm around Rob and said, "You know this fucking guy?"

Then the security guard said, "I'm just making some friendly conversation." I said, "I didn't ask you what you were doing. I'm talking to him." Then Rob said, "No, I don't know him. But it's ok really. Did you know that he's the head of security on this ship?" I said, "How could I forget?" Rob said, "What do you mean?" I said, "Don't worry about what I mean. He told me who he was at least three or four times last night. Now, you're telling me tonight. And you know what? I still don't give a fuck!" Rob said, "Don't you think you should keep your voice down? He's listening to everything you say!" I looked at him and smiled. Then I put my arm around him and said, "That was a stupid question. But I'll answer it anyway. No, I don't think I should keep my voice down. You know why? Because then he'd be sitting even closer to us trying to hear what we're talking about." Rob looked at me and said, "You really are a crazy bastard aren't you? You know he's still listening to you don't you?" I looked back at him and said, "Yes I do and I'm not happy about that. So here's what I'm gonna do." Rob said, "Maybe you should just ignore him." I said, "If I do that he's gonna stay here." Rob said, "I just don't think it's a good idea for you to piss him off!" I said, "Piss him off? First of all, I'm the one who's getting pissed off. You know why? Because I'm hanging out with my family and this guy is asking you stupid fucking questions about me. What he's trying to do is to get you to think like him. Like maybe we're doing something wrong. But I ain't gonna do that. What I'm gonna do is introduce a different kind of scenario, one that suggests complete defiance towards his way of thinking. In other words I'm gonna give him something else to think about. Now, whether or not I follow through with any of this really doesn't matter. The only thing that does matter is that he is going to have to consider it. Plus, he's a fucking idiot. You know what I'm saying?" Rob said, "Not only do I not know what you're saying; now I'm not worried about him understanding you either." We both started laughing. I said, "That's great." Then I put may arm around Rob's shoulder and turned him around until we were both facing the asshole security guard. Then I said, "You see this guy here? He's my cousin. I've been trying to talk him out of it but he's just dying to punch you right in the fucking mouth, man!" They guy just looked at us. Then Rob said, "Well, I'm not dying to punch you in the mouth. I'm just considering it." Then Joey walked over and said, "Considering what, man?" I said, "Man, nothing. Rob was just thinking about hitting this guy, that's all." Joey said, "What guy?" I said, "This guy right here. Right in front of us." Joey looked at the guy and said, "This is unbelievable. He's the same guy you wanted to hit last night!" I said, "Yeah, small boat." Then Joey said, "How many times is that gonna happen, man?" Now we were all laughing. Everybody but the security guard. He just sat there, we were all laughing. Everybody but the security guard. He just sat there looking at us. Then he said, "I guess there's no harm done. Gentlemen, enjoy the rest of your trip." Then he got up and walked away. Rob said, "He called us gentlemen." Joey said, "Yeah, what does he know." My cousin Donna walked over and put her arm around me. Then she said, "Hey cuz! Nice to see you still have that same healthy respect for authority." Donna was 'Good People'. She always called me cuz. And she never tried to judge me, thank God. She probably doesn't know this but she was always one of my favorite relatives. Someday, I'll tell her. Anyway, the asshole was gone. I gave Donna a hug, and then Joey and me drifted back over to our wives. Barbara handed me my drink and said, "What?" Then Tora handed Joey his drink and said, "What did that security guard want?" Joey said, "Fuck him, who cares?" Barbara said, "Is everything ok?" I said, "Barb, don't worry about it. If there was a problem, don't you think I would tell you?" She said, "Oh, yeah! Now I'm totally relaxed." I said, "Good, let's just have a drink and relax. How many times is this gonna happen?" She said, "If I knew that, maybe I could relax." I said, "Ok, nothing else is gonna happen. I promise. Let's just enjoy the rest of the night." So that's what we did. We all had another round of drinks and hung out for a while. We all had a good time, and then we went back to our cabins. Somehow, nothing else happened. The only thing that did happen was something that didn't happen. It was the first and only night I didn't get a headache. The only night on the entire cruise.

I woke up the next morning with a blistering headache. There was the usual chaos in our tiny cabin. The baby was crying and Danny and Maria were arguing, as usual. Barbara was trying to keep everybody happy but it was no use. I knew I had to get the fuck out of there. I climbed down from the top bunk and got dressed. The noise in the cabin was unbelievable. By now, Barbara was screaming at Danny. Telling him to leave Maria alone and Natalie was still crying. Barbara was saying something to me as I headed for the door but I just ignored her. I had to. The blinding pain above my left eye was so fierce I barely heard her. I opened the door and walked out. I started walking down the corridor towards the elevator. Seeing and hearing nothing as I walked. I was in my own little world again, fighting the pain. Although I had become so used to this kind of situation, it was always strange. Even though I was always in so much pain, I always noticed the contrast from what I was going through and what was going on around me. And as you can imagine, being on a cruise ship only intensified that contrast, because everybody but me was in such a great fucking mood. Which of course, pissed me off even more! I couldn't blame them and I didn't. They were on a cruise ship, so of course they were going to be happy.

So there I was, waiting for the elevator with all these happy fucking people. The pain was so bad, I had to keep my left eye closed. The elevator finally came and we all got on. They were all yapping away about what they were going to do that day. It was only three floors to the top deck, thank God.

We got off the elevator and I headed straight for the coffee station. There was a fat broad in front of me that couldn't figure out which lever to pull for decaf. I said, "The orange one is for decaf. Can you hurry up or what?" She looked at me and said, "My god, can't you wait a minute?" I said, "I'm sorry, it's just that I got a real bad headache and need to take some pills." She said, "That's your problem, I was here first." It was my first and last attempt at being polite. I leaned over, tapped her on the shoulder and said, "Listen to me you fat bastard because I'm only going to say this once, get the fuck out of my way." She stepped back and said, "Oh my God! Are you some kind of animal?" I ignored her and poured myself a cup of black coffee. Then I picked her coffee up, threw it in the garbage and walked out onto the deck. As I walked away, I could hear her telling somebody about what I had done. I couldn't care less. If my head weren't killing me, I would've laughed.

I walked to the back of the ship and leaned on the railing. I stared out at the ocean as the ships propellers turned it into white foam. My head was pounding. I put three codeine pills in my mouth and washed them down with the hot coffee. I didn't know if the pills would help or not. Sometimes they did, sometimes they didn't. When they didn't I'd just take some more. I knew it was crazy, but I had to do something. I drank the rest of the coffee as hot as I could stand it. I knew it would break up the pills faster that way. I leaned over the railing and stood there looking at nothing. I just stared out at the ocean as hundreds of seagulls filled the sky. I was in a zone. I remember thinking that I would trade places with anyone of those seagulls in a heartbeat just to not have a headache. The pain was still with me, so I decided to get another cup of coffee. Just in case I had to take some more pills. When I went inside there was nobody on line thank God. I got another cup of coffee and went back outside. I took another couple of codeine pills and went back to my spot at the back of the ship. Once again, I drank the coffee as hot as I could stand it. I had about a half cup of coffee left when I realized that the pain was starting to subside. It was a feeling I had come to know too well. It was such a relief that it almost sounds crazy, but it's the truth. Anyway, I stood there as the pain subsided and just enjoyed the moment. I kept looking out over the ocean and finally started to relax. That's when I heard her voice. "That's him," she said. I didn't realize it at first, but it was the fat broad that was ahead of me on the coffee line. I turned around and looked at her. She was standing there all pissed off. The guy standing next to her looked like a high school English teacher. I hated him already. I said, "What do you want?" She said, "You have some nerve." Then the guy said, "I'll handle this Clara. I think you owe the lady an apology." I turned around and leaned back against the railing. Then I looked at him and said, "You know what? I don't give a fuck what you think. So, what do we do now?" He just looked at me and didn't say anything. Then the fat broad said, "I told you he was an animal." I said, "That's it. I'm sick of both of you now." I looked at the guy and said, "What's your name?" He said, "My name is Charles." I said, "These are your options, Charles. There's nothing else to say. You and your fat friend can walk away or you and me are gonna go at it. You have to decide if she's worth it. Because I'm in the mood to hit somebody and it might as well be you." Then I walked over to where he was standing and looked into his eyes and said, "Time's up, Charles. Make your move. I don't want to hear another word out of you. Walk away now or I'll kick your fucking ass." He said, "I'm not going to stoop to your level. So I'm just going to walk away. And just maybe, you'll learn something from all of this." I said, "What a relief." Then I grabbed his shirt and pulled him toward me. I looked into his eyes and said, "Listen to me, just so you know if you want to get to my level you don't have to stoop, you have to climb. And there's nothing I could ever learn from somebody like you unless you make a move right now. But you ain't gonna do that are you Charles?" He looked at me and said, "Let go of my shirt or I'll have to report you to security." I pulled him closer to me and said, "Hey, fuck you and security." Then I pushed him away and said, "Take a walk asshole. And don't come back." He turned around and started to walk away. Then he looked at his girlfriend and said, "Let's go honey. We'll see what security thinks about all of this." Then I said, "Hey Charles. If anybody breaks my balls about any of this, I'll turn the rest of your trip into a nightmare." I walked back out onto the deck and leaned over the railing again. The seagulls were still circling behind the ship. I looked up at them and said, "Can you believe this fucking shit?" Then I turned around and went back inside the ship. With my headache now a distant memory, I went to find my family.

    I had to walk through all the buffet lines to get to the other side of the ship. There was food everywhere. I remember thinking that there were two constants on a cruise ship. The unbelievable amounts of food, and all kinds of fat bastards. I guess it was a natural combination. I just kept walking. Besides being happy about not having a headache, I was really worked up about something else. The ship was heading back to New York Harbor. I realized something that day for the second time in my life. Something I hadn't thought about since I was leaving California. Even though that was twenty years ago, that feeling was crystallized in my mind.

And it was the same now as it was then. I was going home. And nothing has ever made me feel like that. I'm not saying it was the most important thing in my life. My family, my wife and seeing my kids being born will always be my best memories. But getting back to New York was always special for me. I loved getting back to the city and especially the Bronx.

I got to the other end of the ship where the swimming pool was and found my wife. She was in the pool with my two daughters. My son was on the buffet line. Every time I saw him he was eating. And this was the seventh straight day. I stood there for a minute and just watched him. He was balancing two plates in his left hand and loading them both up with his right. Somehow he managed to pour himself a soda and not drop anything. He got off the line and walked straight toward me. I watched him as he got closer. We looked into each other's eyes, as we always did. As far back as I can remember whenever we make eye contact we never broke it until we were face to face. I don't know if he knows it or not but I love that part of him. His confidence and that look in his eye. Whenever it happened I always felt the same way. He reminded me so much of myself. It was like I was looking into my own eyes. Anyway, we were face to face now, eye to eye. Then he said, "What?" I just laughed and said, "Nothing. Are you gonna eat all that?" He said, "Yeah." Then he walked toward a table and sat down. That was him. Whenever you talk to him, if you get two or three words it's a lot. It didn't matter to me at that point. I didn't have a headache so I was in a good mood already. And seeing him always puts me in a good mood. He has a certain way about him. A confidence in himself that is always there. You can see it in his eyes. I guess he gets it from me and I am proud of that. But even more than that, as good as that made me feel, there was something even more important. I know that confidence. That look his eyes will allow him to stand up to anybody or anything. It will be something he can draw strength from and that gives me a feeling I can never put into words. I am proud of him.

I walked over to the pool. It was right in front of one of the bars at that end of the ship. Sometimes things just work out right. Barbara came over to me and asked how my headache was. I told her it was gone. Then I leaned over gave her a kiss and waved at my daughters. They were on some kind of giant float, splashing and laughing. I was glad they were having fun. They waved at me and kept on splashing. I told Barbara I was going over to the bar and asked her if she wanted anything. She said, "I'm fine but get some iced tea for the girls." I said, "No problem, I'll be right back." I walked up to the bar and sat down on one of the stools. I was finally able to relax and decided to have a beer. The bartender was busy making some kind of stupid fucking blender drink for somebody. I just sat there and watched him. I refer to him as a bartender only because he was behind a bar. To me, he was no bartender. I had been tending bar for the past fourteen years, in all kind of places. In my eyes he was a fat guy wearing a stupid shirt. Anyway, he finished what he was doing and started walking toward me. I just watched him. When he got to where I was sitting, he leaned on the bar and said, "So how're we doing today, buddy?" I looked back at him and said, "You got Bud in a bottle?" He said, "Sure do!" I said, "That's great. I'll have one of those, no glass." He said, "Sure thing, coming right up." He came back and put the bottle down on the bar. I said, "Thanks. You got any iced tea behind the bar?" He said, "We got some great tasting plum punch." I took a sip of my beer and put it back down on the bar. Then I looked at him and said, "I didn't ask you that." He said, "I know, I just wanted to tell you about the plum punch. We don't always have it but we have it today." I lit up a cigarette and said, "Hey, fuck you and the plum punch. What did I ask you for?" He said, "You asked me if I had any iced tea." I said, "That's right. So why the fuck am I hearing about plum punch? Do you have any iced tea back there or not?" He looked at me and said, "Yes I do sir. Please calm down." I looked at him and said, "You're unfucking believable. Bring me two iced teas for my girls. Then I'll calm down. You think you can do that?" He said, "I sure can pal. I'll be right back." I was sitting there watching him pour the iced teas when I heard Barbara say, "Is everything ok?" I was keeping an eye on you while you were at the bar. I've never seen you take that long to get a drink. So I figured I'd come over and see what was going on." I looked at her and said, "Are the girls ok?" she said, "Yeah. They're ok. Are you?" I said, "Yeah, I'm ok. Except for this fucking idiot behind the bar." She said, "There's my favorite line again." We both started laughing then I said, "Barb, I know what you're thinking but this is different." She said, "Oh, I know! They're always different. You always give me variety in this kind of situation. I'll give you that." I said, "Barb, what do you want from me? Can I help it if this guy is a fucking idiot and every thing he says is stupid? That ain't my fault. I'm gonna react to that in my own way." She looked at me and said, "That's what I'm worried about." I said, "There's nothing to worry about. Seriously, I'm just glad I don't have a headache right now. I'm in a good mood and I'm not gonna let anything ruin it. Go back over to the pool with the girls. I'll get the drinks and meet you there." She said, "Ok. Just don't take too long. And leave the bartender alone, he's just doing his job." I said, "Ok, I'll be right there." But what I was really thinking was, if he were doing his job he would have given me what I ordered. But somehow, that didn't matter. Women just have a different way of looking at things. I knew Barbara was just trying to put an end to the problem. But so was I. We just had different ways of doing that. Barbara walked back over to the pool where the girls were playing. While I was waiting for our drinks, I watched her and thought about what she said. I knew she had a point because she always did. I also knew that because of my state of mind and what I was going through with my headaches I was probably part of the problem. I understood that and I did try to factor that in while these things were happening. But I was also dealing with a lot of fucking idiots. I mean, I wasn't just imagining all this shit. These people were all over the fucking place. As I'm sitting there thinking about all this bullshit the bartender comes back and says, "Here you go, buddy. I put some extra cherries in the iced teas. Maybe that will put you in a better mood. You know, cheer you up a little bit." I said, "Who puts cherries in iced teas?" He said, "I do." He looked at me for a second and walked away. I watched him and said, to myself, what a fucking idiot. I knew it didn't matter how stupid he was and I did have more important things on my mind. But there is something that always amazed me and it is worth pointing out for whatever it's worth. And that is the dumber the person is, the surer of themselves they are. It's unbelievable but true. And depending on what kind of mood you're in you either laugh or want to smack them in the mouth. I wasn't sure what kind of mood I was in but because my wife and kids were there I decided to laugh it off. So I picked up the drinks and started walking towards the pool. Then I heard the bartender say, "I hope they enjoy the extra cherries." I turned around and looked at him. He smiled at me and I said, "Whatever asshole!" When I turned back around, Barbara was standing in front of me. She said, "I thought you were going to leave him alone." I said, "I thought I was too, but he didn't leave me alone." She said, "So you had to curse him out." I said, "I don't look at it that way. I just told him what I thought he needed to hear. It's no big deal. You don't hear him complaining, do you?" She said, "He's probably afraid to complain." I said, "That's exactly how he should be thinking." Barbara just looked at me and laughed. Then she walked away. She did that a lot on this cruise. Especially the last couple of days. I understood why and I couldn't blame her. She was going through a tough time and under so much pressure with dealing with the kids and all of that. So I was sure she was sick of putting up with me and all of my shit. And I understood that, too. But I was dealing with so much pain on an everyday basis by that time, that I just didn't give a fuck anymore. I cared about Barbara and what she thought, but I definitely didn't give a fuck about some stupid bartender. And that's what he was, no doubt. Believe me, that's one thing I know about. There are bartenders and then there are people that work behind the bar. And you are either one or the other. There is no in-between. Anyway we found a way to get through the rest of the day.

When I opened my eyes the next morning, I realized that I had somehow gotten through another night of extreme pain. With the bottle of water still in my hand I reached under my pillow to see how many pills I had taken during the night. I didn't know how many I had put under there the night before. But there were no pills under the pillow. I must have needed them all. I didn't care for two reasons. As I lay there I didn't have a headache and it was the last day of the cruise. No matter what else happened on this day, I knew one thing, we were heading home. And that always made me happy. As I thought about it, the feeling was always the same. Wherever I had been, California, Maine, Syracuse or Vegas. Going home was the one thing that always made me happy. Although I probably always knew that it was this particular moment that it really hit home for me. I couldn't wait to get back.

It was the last day of the cruise, finally! I know that sounds strange but if you've been paying attention, you know what I mean. It was after dinner. Somehow we had gotten through another one of those. We were all hanging out on the front deck of the ship. It was before the kids went to sleep and after I had gotten rid of another fucking headache. So I was in a pretty good mood. I always was, when the pain had left me. Plus, we were on our way home. So, I didn't see it coming. It was taking shape all around me. The moment that would define the entire trip. Barbara was sitting on a lounge chair with our daughters. My brother's wife and the rest of the women were gathered around them. They were talking and taking turns playing with the kids.

I was standing at the front of the ship with my father, my brother, my son and my uncle Tony. We were having a beer and looking out over the ocean. My father let my son take a sip from his beer, just like he did with me when I was his age. As I watched them I was lost in the moment. The five of us were leaning on the rail at the front of the ship. We were all talking about how intimidating the ocean was. How it made everybody and everything seem so insignificant. That's when it hit me. I walked over to my father and stood between him and my son. I reached out and put one arm around each of them. And with my uncle and my brother behind us, everything fell into place. We were all staring out at the ocean. The same ocean my father and uncle had traveled across all those years ago. Two kids, alone with their fears. Trying to cope with something they had no ability to understand. Their only companion, a father who was forcing an ocean between them and the love of their mother.

As I stood there, my mind began to wander. Emotions and memories, slamming around inside my head. Time kind of stood still for a while, almost conveniently, as I struggled to harness my thoughts. The black expanse of the ocean and the sound of the waves crashing into the hull of the ship compounded my trance. I stood there, my mind alternating between what I was looking at and what my father might have been feeling looking at the same thing all those years ago. That intimidating ocean and the feeling of uncertainty it exuded was all I could think about. I loved my father and always respected him for all he had been through in his life. But this was something different. As I said, the ocean was scary and it made me nervous. But we were on a fucking cruise ship! With almost everybody in our family around us. When I thought about what he must have felt like. At his age and with nobody around, it made me feel kind of stupid. After all, my father and my uncle had no idea where their lives were leading them at that point. And to really grasp the whole scenario you have to remember that these were two very young children. An eight year old and a three year old. My God! They were really still just babies. When you thought about the toughest thing you had to deal with at that age, it's really fucking unbelievable. I mean really. How the hell did they do it?

Anyway, we were all still standing at the front of the ship. As I said, my mind was all over the place. That's when it hit me. A single thought that had been taking shape in the back of my mind. Almost without me even realizing it. It was simple and over powering at the same time. If my father hadn't been able to overcome the trauma that was shoved down his throat, at that young age, and all the challenges he faced after that, none of us would even have been standing there that night. As that feeling washed over me, I felt as I never have before. Yeah, I was happy. But there was something else and we all knew it. We stood there taking in the power of the ocean and the darkness of the night. Each of us with our own feeling about what we knew about our story. And it was our story. It belonged to all of us. But not just to us. There were other family members that were directly affected, no doubt. My mother, grandma, grandpa, La-La, Ann Marie, Donna, Linda, Peter, all of us. And now, our kids too. They were all on everybody's mind, as we stood there. Nobody had to say a word. We all knew it. Obviously, we all drew something different from that experience. But there was one constant. A kind of common denominator that was felt by all of us. The ocean. That dark, powerful presence. That body of water that had taken so much away from all of us. And then somehow drew us all back to it. Reeled us all back in on that night, for this moment. We all felt the same way. Like we were supposed to be there. Had to be there. Almost like it wasn't really our decision. I looked at my father then I smacked my son in the back of the head. They both looked at me and said, "What?"

    I wish I could explain the feeling I had at that moment but I know I can't, so I won't even try. As we all stood there I felt my eyes well up with tears. My emotions were out of control. I couldn't help myself and I knew it. So I just let it all happen. I guess, deep down, I knew it was gonna happen at some point anyway. So I just stood there and cried. As the tears rolled down my face, my son looked at me and said, "What's wrong Dad?" I still had my arms around him and my father. I held onto both of them as tight as I could and stared straight out at the ocean. Then I said, "Nothing's wrong, man. We're all ok."